DATE DUE

Twenty Years of Nationalisation

Twenty Years of Nationalisation

THE BRITISH EXPERIENCE

R. Kelf-Cohen, C.B., M.A., B.Sc.(Econ.)

MACMILLAN

ST MARTIN'S PRESS

First published 1969 by
MACMILLAN AND CO LTD
Little Essex Street London WC2
and also at Bombay Calcutta and Madras
Macmillan South Africa (Publishers) Pty Ltd Johannesburg
The Macmillan Company of Australia Pty Ltd Melbourne
The Macmillan Company of Canada Ltd Toronto
St Martin's Press Inc New York
Gill and Macmillan Ltd Dublin

Library of Congress catalog card no. 69-13689

Printed in Great Britain by
R. & R. CLARK LTD
Edinburgh

TO THE MEMORY OF

MY FATHER

Contents

A 2

Preface

ALL the nationalised industries (except, of course, steel) have been functioning for twenty years. This is a period sufficiently long to enable stock to be taken of what has been happening in the industries and to assess their achievements.

During the 1960s developments in the Public Corporations have been many and substantial. Their position as the decade nears its end is vastly different from what it was in 1960. The framework of the Nationalisation Acts, within which they operate, has been subtly modified time and again. The most substantial modifications have been carried out by Labour Governments since 1964; but their work has been the acceleration of a trend which was already apparent in 1961 when the White Paper appeared on The Financial and Economic Obligations of the Nationalised Industries.

The fact is that these industries have steadily become a more and more significant part of the national economy, and Governments struggling with increasing economic and financial problems must pay considerable attention to the public sector, in which these industries are so important. As a result they are frequently in the news. As the issues raised are often complex and are not very clearly presented, the public are naturally confused as to what is happening.

This book is an attempt at comprehensive cover of a wide and complex subject. Within the limits of size agreed with the publishers, this comprehensiveness has involved careful selection and substantial compression. We have many partial studies on these industries, and as their careers lengthen the difficulty of covering all their activities increases. Even to keep abreast of the flood of publications concerned with Public Corporations has now become a major task. A concise and comprehensive book on the subject has therefore become a necessity.

It is hoped that this book will be useful not only to the student at school or college, where public ownership of industry may be a compulsory subject for study, but also to the general reader and student of affairs. Hardly a week goes by without one or other of the nationalised industries coming under discussion in the news-papers—sometimes in a not very informed manner. This book might be useful as supplying background information.

The scope of the book has been limited to the five great industries under public ownership – coal, transport, electricity, gas and steel. The Airways Corporations have special problems of their own – operating as they do worldwide in a sphere where government control is paramount. The National Health Service I regard as a social service and not a nationalised industry. But any writer on this subject in the 1970s will have to include the Post Office, which will shortly join the ranks of the nationalised industries.

It is unfortunate that the text has gone to the publisher in April 1968 while the Transport Bill is going through Parliament. A brief summary of the Bill is provided in Chapter 3, but there may be substantial changes in the Bill before it becomes an Act.

Statistics for the year 1967–8 have been added to the tables in proof, but changes have not been made in the text.

I am grateful to Mr H. Pitchforth, Controller of Her Majesty's Stationery Office, for permission to quote from official publications.

Mrs Monica Coupland has carried the whole burden of typing the successive drafts of the book and the numerous changes and amendments. My writing becomes more crabbed as I get older, but nothing seems to defeat Mrs Coupland. Her keenness and cheerfulness in collaborating have made my task much lighter and I shall always remain deeply in her debt.

I am also grateful for the willing help given by the Library Staff of my old Department, the Ministry of Power.

The Statistical Tables are to be found in the relevant chapters.

R. KELF-COHEN
Upper Norwood
London

PART ONE

1 Socialist Thought on Nationalisation to 1945

THE concept of public ownership of industry is very old. The Athenian State made a handsome profit from the silver mines of Laurium. But the modern belief in public ownership is the result of the Industrial Revolution and the doctrine of *laissez-faire* which went with it. The tremendous social upheaval which followed gave rise to Socialism, and a fundamental doctrine of Socialism is the public ownership of the means of production, distribution and consumption.

To the Socialist the capitalist who owned the instruments of production was an exploiter. He paid the worker the minimum wage necessary to enable him to live and reproduce himself, and the 'surplus value' between that wage and the price of the product was appropriated by himself in the form of profit. If you expropriate the capitalist, the worker will receive the full return for his labour, which is, of course, considerably higher than the minimum wage on which he just contrives to subsist. Socialists looked at the capitalist and found him a harsh and unconscionable exploiter of his fellow men: he worked hard himself and made his employees work hard. But he became wealthy and they remained poor.

The revolutionary fervour of the mid-nineteenth-century Socialists in Europe found little support in England, which was the classic home of the capitalist. English hospitality to the foreign revolutionary gave him the opportunity of studying capitalism at close range.

But Marx had few followers in England. The Social Democratic Federation formed in 1882 by Hyndman, a disciple of Marx, made no impact on public opinion. Ramsay MacDonald described it as 'haughtily dogmatic and intransigent; it occasionally broke out with open hostility against the trade union movements; it never appealed to the average British mind though it had a faith and an energy which ought to have moved mountains' (*The Socialist Movement*, p. 232).

In the winter of 1883–4 the Fabian Society was formed from a small idealist group, with the ambitious object of 'reconstructing society in accordance with the highest moral possibilities'. The Fabians were Socialists but they rejected the Marxian doctrines both in politics and economics. They held that Socialism was a principle already to be found both in central and local government and that it could be extended further by actions of existing political parties. As Ramsay MacDonald put it, their policy was to 'permeate' rather than to 'organise'. They rejected, therefore, the idea that a political party should be formed by the adherents of Socialism.

The Fabian Society, as Socialists, worked unceasingly for the development of public ownership. Soon after it was formed it received several recruits whose work was to make the Fabian Society a great national force. Among them were Sidney and Beatrice Webb. It is not always easy to distinguish which member of the famous partnership was the major contributor in a political work. But Sidney's amazing ability to 'plan' (as we now call it) and to set out his 'plans' with great lucidity, points to him as the main contributor in their writings on public ownership.

Another reason for the failure of Karl Marx to capture English Socialism was the growth of the trade unions. As instruments for defending the interests of the working man, the unions developed in a typically English manner, slowly winning year after year a stronger position; their leaders were desperately anxious to prove that the unions were respectable and free from revolutionary taints.

In this development of the trade unions, the work of the Webbs was most important. They were most skilful at explaining to English public opinion the true meaning of these little-known working-men's organisations. With great skill and clarity they wrote pamphlets and books which educated the middle class in the activities and aims of the working class; this massive effort was completed in two classic books – the *History of Trade Unionism*, published in 1894 and *Industrial Democracy*, published in 1897.

As trade unions persisted in being English in the gradualness of their approach and refused to become revolutionary, the Webbs, who fully understood their attitude and indeed helped to form it and give it an intellectual basis, naturally looked elsewhere for their instrument to bring about the public ownership of industry. They found it in the municipality. The Webbs were the protagonists of 'Gas and Water Socialism'. Electricity, of course, was still too young and unimportant. Nevertheless, Parliament, in the first Electricity Act in 1882, laid it down that electricity franchises were to revert to the local authority after a period of twenty-one years. As this was found too restrictive, the period was extended by the 1889 Act, to forty-two years. The 1882 Act was the work of a Liberal Government, and the 1889 Act of a Conservative Government. This goes to show that 'Gas and Water Socialism' had a backing of public opinion far beyond the ranks of the Fabian Society; 'permeation' was working.

'Gas and Water Socialism' was obviously a very slow and gradual approach to the public ownership of industry, but the Webbs had lighted on another economic development which opened up a speedier approach. The 'capitalist' had hitherto been an individual – endowed with most unpleasant characteristics and rightly doomed to suffer for his behaviour. But now the Webbs realised that the capitalist, or rather Capitalism, was becoming impersonal. On page 112 of *Socialism in England*, published in 1890, Webb draws attention to the 'elimination of the purely personal element in business management', which had now been replaced 'by the salaried officers of large corporations of shareholders'. More than one-third of industry, measured by the capital employed, was now carried on by joint-stock companies. Why not expropriate the shareholders? This could be carried out by the community with little more dislocation than is caused by the daily purchase of shares on the Stock Exchange. And so, says Sidney Webb, 'this is merely the replacement of the private by the public shareholder'. Nearly seventy years afterwards this proposal was revived by the Labour Party under the leadership of Mr Gaitskell.

During the 1890s the younger element in the trade unions was becoming restive at the lack of a political party of its own. A Scottish 'Labour Party' had been formed as early as 1888 and at a conference at Bradford in 1893 the Independent Labour Party was formed with Keir Hardie as its moving spirit. It was a practical, down-to-earth Party, rejecting Marxian dogmas. Keir Hardie had already been returned to Parliament in 1892 for West Ham (South).

During the period 1893–1900 this Party worked to create a political alliance with the trade unions, and succeeded in February 1900 in creating the Labour Representation Committee which in 1906 became the Labour Party. During the whole of this period there had been strong support among the trade unions for a Liberal–Labour alliance which only ended in 1908 when the miners decided to join the Labour Party. When war came in 1914 the Labour Party had become an important political force with forty-two members in the House of Commons. But as Ramsay MacDonald emphasised: 'The Labour Party is not Socialist. It is the only political form which evolutionary Socialism can take in a country with the political traditions and methods of Great Britain. Under British conditions, a Socialist Party is the last, not the first, form of the Socialist movement in politics' (*The Socialist Movement*, p. 235, written in 1911).

The First World War gave a great impetus to socialist thought. The State took powers to control the economic life of the nation on a scale previously unknown. It discovered ways and means of regulating industry and commerce which had never been suspected. Taxation was raised to unparalleled heights. Income tax, which had been denounced as crushing in 1907 when it had climbed to 1s in the £, was raised in 1918 to 6s in the £. Distribution of many essential commodities was controlled on the basis of fair shares. Unemployment disappeared and the State found work for everyone. Here indeed was a most valuable series of object lessons to the Socialists. Their vision of life had often been denounced as absurd and impossible; under the stress of war most of it had been realised. Naturally enough the Webbs, as the most formative thinkers among Socialists, set out on revision in the light of war-time experience.

Early in 1918 Webb produced *Labour and the New Social Order*, which, with slight modifications, was adopted by the Labour Party.

The beginning of the pamphlet sets the tone. It advocates

the progressive elimination from industry of the private capitalist, individual or joint stock; and the setting free of all who work, whether by hand or brain, for the service of the community and of the community only: and Labour refused absolutely to believe that the British people will permanently tolerate any of the waste and inefficiency involved in the abandonment of British industry to a jostling crowd of separate employers with their minds bent, not on service to the community, but by the very law of their being, only on the utmost possible profiteering.

This is followed up by the statement that 'what the Labour Party looks to is a general scientific re-organisation of the nation's industry on the basis of the common ownership of the means of production'.

The sweeping statement that the whole of private enterprise is to disappear is rather startling coming from the Webbs. The programme is vast; but this was an ultimate programme, part only of which was to be put immediately into force.

For on the same page the demand is made for the immediate nationalisation of the railways, the mines and electric power – in the last case with municipal co-operation in distribution. There was also the suggestion, revived thirty-one years later, that industrial insurance should be nationalised.

It is not surprising that the Webbs put in a plea for the maintenance of the war-time controls which had developed since 1914. They were in favour of maintaining the

present profitable centralisation of the purchase of raw materials; of the present careful 'rationing' by joint committees of the trades concerned; of the special establishments with the materials they require; of the present elaborate system of costing and public audit of the manufacturers' accounts; of the present salutary publicity of the manufacturing processes and expenses thereby ensured . . . ; and of the present rigid fixing of the prices of standardised products to a maximum at the factory, at the warehouse and the wholesale store, and in the retail shop.

When the Labour Party met in London six months after this manifesto was published, they endorsed it: and it was issued under the same title in a revised form. This revised *Labour and the New Social Order* demanded the 'immediate nationalisation of the railways, mines and electric power'. The Labour Party pressed unhesitatingly for the

national ownership and administration of the railways and canals, and their union along with harbours and roads and the posts and telegraphs – not to say also the great lines of steamers which, if not at once owned, should be immediately managed by the Government – indeed a combined national service of communication and transport; to be worked, unhampered by Capitalists, private or purely local interest (and with a steadily increasing participation of the organised workers in the management both central and local) exclusively for the common good.

On coal the revised manifesto demanded the immediate nationalisation of the extraction of coal and iron. Retail distribution of coal as a local public service was to be handled by municipal or community councils.

Among the trade union leaders of that time, Arthur Henderson was rapidly coming to the forefront. There is a most interesting passage in Beatrice Webb's *Diaries, 1912–24* (p. 167) which shows the strong belief of the trade union leaders in the virtues of nationalisation.

The passage reads as follows:

He [Henderson] wanted Sidney to draft a complete scheme for 'socialising industry' – the whole of industry – said that 'we must come down to bed rock and show that the principle of socialisation was applicable to all industries.

Why should the miners and railwaymen have the privilege of being socialised? The engineers and other operatives resented this; it would be far better electioneering to have a complete scheme for all industry and get it accepted by the Labour Party conference.' We pointed out the difficulties – the discrimination between one industry and another, the absence of brain-power and goodwill in the government service, the peculiar technical requirements in each industry, the universal alarm that any such scheme would arouse – considering the inaptitude of labour for the every-day working of their own organisation.

Obviously Sidney Webb's facility for drafting programmes had overreached itself and had been all too successful; his clarity had made it all so simple.

In July 1920 the Webbs produced *A Constitution for the Socialist Commonwealth of Great Britain*. The book, as was explained in the preface, was written in reply to 'a request from M. Huysmans, the Secretary of the International Socialist Bureau, to all the constituent bodies of the International Socialist Congress that they should furnish reports upon the "socialisation" of industries and services and upon the Constitution that should be adopted by any nation desirous of organising its life upon Socialist principles'.

This is one of the least successful of the Webbs' books. It is too doctrinaire. Its fundamental defect is the proposal for two parliaments, political and social. The socialisation of industry and services was to be carried out under the aegis of the Social Parliament. The proposal to split Parliament in two arose from the Webbs' dislike of the great power which had been centred in the hands of Parliament, or rather in the hands of the ministers who control Parliament; it seems remarkable that such intelligent people should have believed that the citizen would wish his political and economic activities to be handled by two different groups.

As a result of this futile proposal for two parliaments, the book had little effect on public opinion. But it is important in the history of Labour Party views of nationalisation, because in it the Webbs made a serious effort to grapple with some problems which they foresaw were bound up with the change-over in ownership. Their conscientiousness drove them to consider in detail how they were going to 'socialise' industry.

They were conscious of some of the dangers. On page 140 they point out that 'if the present force of the Crown, Cabinet and House of Commons and the special services were to be applied to the ownership and administration of industrial capital, the individual might easily find himself helpless'.

They foresaw the great powers of a national monopoly with the authority of the State behind it. From the workers' point of view they were concerned at the possibility of the workers being employed directly by the Government, who might treat a strike as a rebellion (p. 141), and they tried to get round this by postulating that the strike would be against the National Boards and not the State itself.

By July 1920 they were unhappy at the suggestion that Socialists might wish to 'socialise at one blow and in any one way the whole of industry and all services' (p. 147). They had obviously been taken aback at the swift acceptance by the trade unions and the Labour Party of their 1918 manifesto; the sweeping developments in Soviet Russia probably contributed to their hesitation.

They proposed therefore to provide the 'most advantageous form of administration for each industry or service as, one after another, in the course of industrial and social evolution, each passed from capitalist to public ownership and control' (p. 147). The Webbs were following Karl Marx with some hesitation.

So they set to work to devise a form of national administration 'for those industries and services, probably fewer than half a dozen, which required to be dealt with primarily on a national basis'. They proceeded to consider some of the problems involved in changing the ownership and organising a new control of these basic industries. They were concerned how to select the managers of these public industries and came to the conclusion that appointments and promotions 'should be made on the well-considered and authoritative recommendation of a selection committee or appointments board'.

This was to be a standing committee specialising in the art of selection, but there were to be added to it, for particular appointments, representatives of those from whom the person to be appointed will receive orders, of those to whom he will give orders, and sometimes outside experts. The Webbs were definite that appointments made by individuals such as ministers were to be deplored.

When this book was produced there was developing a Guild Socialist Movement which was the mild British version of the Syndicalist Movement which had swept the Continent somewhat earlier. The Webbs were very anxious to improve the status of the producer, but they could not stomach the proposals of the Guild Socialists, whereby industries were to be run by associations of the producers in each industry.

So instead they attempted to give the producer an important part in the organisation of the nationalised industries, but the clarity of their outlook could not eliminate the consumer from the picture in the sweeping manner of the Guild Socialists. Therefore, in the administration of the nationalised industries, they always balanced representation of producers by representatives of the 'citizen consumer'.

In chapter 3 of part 2 of the book the Webbs grapple with the problems of nationalising industries. They start by suggesting that only about half a dozen industries 'out of all the many hundreds of industries and services which go to make up the social life of the nation' will have to be nationalised.

Immediate nationalisation is demanded for railways and canals on the one hand and the mining industry, including oil, on the other. Additional candidates might be afforestation, insurance and 'the service of keeping current and deposit accounts which is the basis of British banking'. They did not mention electric power, nor the gas industry, which were partly in public ownership already.

The objects of nationalisation are defined as centralisation and improvement of services, the fullest participation in management by the workers, the most effective safeguarding of the interests of the consumers, and the permanent welfare of the community as a whole.

At this point they bring in a suggestion which has found great favour, and which is to be found in the Nationalisation Acts. There is to be a separation of policy and of day-to-day administration. Policy was to be the concern of the appropriate standing committee of the Social Parliament, but there should be no parliamentary interference in the 'day-by-day administration in the widest sense, including appointments and promotions, purchases and sales, and the choice between this and that method or technical device of the service'.

Just as local authorities are left to carry on their own services, so would the nationalised industries be left to themselves. This important distinction between policy and day-to-day administration which, as will be seen later, is today an important issue, obviously worried the Webbs in 1920. Their definition of day-to-day administration is rather narrow and, in fact, power is left largely in the hands of the standing committees of the Social Parliament.

The Webbs distrusted the increasing powers of ministers; so they objected rather strongly to ministerial responsibility. 'What has happened, in fact, during the past half-century with the continuous increase in the functions of government has been the gradual establishment of a largely unselfconscious bureaucratic conspiracy against Parliamentary interference or control' (p. 172). They came to the conclusion that ministers, assisted by their able civil servants, were successful in evasion and denial of information; and they end up with the startling conclusion that 'Parliamentary control, even over policy, has become an illusion and a sham' (p. 172).

Their remedy, therefore, would be not to organise the nationalised industries on the lines of the Post Office, and they avoided ministerial control by providing that each nationalised industry would be supervised by a standing committee appointed by the Social Parliament.

But the Webbs realised that this is not enough, because

the community needs a much more effective democratic control over its affairs and some adequate safeguards for both efficiency and improvement – not to say more protection against the evils of uncontrolled bureaucracy – than can be given by the amateur supervision of busy members of Parliament, advised only by heads of departments who are themselves part of the very administration to be directed and controlled (p. 174).

Despite their complaint about the efficiency of the Civil Service in helping ministers to conceal everything from the members of Parliament, the Webbs plump for a more efficient Civil Service and the development of various departments of 'control'. Each standing committee will have allocated to it a Department of State which will be 'always inspecting, costing, auditing and researching' (p. 190). These new civil servants would have to develop a new technique. All this is rather vague and shows that the Webbs are groping in the dark. They also overlook the important fact that civil servants are responsible only to their ministers and that their position would be intolerable if they were the servants both of ministers and standing committees, who might well be at variance.

The 'current administration' of the nationalised industries was to be carried on by National Boards. Such a Board should consist of sixteen members – a chairman, five from the principal branches of administration in the service, five representatives of the workers and five representatives of the community, who are the consumers of the products of the nationalised industry. They admit that the majority of this Board would be producers and that the consumers would be, therefore, at a disadvantage. It is interesting that this tripartite representation on the Boards was subsequently adopted in France.

The selection of the sixteen members would be made by the appropriate standing committee of the Social Parliament, who would advise the Crown, who would make the appointments.

The Webbs also anticipate a later development in suggesting that the National Board would have full power of administration, in its widest sense, but would be subject 'to such specific directions as to policy as it may from time to time receive from the Social Parliament itself' (p. 176).

If we delete their Social Parliament and substitute the Minister in Parliament to whom the Webbs so violently objected, we arrive at the appointment of a Board by a Minister who has the power to give directions on general policy. In later Acts there was no provision for a selection committee, except in the London Passenger Transport Act of 1933. The tripartite structure of the Boards proposed by the Webbs never found favour in this country, and the Nationalisation Acts gave complete discretion to the Minister, subject to certain general qualifications of the appointees.

The Webbs, with their great interest in trade unionism and impressed by the unsatisfactory position of the workers in the industries to be nationalised, devoted much attention to the treatment of the workers in the new organisations. There were to be collective bargaining arrangements. There were to be district councils and workers' committees which would deal with local matters of a limited kind. These foreshadowed the Joint Consultation arrangements described in Chapter 11 of this book.

Optimistically they believed that collective bargaining conducted by Joint Boards, on which representatives of the National Boards meet equal numbers of representatives of the trade unions, would remove all the familiar troubles and industrial disputes inherent in capitalism. When the capitalist went he took industrial friction with him.

As 'no more can be shared among the producers than is produced' (p. 186), sweet reasonableness backed by full information would ensure the settlement of industrial disputes. There would be a 'full use of the essential instruments of Democracy, Measurement and Publicity', which are cardinal doctrines in the philosophy of the Webbs (p. 186).

They completely overlooked the fact that an industry which was a statutory national monopoly, dominated under their scheme by the producers, could increase the relative value of the products of that industry by making the consumer pay a higher price. There would be strong temptation for the management of the nationalised industry, freed from competition, to conciliate the workers in the industry in this manner. The influence of great bodies of workers employed in the nationalised industries would be so strong that management would find it desirable to buy industrial peace at the expense of the consumer.

Finally the Webbs made some attempt to describe the administration of the nationalised industries.

This part of their book is very thin, as the Webbs had slight experience of the detailed work of managing industry. They placed great reliance on 'independent and disinterested experts who will keep on turning the searchlight on to the industries and will thereby bring public opinion to bear'.

They had great faith in the reasonableness of the human being, who could always be swayed by facts duly collected and published. Alas, human beings are rarely as intellectually fairminded as the Webbs. They, of course, believed that, once the personal element represented by the capitalists had disappeared, the character of all persons connected with these industries would be so profoundly changed that the industries would in fact represent a new way of life. This naïve optimism, as we shall see, was shared by members of the Labour Government of 1945–50.

As the Webbs had little understanding of the function of management and the responsibility for making decisions, which is a vital part of that function, they failed to realise that a conglomeration of committees and disinterested experts would still leave it necessary for responsible management to do its work. They tended to identify at the back of their minds the responsibility of management with the greed of capitalism.

The work of the Webbs was valuable. They were intellectually honest and did their best to plan the future. They realised that the change-over would involve great difficulties and they analysed those difficulties and sought remedies for them. Unlike many Socialist writers they refused to rely on vague shibboleths; their intellectual conscience was far too strong.

The brave vision unfolded by the Webbs and eagerly embraced by the Labour Party was shattered by the horrible economic aftermath of the war. Throughout 1920 the shadows were lengthening and the end of the hectic post-war boom was rapidly coming into sight.

The crucial test of the case for public ownership was the coal mines. Unrest among the coal miners had been a feature of war-time industrial troubles. During the war the State had been forced to take control of the mines and to fix the price of coal.

The end of the war brought great difficulties to the coal-mining industry, details of which are not relevant here. From the Sankey Commission in 1919, which by a majority recommended national-isation, to the Samuel Commission in 1925, the future organisation of the coal-mining industry dominated political and economic issues. The storm burst in 1926. The miners rejected the Report of the Samuel Commission, which the owners had, under pressure, accepted, and demanded a continuance of the wages which had only been made possible in 1925 by a Government subsidy of £19 million. The trade unions felt the justice of the miners' claims so strongly that they called a General Strike in support, which collapsed after a week. The miners hung on grimly through the long summer months of 1926, and finally accepted the owners' terms which scrapped national settlements of wages, which were to be fixed district by district. Nationalisation of the coal mines was, for the present, out of sight.

As the troubles of the 1920s deepened into the depression of the early 1930s, the transfer of industries to public ownership became an academic issue. But there were developments in the period 1926–39 which are of importance.

In 1926 the Baldwin Government secured the passing of the Electricity (Supply) Act, which created a public corporation known as the Central Electricity Board. Its purpose was to co-ordinate and standardise the generation of electricity, and to construct and own a high-tension grid connecting the power stations. The technical case for such a step was overwhelming, but the Baldwin Government encountered fierce resistance from among their own followers, because the new Board was a public corporation. But, as we have seen, even in the 1880s Parliament had envisaged that electricity supply would ultimately come under public ownership, and by 1926 about two-thirds of the electricity undertakings were in fact in the hands of local authorities. The extension of public ownership to the high-tension grid was hardly, therefore, revolutionary.

The other Board set up in the 1920s was the British Broadcasting Corporation. The advent of broadcasting posed a most difficult problem, on which there is still debate. It is to be noted that the B.B.C. has always operated under a charter which has meant a periodical parliamentary review, followed by a fresh charter. Broadcasting is, of course, a powerful social and cultural and political factor in our lives, and can hardly be compared to an industry. Furthermore, it was new and its scope ever-changing; therefore, a periodical review of its organisation is inevitable.

During the 1920s Labour policy on plans for nationalisation was in a state of flux. The Labour Party and the T.U.C. submitted proposals to the Samuel Commission of 1925, which were published in a pamphlet *Coal and Commonsense*. These were incredibly complex and unworkable, because they tried to make the best of all worlds. There would be 'expert' direction, combined with limited ministerial responsibility, an element of 'joint control' and finally some representation of and power for the consumers. This was an attempt to adapt to a changing world the proposals of Sidney Webb; it found no favour with the Samuel Commission.

The examples of the B.B.C. and C.E.B. were of interest, and some minds in the Labour Party were turning to the Public Corporation as a breakaway from the balances and complexities of the Webb proposals, which had had their last fling in *Coal and Commonsense*. But though both these new Boards entailed a form of public ownership, they did not constitute precedents for a policy of nationalisation. They were both the result of technical and scientific developments. No transfer of ownership took place. Even the 'selected' power stations operated by the Central Electricity Board remained in the ownership of the electricity undertakings. Though the C.E.B. was hardly known to the public, while the B.B.C. was known to everyone, neither corporation can be prayed in aid, either by supporters or opponents of nationalisation. They were very much *sui generis*.

But during this period there was one case of a transfer of an industry from private to public ownership – London passenger transport. It is not quite correct to describe it thus, because a substantial part transferred was already in public ownership. The L.C.C. and other local authorities owned tramway systems.

In its limited way the problem of London passenger transport had attracted as many enquiries as the coal-mining industry. From earliest days the companies catering for the London passenger had tended to amalgamate and apart from the municipal trams were, by the 1920s, organised in one large group, the main constituents of which were the London General Omnibus Co. and the Underground companies. But there was nothing to prevent new bus companies entering the field and in the 1920s there was an outburst of competition, which the 'Underground' group resented as 'irresponsible'. But their monopoly was *de facto* and not legal, and the public, always resentful of a monopoly, welcomed the 'pirates'.

In the Labour Government of 1929–31, the Minister of Transport was a Londoner, Mr Herbert Morrison (later Lord Morrison of Lambeth), who had already devoted much of his time to the difficulties of London Transport. As Minister of Transport he was also responsible for the Central Electricity Board and was therefore familiar with the working of a Public Corporation.

With this background Mr Morrison set to work to produce a Bill which would unify all passenger transport in London, under the management of a Board which he proposed should be appointed by the Minister of Transport. The story of this effort and his philosophy of public ownership is set out in Mr Morrison's book *Socialisation and Transport*.

The first problem Mr Morrison had to face was to persuade the local authorities, headed by the London County Council, to surrender their trams to the new Board. He was assisted by the fact that the local authorities were realising that trams were finding it difficult to compete with buses, and that their future was uncertain. Many local authorities would, at an early date, have to face large programmes of capital expenditure to renew the out-worn trams. The tram tracks were the responsibility of the tramway undertaking, and with increasing road transport the cost of maintaining the tracks was heavy. In any case, trams and tramlines were under heavy criticism and if trams were to be replaced by trolley buses, heavy capital expenditure would be necessary, not only in replacing the trams but in making good the abandoned tram tracks.

It was obvious that the new Board would be under the same control as the London Underground Group. It was unthinkable that the Chairman of the Board should be other than Lord Ashfield, or that his deputy should be other than Mr Frank Pick. The management, so capable and experienced, of London traffic would remain unchanged. There was no drastic change of management as resulted from the later Nationalisation Acts. The London Passenger Transport Board was the London Underground Group writ large.

Mr Morrison never intended that the new Board would, in any way, be a charge on public funds. It was to raise its own capital, and compensation to all bodies or persons transferring their assets to the new Board would be made in London Transport stock, which would not be guaranteed by the Government. In other words, the new Board, under the same management as the old Underground Group, was regarded, and rightly so, as able to pay its way without any assistance from the Exchequer.

This unification of London passenger transport, although over-due, and very valuable in its way, was therefore a limited and special case of public ownership, the conditions of which gave little guidance for a policy of nationalisation of nationwide in-dustries. But it was used nevertheless, both by Mr Morrison and the Labour Party, as a basis for a new survey of public ownership which was discussed and adopted by the Labour Party Conference at Leicester in 1932.

On page 113 of his book *Socialisation and Transport* Mr Mor-rison points out that his 'Party had never worked out its socialisa-tion proposals in Government Bills. The Party had now [presum-ably 1933] got to the stage of working out socialisation schemes in some detail – in the view of some critics in too much detail. But in the days of the second Labour Government – that is, 1929–31 – its ideas were by no means clear.'

Those who are interested in these various schemes will find them discussed in Mr E. Eldon Barry's book *Nationalisation in British Politics*. Mr Eldon Barry is a Socialist – his book is dedicated 'to the memory of James Keir Hardie'. But, despite his Socialism, his critical analysis of the various schemes for nationalisation cannot be bettered. Some were imaginative and forward-looking, such as the Memorandum submitted in 1926 to the Labour Party Conference, which proposed the transformation of the coal-mining industry into a coal utilisation industry. But all the schemes suffered from the fundamental defect that they were drafted by persons with no experience of managing an industry and it was therefore inevitable that they should be out of touch with reality. It is not surprising therefore, as we shall see in Chapter 2, that in 1945 Mr Shinwell could find nothing on which to base a coal nationalisation Bill.

Mr Morrison was acutely conscious of the defects of these schemes. In his book he explains that he had been for a long time closely concerned in the problems of London Transport and had taken a very active part in many of the discussions on that subject in the 1920s. He could fairly claim to be an expert on the subject and yet, as he says, 'despite this advantage, I soon learned that there was a great difference between drafting a paragraph on London Transport for the London County Council election manifesto, and the preparation of an important Parliamentary Bill incorporating a practical solution of a big and complex problem' (p. 106).

In 1945, as Lord President of the Council, Mr Morrison became the senior minister responsible for formulating and carrying out the policy of nationalisation which he had advocated. Nevertheless the doctrines in his book are in some ways sounder than the doctrines of the Labour Government of which he was an important member.

On the all-important question of finance, Mr Morrison's view was that the proposed London Passenger Transport Board 'would be such that would command the confidence both of the investing public and the users of transport in London' (p. 125). In other words, financially the new Board would stand on its own feet and no Treasury support was required. It would issue its own stock, based on its own assets and financial reputation, and the Bill provided that if the Board did not meet its liabilities, a receiver could be appointed.

The Labour Government of 1945 made no attempt to apply this test to the new Boards which it appointed, all of whom were supported by state finance.

In his discussions on the management of socialised industries, Mr Morrison assumes (p. 141) 'that the management of these industries can broadly be relied upon to get on with its work, and having done one good deed the Minister can let the people put in charge carry on with the work done, while he immediately sets about the other good deeds of socialisation which await his attention'.

In other words, he assumes that the Government of the day will exercise a slight and occasional influence over the nationalised industries. Mr Morrison is opposed to any form of management by the State. That leads to detailed interference and political pressure from groups of interested parties – workers or consumers – which might result in a disguised form of corruption. With a Public Corporation in charge he anticipates that all this can be avoided. As we shall see later, however, even with Public Corporations, political influence on nationalised industries is inevitable – but it takes on a much more subtle form than he contemplated.

In his discussions on the Public Corporation he considers the salaries for the staff of the nationalised industries. He wishes to leave the Boards complete freedom to pay any salaries they think fit, but he ignores one important fact which vitiates his sound principles; when the salaries of the Board members themselves are fixed by the Minister, the salaries of their staffs are bound to be graded accordingly.

On pages 171–4 of his book Mr Morrison discusses the informal relations between ministers and Boards. He draws an imaginary picture of a Minister refusing to defend the policy of a Board, and therefore he says

the Board will wish its policy to be so sound and popular that it should be defended by the Minister in Parliament. It is quite likely when, in certain cases, it is about to make a decision which involves ticklish policy in relation to the general public, that the Chairman will have an informal talk with the Minister in order, not to receive instruction, but to ascertain his views and to keep his mind fully informed in readiness for any public or Parliamentary discussion which might arise (p. 173).

When Mr Morrison wrote these words in 1933, he had only had experience of Boards such as the Central Electricity Board, in which Parliament and the public took a limited interest. The fitful guidance of a Minister on the lines he suggests was not inappropriate in such cases. We shall see how different is the case of national industries in which everyone is interested.

Even so, Mr Morrison does not seem to have appreciated that if the policy of the Boards is to be moulded by informal contact with ministers, which, being informal, was not known to Parliament or the public, ministers might, in effect, be deciding the policy of the Boards, but in a way that frees them from responsibility to Parliament.

On page 250 Mr Morrison has interesting views on compensation. He discusses the concept of net maintainable revenue as a basis. This concept is one of great difficulty. The word 'maintainable' introduces assessments of the future about which there could be legitimate grounds for difference, and unless one invoked arbitration of a high order, no decision by Government on maintainability would be likely to be accepted. In fact, such arbitration was adopted once by the Labour Government after the war – in the case of coal.

An example of this difficulty is his view that 'a factor of maintainability to be borne in mind is the efficiency of the Capitalist management and the probability or otherwise of considerable capital expenditure being required in order to put the undertaking into an efficient state' (p. 251).

One could picture endless difficulties in determining the 'efficiency' of past management. How was it to be measured, what was to be the yardstick? Was there to be comparison with other industries? If so, how were they to be selected, and so on?

His final sentence on that subject reads as follows:

There is another aspect of maintainability which must be considered, namely the case of undertakings which are making unreasonably high profits, which it is reasonable to suppose would not be maintainable, either because of potential competition, or because of the probability that the State, even under private management, would in the future restrict such profits in order to protect the consumer or user of the service (p. 251).

He admits in the next paragraph that the word 'reasonable' has certain aspects, and 'ethics are at times a complication in these business matters'. But Mr Morrison goes on to assure us that 'the practical definition of the word "reasonable" would present no insuperable difficulties to a Socialist Government with a majority of the people behind it' (p. 252). So he devised the formula 'net maintainable, reasonable revenue', which he was unable to persuade the Joint Select Committee of Lords and Commons to accept. Mr Morrison is fair enough to admit that this phrase contains 'no real guiding principles' and that a decision of an arbitration tribunal would therefore depend on the personal opinions of its members (p. 256).

He goes on to suggest that he 'would much prefer that the actual sums to be paid in compensation, or a concrete basis of compensation, should be set out in the statute or other instrument which effected the socialisation. This would mean that whilst ministers could negotiate and argue as to the amount of compensation, they and Parliament would have the last word, which would be a very healthy factor conducing to voluntary agreements' (p. 260). In fact, with the exception of the Bill nationalising the coal industry, the Acts passed during the Labour Government of 1945–50 did set out the basis of compensation. Had they not done so, the country would have been hag-ridden with this problem of compensation for many years. The valuation proceedings in connection with the take-over of the coal industry took ten years, and cost £6½ million.

Mr Morrison is very unhappy about a state guarantee for finance. This is most important and it is worth while setting out his views verbatim.

The Government did not wish to do this [give a State guarantee] for it might well have encouraged a spirit of slackness, or even recklessness, on the part of the Board in matters of management, on the part of the travelling public in demanding lower fares, and uneconomic facilities, and on the part of the work people in asking for big concessions as to conditions of labour; all might be tempted to say, 'Well, after all, the Treasury is behind us'. As I have shown from the Russian experience, this is a dangerous frame of mind (p. 272).

One wonders how often Mr Morrison had these views in mind as he was engaged in putting through Parliament a series of nationalisation measures, all of which provided for state guarantees of the type which, he rightly felt, were so dangerous.

Towards the end of the book (p. 284) Mr Morrison sums up the benefits of nationalisation. Ten of these benefits are listed. They might well be described as pious hopes, rather than benefits. For instance, what evidence had Mr Morrison that an industry, once nationalised, 'will be more efficiently and economically conducted'? He just did not know. What made him assume that the 'quality of service would tend to advance and the prices charged tend to fall'? Did he not anticipate the possibility that large nationalised industries would develop bureaucratic organisations and that, being monopolies well protected from criticism on 'day-to-day administration', might have a standard of service lower than that of private enterprise?

One of the benefits he lists is that 'socially necessary but, narrowly regarded, unprofitable particular services, or pieces of work, may be carried on by a public corporation aiming at public service which would not be looked at by a profit-seeking Capitalist undertaking'. This conflicts directly with the concept of a nationalised industry being run by a Public Corporation on commercial lines.

The same conflict is shown in the next benefit which is 'that the security and status of the work people employed will be greater because the shocks of destructive competition will be avoided'. Mr Morrison does not pause to reflect on the effect of this doctrine on the workers in the nationalised industries. What inducement have they to give better service in return for their improved security and status? Is it not asking too much from human nature to expect a change in outlook among workers because Parliament has passed an Act?

But Mr Morrison seems to have some doubts about these privileged workers, because he goes on to suggest that improvements in the position of the work-people should have due regard to the rights of the consumer and user, the sound financing of the undertaking and to the interests and position of the workers employed in other industries, including those which are still conducted as capitalist enterprises. This delicate set of balances can hardly be formulated in sufficient detail to provide a policy.

The structure of English trade unions, he should have known, makes such a privileged position difficult to maintain. If engineers employed in a nationalised industry are fortunate enough to obtain higher wages than the corresponding engineers in private enterprise, the trade unions concerned, which are responsible for both sets of workers, will make it their policy to level up the conditions of the workers in private enterprise to those enjoyed in the nationalised industries. This view that a prime purpose of nationalisation is to protect the workers in the industry concerned is still common to the Labour Party.

Not much comment is required on the last benefit, which reads as follows: 'and for everybody the industry will be lifted above the gamble with life and money involved in capitalist competition' (p. 285). No doubt this could always be assumed for national monopolies backed by the authority of the State and financed by Treasury guarantee.

The publication of Mr Morrison's book in 1933 was the prelude to discussion over several years among the Labour Party and the trade unions on future programmes of nationalisation and on the organisation of the industries taken into public ownership.

Incidentally, during the inter-war period, the term 'nationalisation' was pushed on one side by the term 'socialisation' as is shown by the title of Mr Morrison's book. 'Socialisation' has a wider significance than 'nationalisation' and can be used for various forms of collective ownership which might be regarded as tending towards socialism – such as co-operative or municipal. It was particularly suitable for a localised project such as Mr Morrison's reorganisation of London passenger transport. The term was originally employed by Marx and Engels in contrast to 'individual'; for instance, joint-stock companies had 'socialised' capital in contrast to privately-owned companies.

The word 'socialisation' was adopted abroad, and particularly in Germany and in Britain came to be used by writers other than Socialists, such as Keynes and the authors of the Liberal *Britain's Industrial Future*. To them the word simply meant that the 'socialised' industry had moved out of individual control. Keynes in his book *The End of Laissez-faire* spoke of the 'tendency of high enterprise to socialise itself' – merely referring to the divorce of ownership from management.

For the Labour Party the use of the word 'socialisation' was a mistake. It might be regarded as evasive and disingenuous. No one quite knew what it meant. Because of its vagueness, persons holding widely divergent views could all agree that more 'socialisation' was required. The difficulties of hammering out a clear-cut policy for transferring industries to public ownership were sufficiently formidable without being misled by key terms which lacked clarity and definition – which therefore led to confusion of thought and misunderstanding.

In the discussion following Mr Morrison's book there were two main schools of thought. On the one hand there were the socialist theorists who hankered after 'industrial democracy' and who pressed for labour representation on the Public Boards of industries taken over; this was a watered-down version of the doctrines of Guild Socialism. Opposed to these left-wing theorists were the trade unions, who were not anxious that their members should take on responsibilities in running publicly-owned industries, and were quite content if these Boards included trade union officials who would attend to 'industrial relations'. Indeed a precedent for this had been created when the London Passenger Transport Board was set up. The trade union point of view was so well put at the 1934 Labour Party Conference by Mr James Walker, an official of the Iron and Steel Trades Confederation, that his remarks deserve quotation. He wanted a Public Board manned by 'people who are experts in the industry and not mere politicians', because the purpose of socialisation was to create 'an efficient machine under the control of the community'. Efficiency demanded reorganisation. 'If you do not reorganise industry – your industry will go out of existence: and the men and women who are dependent for their living on the industry are not going to thank you because you think by mere phrase-making you are going to make the industry effective.'

The trade unions got their way. In 1934 the Labour Party adopted a sweeping nationalisation programme 'For Socialism and Peace'. This was modified in 1937 by 'Labour's Immediate Programme' which cut out from the list joint-stock banks, cotton and iron and steel. We can only assume that the trade unions in the latter industries had lost interest. But in 1944 the T.U.C. in its *Interim Report on Post-War Reconstruction* put iron and steel back on the list. These proposals of the T.U.C. were incorporated in the Labour Party's programme for the 1945 General Election, *Let us Face the Future*, and were therefore the basis of the Nationalisation Acts of 1945–50.

The chairman of the National Executive's Policy Committee, which drafted *Let us Face the Future*, was Mr Morrison (p. 247 of *Government and Parliament* by Mr Morrison). When Labour came into office in 1945 the Prime Minister set up a 'Committee on the Socialisation of Industries', which was responsible for the supervision and co-ordination of schemes for taking industries into public ownership (*Government and Parliament*, p. 22). Mr Morrison obviously got his way with the title of this committee. He became its chairman and thus the main architect of the nationalisation of the Labour Government.

In this chapter I have concentrated on the theories and writings of the Webbs and Morrison, because they were much the most valuable of all the efforts to plan the nationalisation of industries. The value of their work can be judged if it is contrasted with the efforts of another great Socialist writer, R. H. Tawney. In his essay on the 'Nationalisation of the Coal Industry' (1919) Tawney is an optimist about every facet of the scheme for coal nationalisation which emerged from the Sankey Commission Report. It forms a contrast to the contemporary doubts and questionings of Sidney Webb. With Tawney there are no doubts of any kind.

Thirty years later (1949) Tawney wrote an essay on 'Social Democracy in Britain' from which the optimism has vanished. Listing the great and difficult problems which then faced the newly nationalised industries, he concludes: 'In matters of this kind, socialists, no more than their critics, can pretend to the possession of an infallible formula' (*The Radical Tradition*, p. 163). His earlier belief in the overweening power of an Act of Parliament was fading: 'the evil legacy of suspicion left by Capitalism among the rank and file of workers cannot, unfortunately, be wound up by the sections of an Act of Parliament.'

In the doubts and questionings of this later essay, Tawney shows a greatness and intellectual honesty comparable to that of Sidney Webb. In a still later essay, 'British Socialism Today' (1952), Tawney's comment on nationalisation is 'the mere transference of property-rights involved is not by itself tidings of great joy' (*The Radical Tradition*, p. 182). When Tawney died ten years later in 1962, he must have had grave doubts how far the nationalised industries could be regarded as Socialist achievements.

PART TWO

The History of the Nationalised Industries

TABLE I: COAL 1947–67

	1947	1950	1953	1956	1959	1960	1961	1962	1963	1964	1965	1966	1967
Output (million tons)*	197	216	223	222	206	194	191	197	196	194	187	175	172
Inland coal consumption (million tons)	184	203	208	217	189	197	192	191	194	187	185	175	164
Average number of wage-earners on colliery books (ooos)	701	687	707	697	658	602	570	551	524	498	466	427	401
Average output per man year (tons)	265	295	298	298	294	306	316	342	359	372	384	390	409
Average number of shifts per week per underground worker	4·54	4·59	4·56	4·57	4·14	4·17	4·16	4·13	4·11	4·08	4·02	4·02	4·03
Absence percentage underground	13·74	13·05	13·48	13·98	15·76	15·8	16·43	16·32	16·93	16·75	18·43	18·59	17·78

Source: Ministry of Power Statistical Digests.

	1947	1950	1953	1956	1959	1960	1961	1962	1963/4	1964/5	1965/6	1966/7	1967/8
Total costs per ton	41/3	45/5	59/2	74/5	82/5	84/2	88/5	87/2	87/5	88/5	92/6	98/5	95/11
Wages costs per ton	26/11	29/5	36/11	44/9	47/5	47/1	48/1	46/4	47/1	47/9	49/-	50/6	49/3
Proceeds per ton	40/3	47/10	61/2	77/-	83/5	86/1	90/10	91/9	91/8	91/9	92/6	100/7	98/8

Source: Annual Reports of N.C.B.

In 1963 the National Coal Board changed its accounting year from the calendar year to the year April–March.
* This covers both deep-mined and opencast coal.

2 Coal

In July 1945 a Labour Government took office for the first time, with a parliamentary majority. Nationalisation of the mines became inevitable. For a generation this industry had been the subject of bitter political controversy and in the moment of victory Labour naturally declared that it would carry out the policy it had advocated since 1919.

Despite propaganda for the nationalisation of the mines since the 1890s, not enough thought had been given to the problems of the take-over into public ownership. Many proposals, memoranda and even draft Bills had been produced in the preceding fifty years, but they were all inevitably theoretical and lacking in substance. Mr Shinwell, as Minister of Fuel and Power, was now responsible for laying a Bill before Parliament to nationalise the coal-mining industry, and in a candid revelation in his autobiography he has revealed the emptiness of Labour thought (*Conflict Without Malice*, p. 172):

I immediately took up the task of preparing the legislation for nationalisation of the mines. The miners expected it almost at a wave of the ministerial wand. The owners were hardly less anxious to get out of the pits – on terms. For the whole of my political life I had listened to the Party speakers advocating State ownership and control of the coal mines, and I had myself spoken of it as a primary task once the Labour Party was in power. I had believed, as other members had, that in the Party archives a blue print was ready. Now, as Minister of Fuel and Power, I found that nothing practical and tangible existed. There were some pamphlets, some memoranda produced for private circulation, and nothing else. I had to start on a clear desk.

Mr Shinwell had throughout his parliamentary career been closely identified with the mining industry. He had been Secretary for Mines in two Labour Governments and sat for a mining constituency. In 1928 in company with Mr John Strachey he had circulated a Memorandum proposing a 'Mining Corporation' run by directors with 'industrial experience' and trade union

B 2

participation in running the industry was described as 'nothing short of disastrous'. For this reason it was rejected by the Miners' Federation.

The announcement by the Labour Government of their intention to nationalise the coal industry was made in the King's Speech on 15 August 1945, immediately they took office. On 19 December 1945 the Bill was published. In all there were four months for preparation, drafting and printing and, however quickly everyone worked, in that very short period nothing but a very crude scheme was possible.

The Coal Industry Nationalisation Bill contained little detail. Its main provisions were in the first three clauses, which created a National Coal Board of nine men to take over the coal-mining industry. The greater part of this fairly short Act was concerned with the transfer of assets, compensation for the transfer, and consequentials.

The aggregate amount for the colliery assets compulsorily taken over was to be determined by a tribunal, whose terms of reference were to be settled by agreement between the Minister and the Mining Association. This aggregate sum was to be apportioned between the districts, in proportion to a valuation to be made for each district. These district valuations were, in turn, to be apportioned between the different colliery companies, the assets of each of which would be valued. A tribunal of three eminent men fixed the total values of the assets thus transferred at £164,600,000; no explanation was given how this sum was determined.

Compensation for subsidiary assets which were not used directly in the winning of coal was determined on an individual basis by valuation boards.

The Government employed two main arguments in advocating the Bill. The first rested upon the Reid Report (the Technical Advisory Committee on Coal Mining), which had appeared a few months before the Labour Government took office. This was a committee appointed by Major Lloyd George when Minister of Fuel and Power and consisted entirely of mining technicians. The Report made a thorough analysis of the technical weaknesses of the industry and made many detailed recommendations.

Much of the industry was out of date. Methods of coal-getting and haulage had to be modernised. Coal leases were not adapted to the requirements of coal-getting. There was an acute shortage of technical ability, and an acute shortage of finance. The industry required reorganisation into larger units which would enjoy the benefits of large-scale production.

The Report, being strictly technical and non-political, did not, of course, propose national ownership. But it did propose that an Authority be established to organise the industry into larger units and to stimulate and supervise reorganisation. This Authority would be endowed by Parliament with powers for this purpose.

On technical grounds, therefore, the case for reorganisation of the industry was clear. The Labour Government contended that only by taking the whole of the industry into national ownership could the objectives of the Reid Report be obtained.

The second main argument was, of course, political; coal was the first industry to be nationalised by a Socialist Government. The National Coal Board was the first of the giant Boards created by Parliament to run a nationwide industry. There was no precedent. The Coal Industry Nationalisation Act gave the Board no guidance how to run its affairs. It took over responsibility on 1 January 1947, in the midst of an appalling crisis; a few weeks later shortage of coal shut down more than half the country's power stations. But the Board's most serious handicap was that it had to create a brand-new organisation and management for the coal-mining industry. Many of the ablest men left the industry either because they found the new environment unpleasant or because they were not offered posts by the new masters. As the Reid Report pointed out, the industry was already short of technical and managerial skill; to deplete it still further of some of its ablest men was disastrous. Eight years later the Advisory Committee on Organisation (known as the Fleck Committee) could write this damning comment (para. 109):

When the industry was nationalised, it lost many of its administrators. In particular, most of the managing directors of the larger undertakings did not choose to come into the service of the Board. Thus the industry lost virtually a complete level of management at the moment when, because of the great size of the new undertaking, managerial and administrative talent was needed more than ever before. The gap has not yet been filled.

The Coal Board started with a labour force of over 700,000 miners working in the most diverse conditions in pits ranging from Fife to Kent. In addition it owned a miscellaneous collection of coke ovens, brickworks, by-product plants, houses and farms. All were in run-down condition after six years of war and inadequate capital injection during the thirties. Above all, the country was desperately short of coal and every ton produced by the Board – regardless of cost – was urgently needed. At a time when over 90 per cent of the nation's fuel requirements was represented by coal, the responsibility laid upon this new, vast and untried organisation was stupendous.

The main features of the Coal Board's record since 1947 are set out in Table I. In its first ten years up to 1956 the Board was fighting desperately to maintain supplies, and 1955 and 1956 were years of heavy imports of coal. In 1957 the tide turned. Demand fell off slightly, more sharply in 1958 and still more in 1959. Inland consumption of coal fell between 1956 and 1959 by no less than 28 million tons. At the end of 1959 unsold stocks of coal (in addition to those held by consumers) amounted to a staggering 36 million tons.

In 1958 when the first sharp fall in coal consumption took place, the image of the Coal Board and its product – coal – was very poor; goodwill from the consumer was non-existent. Since 1939 the domestic consumer had been restricted in his use of coal, which steadily became dearer and remained uncertain in quality. The Coal Board did not sell its coal; it sold itself. Though the Board was aware of consumers' grievances and struggled hard to improve quality, its difficulties were very great. It might issue directives, but these lost much force when they reached the miner at the coal face. His interest was to maximise 'saleable output' – being paid on piece rates based on tonnage. Increased mechanisation, increased shot-firing, and thinner seams all tended to produce degradation of quality. Saleable coal per pound of explosive used in shot-firing fell from 7·6 tons in 1938 to 4·1 tons in 1957. The result was that a steadily increasing proportion of output was small coal, i.e. coals which are officially defined as 'coals with no lower size limit and with a maximum upper limit of 2 inches'. These coals were not suitable for many consumers and could only be satisfactorily burned under the huge boilers of power stations.

During the period 1956 to 1959 total home fuel consumption was static allowing for temperature adjustments; in fact it declined slightly from 253 to 245 million tons of coal equivalent. This decline has never been fully explained. But the increased cost of fuel – especially coal – and the impact of fuel efficiency were contributory factors. As mentioned above, inland coal consumption in this period declined by 28 million tons. Inland consumption of black oils – which are directly competitive with coal – increased from 15 million tons in 1956 to 28·8 million in 1959; this increase of 13·8 million tons – using the conversion factor of 1·7 tons of coal per ton of oil – is equivalent to 23½ million tons of coal. The three major markets where coal declined were industry, gas and railways, in all of which oil was taking its place. There were technical reasons for this, such as the start of railway dieselisation and the decline of carbonisation; but even on straight heating, as in industry, oil had great advantages. The oil companies competed for custom and once they had it they gave good service. Oil therefore naturally increased its share of the fuel market, even after 1961 when the Conservative Government put on the oil duty referred to below.

It is not surprising that the Coal Board took some time to adjust itself to the new situation of reduced demand – which at first it believed to be temporary. With 36 million tons of unsold coal at the end of 1959, production would obviously have to be reduced; further stockpiling was unthinkable. So both deep-mined and opencast output were cut back. Opencast has always been the more profitable, but it did not entail the social obligations of the collieries.

Early in 1961 Lord Robens became Chairman of the Board. He set himself to improve the sorry image of the National Coal Board and to woo the consumer – with considerable success. With this he combined a stout campaign to influence public opinion and Government to maintain a market for coal at 200 million tons.

An early success in his campaign was the imposition in the 1961 Budget of a duty of 2*d* a gallon (equivalent to about 30 per cent) on oil used for burning. This must have had some effect on the rising consumption of oil, which nevertheless, apart from transport and refinery fuel, increased from 43·2 million tons of coal equivalent in 1961 to 74 million tons in 1966. This was a concession wrung from a Conservative Government, who at first claimed that the duty was imposed for revenue purposes and not to assist the coal industry.

But in 1965 the campaign suffered a serious reverse. Both the 'National Plan' and the White Paper on 'Fuel Policy' contained estimates that by 1970 the market for coal was not likely to exceed 170–180 million a year. This forecast, which is likely to prove optimistic, gave great offence both to the Coal Board and the miners, who protested strongly and demanded that a market for 200 millions should be created by Government action.

The strongest points in the case against oil deployed by the Coal Board was that oil was not indigenous, that the crude oil had to be imported from countries not always friendly and that it cost foreign exchange. The last point is unfortunately somewhat obscure. The Government keeps secret the statistics required to compile an 'Oil Balance of Payments'. *The Economist* has compiled such an Oil Balance for 1963 which appears as Table 15 in the P.E.P. Report, *A Fuel Policy for Britain* (p. 209). This estimated the cost in foreign exchange of U.K. oil imports at £405 million, but that, allowing for all visibles and invisibles, the cost falls to £104 million.

The dependence on imports from doubtful countries is a valid point, as the events of 1956 and 1967 have shown. The remedy, as the oil industry points out, is to diversify operations and sources of supply on such a scale that any interruption can have only a limited effect. After all, substantial oil imports are a basic necessity.

But recently two further serious competitors to coal have appeared. One is North Sea natural gas – an indigenous fuel of high quality. It is a serious competitor because the substantial early discoveries justify the hopes that natural gas may become a major fuel, which might affect the whole pattern of energy use in Britain. Plans of future usage must therefore remain tentative till the full scope of the North Sea gas discoveries are revealed.

The other new competitor to coal is the second generation of nuclear power stations based on the air-gas-cooled reactor, of which Dungeness B Power Station is the first example. It is claimed that these stations can produce electricity more cheaply than the most modern coal-fired station. Dungeness B does not operate till 1971 and the claim has yet to be proved. Many previous claims advanced by nuclear enthusiasts have fallen to the ground. But if the claim is substantiated it will endanger the Coal Board's largest market – electricity generation – which has absorbed the untreated small coals which form about 38 per cent of its output. If the achievements of Dungeness B match the forecast, the market for power stations cannot be expected to grow to 100 million tons as the Coal Board has hoped in the past. The increase in the price of coal from April 1966 which added over £30 million to electricity's coal costs in 1966–7 makes the reliance on Dungeness B more than ever justifiable.

As a result of the Coal Industry Act 1967 the Government are now subsidising electricity to burn six extra million tons of coal per annum up to 1970–1 which they would prefer not to take. If this is merely a stop-gap to keep an orderly redeployment of miners, there is something to be said for it. But temporary subsidies have a habit of lingering on, long after their original justification has disappeared. The maximum of the four-year subsidy is fixed at £45 million.

Under the chairmanship of Lord Robens, the Coal Board set out to reform itself, become more consumer-conscious and adapt itself to a new world where it had to go out and sell its coal in competition with other fuels. This campaign had several aspects. Improving channels of retail distribution and modernising coal depots was one. The production of coal was increasingly mechanised and, in 1966–7, 140 million tons of coal came from mechanised output, compared with 83 million tons in 1960; but the output of large coal had fallen by almost half.

Above all, the Coal Board did everything possible to keep steady the pithead price of coal. Apart from increases in high-cost areas, the general price of coal remained steady from 1961 to 1966. During this period the index of retail prices rose by 17 per cent. As the statistics show, total costs per ton between 1961 and 1965 rose by 4s 1d per ton but proceeds per ton only by 1s 8d.

This change of policy in the 1960s had a substantial effect. Between 1961 and 1965 inland coal consumption dropped by only 7 million tons. Two of its major consumers – gas and railways – had announced programmes of changing over the base of their activities from coal to oil; in railways the rundown was rapid. Fortunately for the Coal Board, between 1961 and 1965 there was an increase of 15 million tons in the use of coal at power stations. Knowing that these bulk consumers were working to national policies, which only Government could influence, the Coal Board concentrated its publicity on the general domestic and industrial consumer. It co-operated with appliance manufacturers in launching new appliances – especially for central heating. As mentioned above, prices were kept steady, and both miners and public were reminded of that fact. The Board introduced a new 'heat service' for small industrial consumers under which it not only supplies the fuel but also undertakes all the work of operating a boiler plant, maintaining the plant day-by-day and providing for ash removal. To help it in these activities the Board recruited fuel engineers who could advise industrialists.

The domestic consumer was also wooed. In 1960 the Board had introduced a 'housewarming plan' under which the Board arranged through a finance house for loans at low rates of interest for the installation of up-to-date solid-fuel-burning appliances. By March 1967 £48 million had been advanced under this plan.

But 1966 was a bad year for the Coal Board. It was forced to put up prices from 1 April, though some types of coal were not affected immediately. Every one of its markets took less coal and inland consumption fell from 181 million tons in 1965–6 to 170 in 1966–7. Even electricity took less coal, partly because the increase in electricity slowed down and partly because a group of nuclear power stations came on stream in 1965–6.

In 1967–8 inland consumption fell further to 165·5 million tons. As a result stocks of unsold coal increased in 1967–8 by 6·4 million tons making a total of 26·8 million tons. Both 1966 and 1967 were years of economic stagnation and the Coal Board naturally suffered when its customers reduced their activities. But the scale of the decline in the demand for coal and its spread to all markets show that what is happening is in effect a 'flight from coal'. This would have been greater but for the subsidy for coal at power stations.

This decline must have a serious effect on the finances of the Coal Board. The advance in mechanisation in the 1960s had greatly increased productivity. Output per man shift at the face had risen from 79·5 cwt in 1960 to 116·7 cwt in 1967; in the same period output per man year had risen from 306 to 409 tons. In a labour-intensive industry such as coal-mining this great improvement gave a breathing space to the Coal Board and had helped it to hold back an increase in price.

Three times in the 1950s the Coal Board had given hostages to fortune by issuing plans for years ahead. In 1950 it published its *Plan for Coal*, which was a programme of capital development for the period 1950–65. It estimated that demand in 1961–5 would be between 230 and 250 million tons. In order to produce 240 million tons in 1965 it proposed to invest £520 million – at mid-1949 prices – plus £115 million for auxiliary activities. It anticipated employing 618,000 men in 1965 as against 698,000 in 1950.

Naturally in preparing a large-scale plan for a period so far ahead the Board had to protect itself by rather vague and sweeping provisos. No more than anyone else in 1950 could it foresee the unrelenting inflation of the post-war period with its drastic effects on levels of costs and prices.

In 1955 the Board, wiser by five years' experience, set about revising the Plan and in 1956 published the revision in the booklet, *Investing in Coal*. The target of 240 million tons for 1965 was reduced to 230 million – described as a 'considered estimate'. Instead of 618,000 men to produce 240 million tons, it now planned for 672,000 men to produce 230 million tons. This envisaged a small increase in productivity as, in 1955, 704,000 men were producing 208 million tons. Yet to achieve this smaller target a round figure of £1,000 million of capital would be required – £860 million on mines and £140 million on auxiliaries. Adding in the capital already spent since 1950, the total for the fifteen years 1950–65 would be £1,350 million – but at 1955 and not at 1949 prices as in the original plan.

But the falling consumption of coal of 1957–9 obviously made the plans of *Investing in Coal* out of date and necessitated a second revision of the *Plan for Coal*. This appeared in October 1959 as the *Revised Plan for Coal*. On 23 July 1959 Mr Maudling had given in the House of Commons the Government's estimate of the country's fuel requirements in 1965, which was important as influencing the Coal Board in revising its plans for capital development. His statement deserves quotation:

Some while ago, I said that the best calculation that we could make of the inland demand for energy in 1965 would be about 300 million tons coal equivalent. To reach that figure by 1965, the expansion that is taking place in the [coal] industry will have to go ahead very fast, but I still think that it is reasonable to take 300 million tons as a rough figure for the total energy demand in the middle 1960's. The amount which the coal industry will secure will depend on its competitive position (*Hansard*, vol. 608, col. 1559).

The Coal Board, spurred on by this statement, consulted all its major consumers and came out with a detailed estimate of demand in 1965 of 196 million tons. It is interesting to see what the experts of these major consumers anticipated they would require in coal five years ahead, and what in fact they did consume in the year 1965. The following table gives the figures – estimated and actual for 1965 – and actual for 1958.

COAL CONSUMPTION (million tons)

	Actual 1958	Estimated 1965	Actual 1965
Coke ovens	27·8	35	25·8
Gas	24·8	21·5	18·2
Electricity	46·2	55	70
Railways	10·4	6	2·8
Domestic	36·2	27	24
Total inland	202·8	196	184·3

(The above figures are for calendar years.)

In fairness to the Coal Board it stated in 1959 that it understood that the estimates for the coke ovens and the railways were on the high side. The Board summed up the *Revised Plan for Coal* by saying it would now work to a flexible plan with a range of outputs between 200 and 215 million tons. The capital expenditure required for 1960–5 was estimated at £535 million (at 1959 prices) and manpower in 1965 would be between 587,000 and 626,000 as compared with 652,000 in August 1959. In fact in 1965 average manpower was 469,000. So great was the increase in productivity that this much lower manpower produced 179 million tons of coal.

Perhaps the most interesting features of these various estimates is the failure of electricity supply to forecast its expansion in demand and the failure of the Coal Board to forecast the great increase in productivity. This increase was a great service to the national economy; it must have saved at least 100,000 men who could usefully be employed elsewhere.

The only important forecast which was accurate was Mr Maudling's. He forecast for 1965 an inland fuel consumption of 300 million tons of coal equivalent (i.e. valuing fuels by various conversion factors as coal). In fact, in 1965 total inland fuel consumption was 296·9 million tons of coal equivalent. In 1958 it had been 247·5 million tons. Between 1958 and 1965 the inland consumption of coal had dropped from 202·8 to 184·3 million tons; oil had risen from 47·2 to 102·8 million tons of coal equivalent (including oil for transport). Coal had not been sufficiently competitive to secure a share of the national increase in fuel consumption, all of which had gone to oil and nuclear power.

By 1965 it was obvious that the National Coal Board was carrying a volume of capital designed for a scale of operations which was not likely ever to be reached. A private company, finding itself in such a position, would go to the courts for authority to cut down its capital. A nationalised industry can only achieve this object by obtaining an Act of Parliament. The Government announced its proposals in a White Paper of November 1965 (Cmnd. 2805).

It might be useful to set out the capital structure of the National Coal Board at this date, after nineteen years of operation. Unlike other public Boards it had never issued any stock, because it was felt that the miners would object to paying interest to stockholders. Instead the Government paid out compensation in ordinary gilt-edged stock – not tied to coal in any way – and in turn the Coal Board repaid the Government in annuities which were to run for fifty years. This period was much too long. It meant that the repayments would be low but fifty years was far too long a period in relation to the life of the assets taken over by the Coal Board in 1947. They would be obsolete, if not physically worn out, at an early stage in the fifty-year period. That in fact proved to be the case. The total original liability for stocks and assets taken over was £388·1 million; at end March 1965 only £53·6 million had been paid off, leaving an outstanding liability of £334·5 million – a figure greatly in excess of £116 million, which was the written-down value of these assets.

This method of fifty-year terminable annuities was (apart from compensation) used for financing the Board till 1956. In 1957 the system was changed. From then on capital expenditure was financed by advances repayable in equal instalments over fifteen years, which as the Board says is 'a period which corresponds more closely with the average period over which depreciation of the Board's assets is provided' (1964–5 Report, vol. ii, p. 22). Advances to finance stocks of products were provided by short-term loans – any period from two to five years. These short-term loans became important in the late fifties when the Coal Board was compelled to stock huge quantities of coal and coke; at the end of 1959 these loans amounted to £125 million. As the stocks of unsold coal moved much more slowly than anticipated, it was realised that these short-term loans could not be repaid from the proceeds of the coal lying on the ground. So they were formally repaid and the Board was granted fifteen-year loans in lieu. By March 1965 the £125 million short-term loans had shrunk to £10 million.

At the end of March 1965 the capital structure of the Coal Board was as follows:

1. £334½ million owing for assets vested on nationalisation.
2. £220 million long-term debt – repayable over fifty years.
3. £333 million medium-term debt – repayable over fifteen years.
4. £10 million short-term debt.
5. £62½ million overdrafts, etc.

Total: £960 million.

In addition the Board, since its inception, had incurred an accumulated deficit of £91 million. The White Paper (para. 5) states that 'this deficit is attributable in large part to the action of successive Governments in not allowing the Board to increase inland prices at times and by amounts the Board considered desirable.' This is an exaggeration. In 1947, the first year of its life, the Coal Board incurred a deficit of £22·3 million. The two large deficits of £24 million in 1959 and £21·3 million in 1960 were due to the heavy cost of raising a large tonnage of coal and putting it on the ground unsold; at the end of 1959 these unsold stocks amounted to 36 million tons. The deficit of £19·6 million in 1955 was caused by large imports of coal sold at inland prices which were below cost of import. The deficits of these years amount to £88·8 million out of a total of £90·8 million. These figures are given because there is much emotive talk about the Coal Board's deficits which is not based on any analysis, and this statement in the White Paper repeats this talk.

The Government accepted the contention that in the 1950s the Coal Board had planned and incurred capital expenditure for an industry with a capacity for 240 million tons in 1965. 'As a result of the investment embarked upon, it now has to carry a burden of debt which hampers its efforts to hold its markets and contain its costs' (White Paper, para. 3). The Government therefore proposed to cancel about £400 million of the Board's outstanding liabilities, adding thereto £15 million to compensate for the Board's loss of revenue because the Government would not allow it to increase prices before April 1966. The effect of this would be that the Board would cease to be liable for £21·5 million of interest charges and for depreciation charges of £14·1 million. As the White Paper puts it (para. 8), 'the effect of relieving the Board of debt is to transfer the burden to the taxpayer, since the Exchequer will cease to be entitled to interest.' To put it another way, all the Board's liabilities to the Treasury in respect of vested assets and advances made from nationalisation to 28 March 1965 would be extinguished and replaced by a new loan amounting to £545 million dating also from 28 March 1965.

This loan was to be repaid in thirty-four equal annual instalments from March 1965, at the favourable interest of $4\frac{1}{8}$ per cent. This repeated the earlier mistaken arrangement of fixing a period which was far longer than the life of the assets; but of course the object was to reduce the annual burden of interest charges.

The method of treating the cancelled £415 million in the Board's accounts would be as follows. It would appear in the balance sheet as an increase of £415 million in the Board's reserve fund. The Board would have to secure the Minister's consent to make any debits against this £415 million – an arrangement to remain in force till March 1971. In the first year of this scheme – within three months of passing the Coal Industry Act 1965 – more than half of this reserve of £415 million was used up as follows:

	£ million
Accumulated deficit at 27 March 1965	90·8
Allowance for delay in price increases	24·8
Coke-oven assets	8·3
Colliery assets	99·2
	223·1

It will be observed that the estimated £15 million to compensate the Board for delay in allowing price increase has grown to £24·8 million. A further sum of £52·3 million was debited to the reserve in 1966–7, making a total of £275·4 million.

Section 2 (3) of the Coal Industry Act 1965 contains the curious provision that if, in any year, the Coal Board makes a surplus on revenue account, the Minister may direct that the surplus shall be handed over to the Exchequer. This is, in a way, reasonable when the Exchequer is carrying the losses. But it lowers the status of the Board and deprives it of all incentive to make a surplus. Incidentally it runs counter to the famous Section 1 (4) (3) of the Coal Industry Nationalisation Act 1946 which enjoins the Board to balance its revenue account 'on an average of good and bad years' – a phrase about which there has been much argument and which was interpreted as a period of five years in para. 19 (a) of the 1961 White Paper on the Financial and Economic Obligations of the Nationalised Industries. It also runs counter to Section 30 of the 1946 Act which allows the Board to decide for itself how to use a surplus – though Section 30 (b) contains a proviso empowering the Minister to butt in and direct the Board what to do with the surplus. Nineteen years afterwards that proviso is made more definite in the 1965 Act, though experience has shown that a Coal Board surplus is an extremely remote possibility and that it will be even more remote in the future with shrinking output and increasing overheads.

Let us now look at industrial relations in the nationalised coal industry since 1947. After all, it was the persistence of the miners which brought about the transfer of the industry to public ownership. Their sufferings and harsh treatment in the inter-war years intensified their determination to such a degree that the whole Labour movement accepted the nationalisation of the mines as their first priority when they attained power.

What the miners expected from the transfer to public ownership was never very clear. The colliery companies would disappear. National instead of district settlements of wages would follow. As the colliery owners would be getting no profits, the proceeds available to the miners would be greater and they would enjoy a higher standard of living.

The arrival of public ownership in a great basic industry aroused hopes and expectations. These are well described in the peroration of Mr Herbert Morrison's speech winding up the second-reading debate on the Coal Industry Nationalisation Bill:

> If the management and the miners do not rise to the occasion, I admit this experience will go crash. Therefore I appeal to all of them, miners and management, and particularly to the miners I would say, emancipate yourselves from the understandable inhibitions created by the past. Emancipate yourselves from the mentality thrust upon you by a crude capitalism. This is vital, this is essential, if this socialised industry is to take with it miners and management, to become co-operators and partners in a great and worthy adventure for the common good. That is the spirit in which we approach the problems of this industry (*Parl. Debates*, vol. 418, col. 972).

Much may be forgiven Mr Morrison's rhetoric, but he must have known that such an appeal could have little effect. If he did not know, he was very ignorant of the conditions of coal-mining.

What could nationalisation mean to the individual miner? What evidence of the change-over would be before him? What benefits would he derive from a National Coal Board instead of a colliery owner?

To begin with, the 'boss' had not gone on 1 January 1947. He was still there but behind him there were other bosses reaching all the way back to London. It was all somewhat bewildering – well put by a miner who described working for the National Coal Board as working for a ghost. The manager of the pit was not in a position to be easier with the workers; on the contrary he had to be more careful. In the past an awkward problem could be put to the managing director on the telephone and some decision obtained quickly. Now it was more difficult with the hierarchy of group, area, division and Board; the manager had to go warily.

The miners found it hard to realise that the National Coal Board was in a more difficult position than the coal-owners. The price of coal was a public issue of importance and the Board could not increase it at will; it had to consult the Government, who were often awkward. Of course the Board made as many concessions as possible and would have been only too pleased to have made more. But concessions were regarded as long overdue and led to further demands. In 1950 Mr Ebby Edwards, N.C.B. member in charge of industrial relations, who had previously been Secretary of the Miners' Federation for fourteen years, told the Miners' Annual Conference that the concessions made since vesting date were costing nearly £125 million a year. He added, 'If goodwill can be bought, the Coal Board have paid for it – sometimes out of future production that we did not get.'

But this was to be expected. In all Western countries the problem of manning the coal mines since the Second World War has been one of great difficulty. Coal-mining is a dirty and dangerous occupation and, in the post-war era of labour shortage everywhere, why should a man choose to be a miner? On the whole Britain was fortunate, if not unique, in having a native manpower to work in the mines; in most countries this work was largely carried on by depressed workers such as refugees and immigrants. The reason why Britain could find local labour was that in the older areas, such as Scotland, Northumberland, Durham and South Wales, coal-mining was highly localised and often the only industry available for the men; they had to become coal miners or leave home. Hence the tradition of son following father into the pit. In the newer areas in the Midlands and Yorkshire, the Coal Board was in competition with numerous industries for labour and was not very successful in recruitment. It did its best by starting in 1962 the Inter-divisional Transfer Scheme for moving miners from the older to the newer coalfields; but this was only a modest help. 8,801 men were transferred between April 1962 and March 1967 (1966–7 Report, para. 138).

Up to the end of 1957 the miners' position was very strong and the Coal Board could do little more by negotiation than delay and slightly modify the miners' demands. Gradually the miners forged to the front as the best-paid workers. Considering the nature of their occupation and the acute shortage of coal, the miners were charging for their labour what the market would bear. Coal-mining is still a labour-intensive industry. Even in 1966–7, with all the developments in mechanisation, wages, salaries, etc., formed just over 60 per cent of costs. But this was a decline on 1947, when these items amounted to more than 70 per cent of costs. This figure was also partly due to the fact that since 1947 the Coal Board has rightly raised the standard of welfare benefits of its workers from a very low to a very high level. So steadily and frequently the price of coal went up in the 1950s.

But improvement in the quality of coal was slow and what seemed to the public repeated hold-ups to ransom did much to create a public opinion adverse to coal, which, as soon as alternative fuels became available after 1957, asserted itself with increasing force to the detriment both of Coal Board and coal miner. This reluctance to use coal did not apply only to individuals but to whole industries; both gas and railways were determined to reduce their dependence on coal. This was a striking example of how even a powerful monopoly must exercise its powers with care and consideration; the coal-mining industry up to the end of the fifties showed little of either.

Occasionally the miners could be roused to understand they were working in a nationalised industry and that their work in producing coal was of national importance and not merely a matter of their pay packet. The outstanding case was the appeal in January 1951 in a letter to each miner from Mr Attlee, the Prime Minister, to increase output by 3 million tons to avert a recurrence of a fuel crisis – as happened in 1947. The appeal was successful. In 1951 the miners obtained a second week's holiday but renounced it for 1952 – obtaining two weeks' pay for the one week's holiday. But such occasional incidents did little to affect the general picture of steady – and successful – pressure from the National Union of Mineworkers for improved pay and conditions.

Despite these improvements the Board had great difficulty in maintaining the manpower in the mines. All attempts to import foreign labour were turned down by the miners – even if their union executive agreed. Between 1947 and 1957 the average number of wage-earners employed by the Board fluctuated around 700,000. One can say that after the improvements in 1947 and 1948, which repaired the obvious damage resulting from the war, the number of men, the tonnage produced and the productivity as measured by output per man shift or output per man year remained fairly static. Peak output was in 1952 at 212·4 million tons; in 1957 it was 207·4 million tons.

During this period of ten years the Board was desperately trying to improve the coal mines by capital investment. But this is a slow business. The Board was badly hampered by the shortage of technical and managerial skill which it inherited and which was brought out by the Fleck Report in 1954. But coal-mining had to run fast in order to stand still; being an extractive industry it loses each year some millions of tons of capacity – four millions have been suggested – by the diminution or exhaustion of seams under exploitation.

After 1957 the picture changes. Coal loses its monopoly and has to fight hard to keep its markets. Output falls and stocks accumulate on the ground, reaching 36 million tons at the end of 1959. The average number of workers over a year falls from 710,000 in 1957 to 401,000 in 1967; by April 1968 they were 362,000. As the shadows lengthened over the industry, the younger men tended to leave. The average age of the workers, which had been static between 1947 and 1957 when it was 40·5 years, increased every year after; in December 1966 it was 43·5. The manpower in coal-mining is therefore ageing. For instance the number of men between 21 and 30 dropped from 133,000 in 1950 (20 per cent) to 50,900 in 1966 (12 per cent). But in the same period the group aged 55 to 65 increased from 88,500 (13 per cent) to 101,400 (nearly 25 per cent). The favoured recruit of the Coal Board is the school-leaver, but in its 1965–6 Report (para. 136) the Board admitted that it 'found it difficult to attract school-leavers and other juveniles into the industry'.

In the period after 1957 severe competition compelled the Coal Board to keep prices steady for several years at a time. The scope for increasing miners' wages was therefore limited. But a new factor now appears – a major increase in productivity. The substantial capital investment of the 1950s begins to pay off. Power-loading output increased from 23 per cent in 1957 to 85·7 per cent in 1966–7 and will move to about 100 per cent in the early 1970s. The average output per man year overall increased from 296 tons in 1957 to 409 tons in 1967; the average output per man shift overall increased from 24·86 cwt in 1957 to 38·18 cwt in 1967.

It will be observed that the percentage increase in output per man shift is much greater than the percentage increase in output per man year; the Coal Board now quotes the former figure only and ignores the latter. By doing so it boosts its productivity achievements. But in fact the output per man year is the more important figure, because it shows not only the average productivity per shift but also the number of shifts worked during the year.

This brings us to the question of absenteeism in the mines, to which little reference is made nowadays. But it is important and becoming more so as the mines become highly mechanised. In the 1965–6 Report the Board broke a silence of some years. Pointing out that absence of all workers in 1965–6 was 18 per cent (in 1957 it was 13·8 per cent), it goes on to say: 'The rise in absence was one of the major factors contributing to the fall in the industry's output and the worsening financial results. The effects of a high rate of absence are becoming more serious because the expansion of mechanisation means that manpower shortage in coal-face teams have an increasingly disruptive effect on production and pro-ductivity' (para. 50). In 1957 the mineworker worked on the average 4·68 shifts per week out of 5; in 1966 the average number had dropped to 4·13 shifts. An interesting sidelight on this is the fact that 'in March 1966 the average running time for all power-loaders was 126 minutes a shift; an increase of 15 minutes a shift would yield at least 15 million tons of extra output at little additional cost' (1965–6 Report, para. 33).

Increasing productivity has made it possible for the Board in the early sixties to meet most of the demands of the miners for im-proved pay, which were in line with the demands put forward by workers in other industries. In 1965–6, for example, increases in pay amounted to £12 million. Though coal-mining is still a labour-intensive industry, overheads are becoming more important. The large capital invested in machinery is not being economically used. The Board is doing everything possible to concentrate operations on the most efficient collieries and the most profitable faces in those collieries. In 1957 there were 4,200 coal faces in operation with an average yield of 195 tons a day. In March 1967 they had been reduced to 1,674 faces and the average output for 1966–7 was 462 tons a day.

Coal-mining in Britain is on the decline, as it is throughout Western Europe. Only in the United States, with their very exceptional conditions, can coal be sold at a price and a quality competitive with other fuels.

The industry has deserved well of the country. From 1945 to 1958 it alone carried the responsibility of providing the British economy with the necessary energy. If for that reason alone, the employees of the industry deserve the greatest care and con-sideration.

In the last ten years there have been great technological changes and discoveries and there are now three other primary fuels in competition with coal. That competition will become fierce, if not overwhelming, in the 1970s. The economic and technical advantages of these three other primary fuels will ensure them a rapidly increasing market. If Britain is to continue as a great modern industrial nation, it is imperative that this diversification of energy uses should take place with all possible speed and with the least possible hindrance. Despite the powerful publicity employed on its behalf since 1961, coal will, in this competition, find it most difficult to retain support.

All this poses a most embarrassing problem both for industry and Government. The diminution in the coal industry must be carried out with a minimum of hardship to all who have given their life to the hard and dangerous work of mining coal. That is now generally accepted and the Coal Industry Act 1967 embodies a policy for such relief up to 1971. No responsible person grudges the public expenditure required for this purpose.

The Government are doing their best to protect coal, by prohibition on imports, subsidies for the use of unwanted coal, by a heavy duty on oil which is about one-third of its value and by slowing down the closures of uneconomic pits. All these amount to a heavy burden on the economy, which should not be increased further. The pressure to step up the protection of coal will intensify, if only because the forecast of a run-down in gross inland coal consumption from 174·7 million tons in 1966 to 152 million tons in 1970 is likely to be optimistic; 1967 has seen a decline of 12 million to 163 million tons and there are still three years to go. The country's economic difficulties in 1968 will not conduce to an expanding use of energy.

Lord Robens continually emphasises the danger to the morale of the staff and workers if the industry is run down too rapidly. He is right to bring this problem to the public notice; though it can be doubted whether repeated emphasis of this problem does not accentuate it and make matters worse. Coal is our oldest industry – older than cotton, which has been declining far longer than coal. But because coal is publicly owned and decisions are centralised, every feature of its changing fortunes is highlighted with great publicity. There is no scope for local and individual decisions, which have been the feature of cotton.

From the broadest national view, if the country can obtain its energy requirements with a much-reduced manpower and a dirty and dangerous occupation cut down in size, it can only be regarded as a great advantage. But the transition is most painful.

Table II: British Railways

	1948	1952	1956	1959	1962	1963	1964	1965	1966	1967
Gross receipts (£ million)	346	414.6	481	457.4	465.1	468.6	474.1	466.2	463.8	438.7
Operating expenses (£ million)	323.7	377.6	497.5	499.4	569.1	550.2	541.6	545.7	542.1	536.1
Net receipts or net deficit* (£ million)	22.3 (surplus)	37 (surplus)	16.5 (deficit)	42 (deficit)	104 (deficit)	81.6 (deficit)	67.5 (deficit)	73.1 (deficit)	71.6 (deficit)	90.4 (deficit)
Railway staffs (oos) (at end of year)	649	601	571	519	476	439	399	365	339	318
Passenger journeys (million)	1024	1017	1029	1069	965	938	928	865	835	837
Average receipt per passenger mile (pence)	1.4	1.31	1.45	1.51	1.94	1.97	2.00	2.2	2.31	2.36
Total passenger receipts (£ million)	122.6	111.9	127.5	140	161.1	161.8	167.2	173.5	179.4	179.7
Total freight train traffic (million tons)	273	285	277	234	228	235	240	229	214	201
Of which coal and coke (million tons)	158	171	168	144	145	151	147	138.3	131.8	122.2
Average receipt per net ton mile (pence)	2.0	2.69	3.18	3.27	3.51	3.67	3.49	3.51	3.51	3.44
Freight train receipts (£ million)	180.5	250.3	284.1	241.1	235.7	235.4	233	225.5	216.9	194.9

* This surplus or deficit is calculated on railway operations, including collection and delivery. The total deficit on the railways is much larger than this operating deficit, which does not include the unpaid interest. E.g. in 1964 the total was £120.9 million, in 1965 £132.4 million and in 1966 £134.7 million; the worst year was 1962 when the total deficit was £159 million. For 1967 the total deficit was £152 million. For 1968 the total deficit was estimated by the Minister of Transport at £153 million.

Source: Annual Reports of Transport Commission and British Rail

3 Transport

NATIONALISATION of transport was the most ambitious effort of the Labour Government. In coal, gas and electricity the industries taken over were definite and the Acts easily determined what units were to come under public ownership. Later on, in iron and steel, the Labour Government had an awkward problem of definition, which could only be solved by a surgical operation.

But in the case of transport there was no surgical operation. Transport was to be taken over as a whole. A great group of transport industries was to be taken over and put under the control of the British Transport Commission. Its writ ran far. Section 2 (1) of the Transport Act 1947 started by giving the Commission power 'to carry goods and passengers by rail, road and inland waterway within Great Britain'. The Section then gave it further powers 'to provide port facilities and facilities for traffic by inland waterway', to store goods, consign goods on behalf of other persons, provide hotels and places of refreshment where required by passengers, and, finally, provide such other amenities as may be required by its passengers. There were other powers which round off these major powers.

But the general significance of the Section was clear. Parliament intended that there should be one body solely responsible for the transport of persons and goods by road, rail and canal. That, at a stroke, made the British Transport Commission into a giant of a kind previously unknown in any country. It launched a vast and novel experiment.

The rail part of its function was clear enough. The four main-line railways – each of which was in itself a major industrial enterprise – were to be taken over. The Act provided that they were to be managed by a body to be known as the Railway Executive, under the control of the Transport Commission. The Executive, like the other Executives referred to later, was to be an agent of the Commission, which delegated powers under a scheme prepared by the latter and approved by the Minister of Transport.

Nowadays it is difficult to believe that the Executive responsible for running the whole railway system of the country was a subordinate body with very limited powers; for instance, it could borrow no money except temporarily for current business and then only when authorised by the Commission. It could only approve expenditure on works up to £25,000, which was later increased to £50,000. The Railway Executive was in all questions of policy subordinate to the Commission. It was to carry out any direction given by the Commission. So far had centralisation gone.

The hotels and catering facilities of the railways were hived off and put in charge of an Hotels Executive.

All canals and the docks owned by the railways were hived off under the control of the Docks and Inland Waterways Executive, which had a mixed bag of responsibilities. What was there in common between canals and docks except water? Canals and docks posed very different problems, and it is not surprising to find that the Docks and Inland Waterways Executive had an undistinguished career. For about a century the canals had languished, and those owned by the railways had languished most of all. What was required was a government policy on canals, but the Labour Government preferred to hand over this difficult problem to the Transport Commission.

The Annual Reports of the Commission constantly complain about canals. It wants to get rid of them, but cannot. It wants to hand them over to other authorities for drainage or water-supply purposes, but find that impossible or very difficult. Before 1947 the Government had been responsible for the Caledonian and Crinan Canals, which had always lost money. The Labour Government took the opportunity of the 1947 Act to hand them over to the British Transport Commission, which frequently refers ruefully to these unwelcome endowments.

The London Transport Executive was a rehashed London Passenger Transport Board. This creation of Mr Morrison, as explained in Chapter 1, had been in existence since 1933, and by 1948 was well established. It had done excellent work because, under the able and experienced leadership of Lord Ashfield and Mr Frank Pick, it had built up a very efficient transport system for the Londoner. With the absorption of the municipal trams, which were to be replaced by buses, London Transport's system was complete. In 1933 there had been preserved continuity of policy and management. The original London Transport was a good example where the effect of change of ownership was trivial because there was no change of management; it is drastic changes in management which have created the problem of the nationalised industries.

In the inter-war years, carriage of goods by road had increased considerably, and the railways complained bitterly about this competition. They were subject to strict control in fixing of charges, and had all the onerous obligations of a 'common carrier'. They could not pick and choose their traffic. On the other hand, the road hauliers could and did choose. The railways fought back. They acquired road haulage interests themselves. As a result of the Road and Rail Traffic Act 1933, road haulage became subject to a system of licensing, and only holders of 'A' and 'B' licences could carry goods for reward. A holder of a 'C' licence could only carry his own goods. Though the railways were assisted by this Act, competition from road haulage steadily increased.

Under Section 52 of the 1947 Act, all holders of 'A' and 'B' licences, operating more than twenty-five miles from their base, had, from an appointed day, to receive a permit from the Transport Commission. The appointed day was 1 February 1950, and from that date an elaborate system of permits developed which caused great resentment because, under Section 52 (2) of the Act, the Transport Commission, in deciding whether to grant a permit or not, had full discretion to act as it pleased, subject to a proviso on certain local interests. The Transport Commission frankly explained in paragraph 7 of its Report for 1951 that under the 1947 Act, which granted it a complete monopoly of long-distance road haulage, it could have regard only to its own interests in granting a permit.

The Commission would then buy out the undertakings, operating under permits, and in due course would thus acquire a monopoly of the long-distance carriage of goods by road as it already had of the carriage of goods by rail. For dealing with the road haulage undertakings, the Commission set up a Road Haulage Executive.

Apart from London Transport, the British Transport Commission did not take over road passenger transport. It did acquire, however, the share capital of important bus companies, such as Tillings and Scottish Motor Traction, which continued to be operated as bus companies. The 1947 Act trod warily on the subject of road transport. After all, great municipalities, many of them under Labour control, operated their own passenger transport systems, and would have fought to the death before surrendering them. There was no technical justification for transferring municipal transport undertakings to a National Board, as there was in the case of electricity undertakings which had to be operated as part of a national system through the C.E.B. grid. Glasgow or Manchester could quite well transport their citizens in their own buses and trams without supervision from London.

In the Transport Bill 1967 Mrs Castle, the Minister of Transport, recognised this and provided that passenger transport of all kinds should be under local control.

The arrangements in the 1947 Act for road passenger transport were therefore different from those for road haulage. Under Section 63 of the Act, the Transport Commission was to carry out a review of passenger road transport services, and determine the areas in respect of which Area Road Transport Schemes were to be prepared and submitted to the Minister of Transport.

The Transport Commission ultimately prepared a road passenger scheme for the Northern Area, that is, Northumberland, Durham and the North Riding of Yorkshire, and started work on two other schemes for East Anglia and south-west England. The change of government policy in 1952 put an end to these schemes.

In a similar manner the Transport Commission was empowered under Section 66 to review all trading harbours in the country and prepare schemes for groups of harbours. The Commission had taken over only the docks owned by the railways, which represented about 40 per cent of total port facilities. The most important of these docks were Southampton, the Humber and South Wales. But the main ports such as London, Merseyside, Manchester and the Clyde had never been owned by the railways, and were administered by public authorities.

In 1949–50 the Docks and Inland Waterways Executive visited various ports, and in September 1951 the Commission published its Reports. A group scheme was prepared to cover the Tees and the Hartlepools. Under this scheme the Commission would become owner of all port facilities in that area, but leave them under local management. In the case of the Clyde and Aberdeen the Commission suggested ownership by Independent Harbour Boards. These schemes also were dropped when there was a change of government policy in 1952.

But perhaps the most onerous responsibility laid on the Transport Commission was in respect of charges schemes. These were to be prepared in respect of all services provided by the Commission, and were to be submitted to the Transport Tribunal. Two years were allowed from the passing of the 1947 Act for the preparation of these schemes. This was subsequently extended for another two years until August 1951, and then for a third two years. The scheme of passenger charges in the London area was submitted to and approved by the Transport Tribunal and came into force on 1 October 1950. A further passenger charges scheme both for London and the country as a whole was lodged with the Transport Tribunal in April 1951, and came into force for London on 2 March 1952, and for the railways as a whole on 1 May 1952. But charges schemes for passengers were simple compared with charges schemes for freight. On these, discussions with interested parties were most prolonged, and were therefore not complete by August 1951.

A scheme for goods charges was a most involved piece of work. The basis of charge for the railways had always been the value of the goods carried. It was now proposed to replace this by 'loading capability', which was a much less definite basis for charge. The Commission, in its Report for 1950 (p. 26), summed up the work in the following paragraph:

The preparation of a Charges Scheme covering all the varying factors relative to the three forms of transport is a big task. During the year, every possible advance was made with the object of submitting a draft scheme for merchandise, including coal and coke traffic, to the Transport Tribunal by the 6th August, 1951; but it is improbable that any such scheme can at present lay down a detailed basis for road haulage rates and charges.

The change of Government at the end of 1951 and the announcement of a change in transport policy put an end to the preparation of these charges schemes.

As the British Transport Commission was acquiring a monopoly in the transport of goods by rail, road and water, some such charges scheme was necessary so that every consumer should know precisely what he was to be charged. But the prolonged discussions and delays in preparing the scheme which in the end was abandoned, showed all the incredible difficulties of operating such a large-scale monopoly. Even if the scheme had been completed and submitted to the Transport Tribunal, the hearings would probably have taken a year or so, and therefore from start to finish the

c

preparation and putting into force of a charges scheme for goods would have taken five to six years. As soon as the scheme had been approved and put into force, some revision would have become necessary and such revision again would have taken a considerable time. After all, we live in a changing world, and new products and changes in products continually appear which would have involved changes in the scheme. Had it therefore been completed, in all its vast mass of detail, the scheme would have been continually subject to change, and argument between the Commission and the traders who were compelled to use its transport facilities would have been unceasing.

To sum up, the Transport Commission had the herculean tasks of (*a*) owning, controlling and reorganising the whole railway system; (*b*) taking over some 3,800 road haulage undertakings and unifying them into a public monopoly; (*c*) owning and controlling all road and rail passenger transport in the London Area; (*d*) reviewing the passenger road transport facilities for the rest of the country, some of which they already owned, and preparing area schemes of reorganisation; (*e*) surveying the harbours of the country and preparing group schemes of reorganisation; (*f*) preparing charges schemes for passenger and freight transport by road, rail and inland waterway. In addition, it had taken over all canals and all the docks formerly owned by the railways. It had also, of course, taken over the ships and hotels formerly owned by the railways. Incidentally it had also acquired the well-known travel agents, Thomas Cook & Son.

In short, the ultimate objective was that no person or freight was to be transported for reward by rail, road or water, except under the jurisdiction of the Transport Commission and its subsidiaries, or under some scheme promulgated by the Commission and approved by the Minister. It was to be the most complete and all-embracing transport monopoly in the world. Even in coastal shipping, Section 70 of the Transport Act 1947 gave the Commission power to enter into agreements with persons engaged in coastal shipping, in order to co-ordinate (blessed word!) those persons' activities with those of the Transport Commission. Section 71 provided that the Minister of Transport should set up an Advisory Committee on Coastal Shipping, half of whose members were to be representatives of the Commission.

When all the schemes envisaged by the Act had been completed, the only transport outside the control of the Commission were taxis, private motor cars and 'C' licence vehicles. Also certain special traffics, such as carriage of liquids in bulk, furniture removing, etc., were left undisturbed.

This was an incredible weight of responsibility to lay on a small group of men. It is true that the Transport Commission operated through Executives, but the Transport Commission was the sole owner of all the undertakings operated by the Executives. These legally formed one undertaking for which the Commission was responsible to the Minister of Transport and to Parliament. In December 1949 that undertaking employed 895,000 persons, or 4 per cent of all those in civil employment in Great Britain. The salaries and wages bill exceeded £300 million (1949 Report, para. 49). The net fixed assets of the Commission at the same date were £1,609·8 million (1949 Report, para. 162).

The Transport Commission was a small group of five men of advancing years. Only one was under sixty: one was over seventy. The task before them required at least twenty years of hard, steady and purposeful effort. Within a year of the start they had suffered a serious loss in the death of Lord Ashfield.

The task of reorganisation, involving the co-ordination and integration of all forms of transport, was undertaken at an especially difficult time, just after the end of a most exhausting war. Many immediate problems required attention, and had to be dealt with before coping with the programme of reorganisation. The Transport Commission had the function of planning a reorganisation of facilities, which were all in a very run-down condition. The public impatiently awaited an improvement in transport services, as they had been led by Labour ministers to expect that the Transport Commission would rapidly bring about a wonderful transformation. The speeches of ministers during the second reading of the Transport Bill in December 1946 showed an incredible belief in the virtues of their 'chosen Instrument' for nationalising transport, and parts of those speeches well deserve quotation.

In his speech in moving the second reading of the Transport Bill on 16 December 1946 (*Hansard*, vol. 431, col. 1623) Mr Barnes, Minister of Transport, said, *inter alia*:

The Commissioners have to carry through the task of integrating all forms of transport covered by the Bill and – this I particularly emphasise – to see that all parts of the country are adequately served. By that I mean the inclusion of rural and sparsely populated areas. These districts have never had the transport facilities they need. It is only by a unified system of which the cost can be spread over the whole system, that we shall be able to overcome this state of affairs.

Later:

The Commission will have to carry out large-scale capital expenditure in rebuilding our railway stations to make them centres of transport. Travel in this country is becoming a disagreeable thing, something to be endured to get somewhere, rather than a pleasure as it should be. I depend on the Commission with its wide powers radically to alter that state of affairs.

Mr Morrison, Lord President of the Council, wound up the debate and elaborated these statements. He said (*Hansard*, vol. 431, col. 2076):

The Commission will have a splendid opportunity to weld an efficient instrument to meet the transport needs of the country. The new concern will be absolutely free to go for sheer efficiency right from the beginning and to use assets in the way that is best. They will be able to write off those miserable rolling stocks in which the lower middle and working classes of Greater London on the Eastern side have to travel. They will have at their disposal ample capital – at low cost and at low interest rates – unwelcome though that is in certain quarters. We can use in these new circumstances skilled minds in this vast industry to the best advantage; and they will enable, with the new conditions, a bold and considered programme of transport development to take place which would have been utterly impossible in the conditions of the transport industry between the Wars.

At the end of his speech Mr Morrison asserted: 'the Government have brought in this Bill as a result, not of abstract dogmatic or doctrinaire belief, but because they believe in it. We believe it will improve the efficiency and public service of British Transport'.

Incidentally it is interesting to note that, earlier in his speech, Mr Morrison had discussed the blessed word 'co-ordination' and had come out with this remark: 'I think co-ordination is a much abused word in Parliamentary and political language in these days. It has varying conflicting interpretations according to the point of view of those who use it.'

What are we to make of the language of Mr Barnes and Mr Morrison? They knew perfectly well that the country's transport system was in a terribly run-down condition – it was a fact patent to all. Had not the Chancellor of the Exchequer, Dr Dalton, pointed out that the nation was taking over 'a poor bag of assets'? Why, therefore, should responsible ministers such as Mr Morrison and Mr Barnes, both well versed in transport matters, promise a complete revolution in transport as soon as the Transport Commission took over?

The most charitable interpretation to be put upon these remarks is that ministers were just uttering vague hopes boldly disguised as prophecies.

Labour Government policy on transport caused an upheaval by bringing all transport under the sole ownership of the Transport Commission. That created problems of organisation which delayed for years essential post-war re-equipment. However able the Commission, it is very doubtful whether it could have moved faster, because the undertaking was so vast that it could hardly be managed at all. In this connection it is worth remembering the famous saying of Lord Stamp, who was head of the largest railway in Britain, the London Midland and Scottish Railway, and who said that 'the efficient management of any concern really rested upon what could be supervised by the brain of one competent person'. If that was his view about the L.M.S. Railway, which formed about one-third of the responsibilities of the Railway Executive, what could be said of the undertaking of the Transport Commission? Could it be described as a manageable undertaking?

The argument that the nationalised industries are units too vast to manage is often countered by the argument that there are many great industrial organisations, especially in the United States. This argument overlooks the fact that these organisations are the result of a slow growth. Accordingly staff and workers have also expanded gradually, and in doing so have developed a tradition and an *esprit de corps*. On the other hand the great undertakings brought into being by the nationalisation Acts were created overnight; they had to build their organisations in the void, so to speak, taking over staffs who were bewildered by the change in loyalties and responsibilities. The break with the past was too drastic. Most of the staff had served in compact units, with strong personal or local characteristics. Now they found themselves part of a vast machine, with an extended chain of command reaching to some remote body in London.

The peculiar difficulty of the Transport Commission was that, in addition to managing the group of industries entrusted to it, the 1947 Act imposed upon it the functions of continuous change and development. This new and untried organisation had to take over and reorganise road haulage and road passenger transport, and

survey and reorganise all the ports in Britain. To some extent the
two latter groups of functions were optional, but the Commission
was very conscious of the duty laid upon it under Section 3 (1) of
the Act 'to provide or secure or promote the provision of, an
efficient, adequate, economical and properly integrated system of
public inland transport and port facilities within Great Britain for
passengers and goods'.

It is not surprising, therefore, that there developed a conviction
that this massive and centralised structure of the Commission
required change. What had not been realised was that the vast
programme of integration of road haulage, road passenger transport
and port facilities with the transport industries already taken over
could only be carried out under great pressure, and was possible
only if strongly backed by Government. The completion of the
programme was optimistically thought to require ten years, but
those ten years would have had to be ten years of determined
Socialist rule. The difficulties and opposition which the Transport
Commission came up against, as it struggled to carry out the
programme of the 1947 Act, brought increasing resentment. Even
ten years would have been too short a period, but had the Labour
Government lasted for ten years, integration might have been too
far advanced to be disturbed. The movement towards integration
meant continuous struggle against many interests – not only
private enterprise such as road hauliers, but public authorities such
as the Municipalities and Harbour Boards. The procedure provided in the Act was slow and lengthy, as all the interests affected
(and they were very numerous) were entitled to be consulted. Even
when all the prescribed procedure had been followed, the scheme
had to be embodied in a Draft Order published by the Minister.
Objections could be raised to the Draft Order, and if they were
sustained, the Minister had to order a public local enquiry on the
results of which he would consider the Draft Order afresh.

No scheme, therefore, could go through without the determined
backing of Government. Even the Labour Government, in the last
year or two of its existence, gently laid on one side schemes of
integration of road passenger transport. They could foresee the
storm which a Draft Order would provoke. It is not surprising,
therefore, that the advent of a Conservative Government late in
1951 put an end to the various schemes of integration on which the
Commission had laboured so hard.

By 1951 it was apparent that the Transport Commission was

making slow progress in the great programme of integrating all forms of transport envisaged in the 1947 Act. Its greatest success was in the building up of a Road Haulage Service. By the end of 1951 the Commission had acquired 3,766 undertakings of which 3289 had been acquired by compulsion (1951 Report, para. 7). This process of large-scale acquisition inevitably took time, and the longer the period, the greater the opposition.

The Conservative Party had always proclaimed their opposition to the nationalisation of long-distance road haulage. It was not surprising that, when they came into power at the end of 1951, they should produce a White Paper (Cmd. 8538) proposing drastic changes in the Transport Act 1947.

Road haulage was to be denationalised and the Road Haulage Executive abolished. The Railway Executive was also to be abolished and a decentralised system to be set up for the railways. The road-haulage vehicles taken over by the Commission were to be sold and the twenty-five-mile limit on the operation of road haulage was to be abolished. The scheme-making powers of the Commission for Road Passenger Transport were to be brought to an end and the Road Passenger Executive abolished.

This White Paper was followed by a Bill, which embodied changes which were the result of much discussion. The most important changes were the freeing of the railways in the matter of charges, which, in future, were to be maxima. Only these maximum charges were to be published and the Commission was under no obligation to publish reductions granted to any one customer. The railways were thus relieved of the obligation to make the same charge for the same traffic and to avoid the giving of undue preference. At last the burden of the common carrier obligations was to be lifted, and railways were now to be empowered to compete with road haulage. The Bill embodied a special procedure for temporary authorisation of increased charges which mitigated the prolonged agony of the enquiries by the Transport Tribunal. This Bill became law on 6 May 1953.

Let us now turn from the planning and co-ordinating activities to the day-to-day operations of the Commission and its Executives.

In addition to the task of reorganising and integrating all forms of transport the Commission had very serious problems of day-to-day management. Transport is a service which failed to achieve recognition. The nationalised fuel industries, on the other hand, particularly coal and electricity, were regarded as basic – largely due to the shocking fuel crisis of February 1947 which put millions out of work because there was not enough coal to keep the power stations working.

Then there were acute shortages of all manufactured goods: clothing was rationed, furniture was scarce and the housing shortage frightful. The nation's resources for investment were strained to the limit and somehow or other investment in railways and roads did not seem so urgent. The railways taken over in 1948 were in poor shape. No substantial investment had been made in the inter-war years when the railways had been very depressed. During the war the railways had been used mercilessly and their assets were worn out.

The Transport Commission took over on 1 January 1948. It did not receive from the Government capital to enable it to carry out reconstruction. In 1949 the Commission concluded that it could 'do little more than preserve their undertaking in a reasonable working condition' and that it was 'impracticable for the Commission to submit to the Minister of Transport a programme of reorganisation and development under Section 4 (2) of the Transport Act 1947, (Annual Report for 1949, para. 23). In these circumstances it seemed absurd to talk of 'co-ordinating and integrating transport', but the Commission had to go on with the task. As we have seen above, the Labour Government seemed to have the queer idea that, because the Commission controlled a vast undertaking, it had vast resources at its disposal. This completely overlooked the fact that the Commission would require great resources to bring its undertaking to a reasonable standard of efficiency, before it could proceed to the co-ordinating and integrating.

It was not only in capital development that the Commission suffered in comparison with the other nationalised industries; it suffered also in the matter of charges. The Coal, Electricity and Gas Acts left their respective industries free to increase their charges as they wished, although Mr Macmillan, in his Budget speech of 1956, seemed to think the contrary. Occasionally, in deference to government policy, these Boards would temporarily hold back increases in charges, but statutorily they had freedom and they used it to revise and increase charges as they wished; both gas and electricity revised their tariffs on a great scale.

But railway charges were treated very differently under the Transport Act 1947. The reasons are historical. The Victorians hated monopolies and to them railways were the most powerful monopolies. Gladstone therefore, in promoting the Railway Act of 1844, envisaged that they might ultimately be taken over by the State. Meanwhile the State was given sweeping rights of intervention in railway affairs. Because of its dread of monopoly, Parliament in the Victorian era was generally opposed to railway amalgamations and right up to 1914 authority to amalgamate was difficult to obtain. Even working agreements between railways were disliked. We must remember that in the nineteenth century railways were the only means of transport, even for short distances. Until the arrival of the electric tram at the end of the century, any journey of more than a few miles had to be made by train. Complaints against railway charges were frequent and Parliament passed several Acts creating machinery to deal with charges. It was not surprising, therefore, that the Railways Act 1921 which amalgamated the railways into four great systems set up the Railway Rates Tribunal to receive representations from traders and the travelling public and to determine rates for goods and fares for passengers. Between 1921 and 1947 the internal-combustion engine had deprived the railways of their monopoly. But it was hardly possible for the Labour Government creating the greatest possible monopoly in railway transport to jettison the traditions of a century; so by Section 72 of the Transport Act 1947 the Railway Rates Tribunal was reorganised and renamed the Transport Tribunal.

The Transport Act 1953 gave the railways greater freedom in charging. They were to have the opportunity of competing with road haulage. In March 1955 the Commission lodged with the Transport Tribunal the Railway Merchandise Charges Scheme. In the Report for 1955 the Commission complains that it is still without a greater freedom of charge and therefore without the power to compete, which Parliament had provided in the Transport Act of 1953. This Merchandise Charges Scheme finally came into force on 1 July 1957.

Meanwhile, the Road Hauliers had been freed from the twenty-five-mile limit and were operating freely the 25,000 vehicles purchased from the Transport Commission, and other vehicles which they had acquired. At the end of 1955 it was clear that not all the road vehicles owned by the Commission could be sold. The Government decided to leave the Commission with about 10,000 vehicles and Parliament gave effect to this decision in the Transport

(Disposal of Road Haulage Property) Act which was passed in August 1956. This ended the procedure of disposals and the Commission organised the fleet into three companies run by British Road Services Ltd.

As we shall see later in this chapter, the Transport Commission was dissolved in December 1962 and so had a life of fifteen years. In the following paragraphs we shall first deal with its achievements during these fifteen years, after which we shall consider its efforts to reorganise and modernise itself.

Table II shows what happened to the trading results of the railways between 1948 and 1966. The finances of the Transport Commission were dominated by the problem of the railways. Its other activities did earn a surplus right up to 1962. Railways always formed 65 to 70 per cent of the Transport Commission's undertaking. Of the remainder, the main constituent was London Transport. Indeed, in the eyes of the general public the Transport Commission tended to be identified with the railways, and accordingly its achievements were assessed by those of the railways. How was a customer of Thomas Cook or a traveller on a Scottish bus to know that he was dealing with the Transport Commission?

The statistics show that gross receipts of the railways increased during the fifteen years of the Commission's life by just about one-third – from £346 million to £464 million. But operating expenses in the same period increased by over two-thirds from £324 million to £542 million. The result, of course, was that the operating surplus of £22 million, with which the Commission started, ended up in 1962 as an operating deficit of £104 million.

The turning point in the finances of the Transport Commission was in 1956 when for the first time the railways incurred a deficit on operation of £16·5 million. The following table shows what happened in the years 1951–6:

	Surplus or deficit on railway operations	Total traffic-operating surplus or deficit of Transport Commission
	£ million	£ million
1951	+31·7	+40
1952	+37	+45·3
1953	+35	+48
1954	+16·6	+31·8
1955	+ 0·2	+15·3
1956	−16·5	− 3·2

Two comments should be made on the above table and on the statistics given in Table II. They all relate to traffic only. The Transport Commission had activities other than carrying goods and passengers; it ran docks and hotels, let land and buildings and had a substantial advertisement revenue. These miscellaneous activities earned a profit which affected the figures shown in the second column above. On the other hand these results were arrived at before capital was serviced. The capital of the Transport Commission, as of all the nationalised undertakings, was in fixed-interest loans, and in 1956, for example, capital charges of the Commission amounted to £58·9 million. For 1956, therefore, after allowing for receipts from all sources, which gave a surplus of £4·5 million, and for capital charges the Transport Commission incurred a deficit of £54·4 million. In fact, right from the beginning the Commission had been incurring a deficit or was just managing to balance its accounts. The Commission's viability was even weaker than that, as it pointed out in paragraph 34 of its 1952 Report. It was not building up any reserves as enjoined by the Act of 1947 and 'depreciation, where provided, is calculated in relation to the book value of the assets and not in relation to current replacement values'. This latter fact became serious as inflation steadily advanced in the 1950s. Throughout, therefore, the finances of the Transport Commission were precarious.

The Commission constantly and rightly complained of the losses it was forced to carry because of the great delays of the Transport Tribunal in authorising increased charges. In paragraph 160 of its 1955 Report, it estimated that the delays in recouping itself for increased costs during the period 1948 to 1955 involved it in a loss of £100 million. It suggested, therefore, that as its accumulated deficit at the end of 1956 stood at £70 million, these delays were the main cause of putting the Commission in the red. This is true on a short-term basis, but over a long period these delays of the Transport Tribunal were only an exaggeration of an already difficult financial position.

At this point reference should be made to another alleged reason for the decline in the Commission's viability – the Transport Act 1953, which denationalised road haulage and forced the Commission to sell off most of its road haulage vehicles. It is true that the road haulage activities of the Commission earned a profit, the two peak years of which were £8·9 million in 1953 and £8·7 million in 1954. Having sold most of its road haulage vehicles, the Commission

naturally earned smaller profits from that source. But it is an
illusion to suggest that, even if it had kept all its road haulage
activities, the profits from them would have been great enough to
offset the losses from the railways, which developed so rapidly in
the later fifties and early sixties. It is inconceivable that the
Commission could have forced road haulage charges so high they
would earn a profit great enough to offset the massive deficits
incurred on the railways.

The explanation of the railways deficit is clear from the statistics.
The fierce competition of the internal-combustion engine –
whether car, coach, van or lorry – draws traffic from the railways.
Table II shows that passenger journeys are down by nearly one-
fifth between 1948 and 1966, despite increased population and
much more affluence. The railways' largest and most important
freight item is coal and coke. The declining fortunes of the coal
industry must be reflected in declining tonnage of coal traffic by
rail. Further the practice of building huge power stations at the pithead has meant a reduction in the rail movement of coal to the
consumer. In 1966 freight train receipts have only increased by
20 per cent over the receipts in 1948, despite the fact that the
average receipt per net ton mile had by 1966 increased by 75 per
cent over the figure for 1948 – in itself a modest increase for
nineteen years of steady inflation. In this period freight train
traffic had declined from 273 to 214 million tons.

The passenger, if anything, has done even better; the average
receipt per passenger mile has risen from 1·4 pence in 1948 to 2·31
pence in 1966 – an increase of only 65 per cent. This will surprise
the public, who are quite convinced that the rise in railway fares
has been so severe that passengers refuse to travel by rail. The
refusal is there all right but it is not due to excessive charges; it is
due to the superior convenience of the motor car together with the
bad name the railways have earned; as with all declining industries
it is a great problem to maintain morale and standards of service
and in transport the latter count immensely.

It will be noted that between 1948 and 1959 the average receipt
per passenger mile hardly increased at all and that the number of
passenger journeys remained fairly static. In that period there was
a decline in travel at ordinary fares, but the volume of passenger
traffic was kept stable by increased travel at concessionary fares.
During the sixties passenger travel has declined as fares and receipts
have increased and the use of the motor car has become widespread.

Even at present-day prices rail travel is cheap; but even so the railways find it difficult to prevent passenger traffic from declining.

The passing of the Transport Act 1953 put an end to the broad concept of the 1948 Act, under which the Commission would have ultimately had an undertaking which covered all forms of transport, as outlined earlier in this chapter. After 1953 the railways became an even more important part of the Commission's undertaking. The railways had received very little capital for development since 1945; as we have explained earlier, transport whether by road or rail was low in the order of priority in the views of post-war Governments.

So at the end of 1954 the Transport Commission launched a railway modernisation plan, estimated to cost £1,240 million.

The main features of the plan were a great improvement in freight services and the substitution of electric and diesel for steam traction, particularly in the services between and in the large cities. The Commission stressed the fact that, during the initial period of the plan, the capital expenditure would

not improve the financial position and the Commission have made it clear that sound railway finance cannot wait upon the fruition of this capital expenditure. A condition precedent to undertaking a bold and far-reaching plan of new equipment, designed to give this country a railway system second to none, is that the enterprise must not be allowed to get into a position of irredeemable unbalance meantime (1954 Report, para. 120).

In 1956 the Commission undertook a reassessment of the economic and financial future of its undertaking. This was published in a White Paper in October 1956 (Cmd. 9880) and was endorsed by the Government. Briefly the reassessment was as follows.

The railways were to be strengthened partly by modernisation and partly by pruning of railway services for which there was no longer any need. Modernisation was still estimated to cost £1,200 million though 'these figures are now likely to be increased, though not greatly' (para. 47). Of this sum, about £400 million would be found from 'internal sources of finance such as depreciation provisions'. Therefore £800 million would have to be borrowed.

Freight modernisation would give an ultimate improvement of £55 million a year on the 1956 position and passenger traffic modernisation an ultimate increased yield of £30 million a year. Total improvement from modernisation would therefore be

£85 million a year. The interest charges on the capital to be bor-rowed – £800 million – was estimated to be £40 million per annum assuming a rate of interest of 5 per cent, though 'on past experience it may be supposed that the long-term rate of interest will, on the average over the years, be less than this figure'. The Commission concluded 'that after 1960/61 their finances will be strengthened by a rapidly increasing net benefit until, by 1970, a net benefit of at least £45 million per annum should be available'.

This memorandum from the Transport Commission breathed a note of confidence that, given the opportunity, the Commissioners could make a success of the great undertaking for which they were responsible. They naturally required that they should no longer be hampered by the obstacles which had been their lot since 1948, and laid down the following conditions for the success of their efforts:

(1) They must be able to adjust their charges without delay.
(2) They must have freedom to operate a flexible system of charging.
(3) Finance will be provided to carry out the Plan.
(4) The Commission will be left alone by the Government.
(5) As soon as possible, special measures will be taken to enable the Commission to exercise 'proper financial discipline'.

In the White Paper the Memorandum of the Commission is prefaced by a government statement entitled 'Proposals for the Railways'. In this statement the Minister of Transport announces the following government decisions, arrived at after examination of the Memorandum of the Commission.

(1) The national interest requires that the future of the railways should be assured. They are essential 'as carriers of passengers over long distances and of suburban passenger in large numbers as well as carriers of bulk freight'.
(2) The Government are satisfied that the general shape of the Commission's investment proposals is sound and the Commis-sion's forecasts of their requirements are reasonable. They therefore 'accept the Commission's plans as practical and neces-sary' and though not subscribing to all the details of those plans, are satisfied that the Commission 'have clearly shown that they can provide the country with a modern and up-to-date trans-port system which will pay its way'.
(3) But until the railway system is revolutionised, the Commission will be incurring 'substantial though diminishing annual deficits until 1961 or 1962', when 'the Commission will achieve a balance on their revenue account'. The Government therefore proposed

that 'until the revenue account of the Commission is expected to be in balance, special advances should be made to the Commission equal to their revenue deficits in these years but limited as to total amount which may be of the order of £250 million.' 'During the period of the special advances the Commission would be authorised to charge to a special account in their books, for subsequent amortisation over a period of years, the net deficits of the railways and interest on the advances.'

These Government proposals under (3) were the 'special measures' referred to earlier to enable the Commission to exercise 'proper financial discipline', and involved legislation. Accordingly in 1957 Parliament passed the Transport (Railway Finances) Act which authorised the Commission to borrow from the Government sums to cover:

(1) Net deficits incurred by British Railways during the seven years 1956–62;
(2) interest on advances in (1) and on the advances to meet that interest;
(3) interest on British Railway borrowings for capital purposes in the ten years 1956 to 1965 during the year of borrowing and three years thereafter.

The limits on borrowing to meet deficits (item (1) above) was fixed at £250 million.

All those loans were to be transferred to a Special Account which would also carry the accumulated debt of the Commission as a whole at the end of 1955; this amounted to £69·75 million. In other words, so far as its own accounts were concerned, the Commission started with a clean sheet on 1 January 1956. From then, all its deficits and interest on borrowing were to be kept on one side in a Special Account, which would be amortised in the future, when British Railways were once again viable.

When the Commission put forward in September 1956 the proposals described above, it was satisfied that this accumulated deficit of about £70 million at the end of 1955 was 'due to time lags in putting up fares and charges . . . rather than to any inherent weakness in the competitive field'. It took the view, therefore, that 'the problem was one with a sound, even bright, future to pass through this difficult period without being thrown into hopeless disarray' (Commission Memorandum, Cmd. 9880, para. 10).

Everyone therefore expected that when Parliament had taken

the special measures to relieve the Commission, its affairs would brighten up and a noticeable trend to improvement would appear. 1957 was not too bad and the Report for 1957 started as follows:

> In view of the competition which has intensified in all branches of public transport, the Commission consider that the year's working results are as good as could be reasonably expected. They see the need to accelerate the pace of modernisation and they are taking steps to secure further economies. They do not qualify the confidence they have expressed in previous Reports in the commercial future of British Railways and indeed of their whole undertaking (1957 Report, para. 1).

£63·5 million, however, had to be borrowed for 1957 and included in the Special Account. This amount 'exceeds that expected when the financial plan embodied in the Act was made, but not greatly' (1957 Report, para. 164).

In the course of 1958 it became evident that the deficit for the year, which had been forecast at £55 million, would be much worse; in fact it proved to be £90 million. This was due to a fall in traffic receipts, mainly in coal and steel; freight traffic receipts in 1958 were £29·4 million down on 1957. As the limit of £250 million would be exceeded in 1959 it became necessary to revise the arrangements for deficit financing contained in the Transport (Railway Finance) Act 1957. The Government therefore laid before Parliament the Transport (Borrowing Powers) Bill which was passed in March 1959. This increased the limits of deficit financing from £250 to £400 million.

In July 1959 there was published as a White Paper (Cmnd. 813) the Reappraisal of the Plan for the Modernisation and Re-equipment of British Railways.

In this document the Commission shows itself as satisfied, on the whole, with its plan for modernisation, the cost of which has, incidentally, risen from £1,240 to £1,660 million. Its main conclusion is expressed in paragraph 118:

> This Reappraisal has shown that the Modernisation Plan drawn up four years ago, and the financial appreciation made in the White Paper of 1956, were soundly based. Subsequent events now make desirable some modifications of the Plan but they are not many and are principally in the direction of accelerating execution. Where the financial forecasts made in 1956 have not been realised, the causes lie predominantly in factors which were expressly excluded from the forecasts as being outside the control of the Commission.

On the basis of this main conclusion the Commission pressed that:

(1) In order to give industry and the travelling public the greatly improved services which modern techniques make possible, modernisation of the railways should, if at all possible, be pressed forward more rapidly than hitherto planned;

(2) the railways must concentrate on those tasks to which they are best suited and slough the remainder, and this process of rationalisation must also be speeded up;

(3) the Commission's financial structure, which is dominated by fixed-interest charges that are large in relation to working surpluses, should be reconsidered;

(4) and subject to these conditions, the railway modernisation plan represents a sound investment from the country's point of view, and indeed the costs which the nation would incur, if in fact it possessed no efficient system of railways, are incalculable (1959 Report, para. 10).

These suggestions in the Reappraisal had not met with any response from the Government by the end of 1959. The Government were clearly worried about the Commission's financial position and were reluctant to introduce a third Bill to increase the limit of deficit borrowing beyond £400 million. At the end of 1959 the Commission had borrowed £280·7 million to cover the deficits for the years 1956–9 and there were three more years to go. The Special Account, which showed the total accrued deficit of the Commission, showed of course at the same date a much larger sum – £417·8 million, because it included also the pre-1956 deficit and borrowing for interest charges both on the advances to cover deficits and on loans for capital purposes. Since 1956 these loans had amounted to £330 million.

The Commission itself was satisfied with the way matters were going and claimed 'reasonable freedom to press on with reconstruction' as it had claimed in 1956. The first chapter of the 1959 Report was entitled 'Another Year of Substantial Progress'. The Commission had certainly done better in 1959 than in 1958 but 1959 was a year of uninterrupted boom in the national economy.

On 10 March 1960 the Prime Minister announced in the House of Commons that the Government had appointed a special Advisory Group of industrialists under Sir Ivan Stedeford to advise them how best the country's railway system could be remodelled to meet current needs, reducing uneconomic services and obligations and securing a more effective distribution of the

Commission's functions and a better use of its assets. Earlier, in December 1959, the Select Committee on the Nationalised Industries, which is described in Chapter 7, had begun at the request of the Transport Commission a massive investigation into British Railways. The Government were, of course, aware of this investigation but as they had no control over the deliberations of the Select Committee and presumably preferred an enquiry carried out by men chosen by themselves, there was no alternative but to allow the two enquiries to proceed at the same time. This put a great strain on the leading men of the Transport Commission, who quite reasonably hinted at their difficulties 'while two enquiries of political origin are taking place' (1959 Report, para. 1).

The conclusion of the Reappraisal was that, by speeding up modernisation, the Commission by 1963 would have gross receipts greater than its working expenses 'leaving a substantial working surplus, which it is considered can reasonably be put at between £50 and £100 million' (para. 111). This result would be achieved by 1963, i.e. seven years earlier than was anticipated in the White Paper of 1956 (para. 101). Naturally the Commission could not say in the 1959 Reappraisal how much it expected the wages and salaries bill to increase; but the reference to 'some provision for improvement' shows that it had only some marginal amount in mind. Yet within twelve months of writing those words the Commission had to find £40 million more each year as a result of the Guillebaud Report. This sum was large enough to destroy the optimistic estimates in the 1956 White Paper and still more in the 1959 Reappraisal.

In a Memorandum submitted in February 1960 to the Select Committee on Nationalised Industries (H.C. 254 (1960), appendix 17, para. 38) the Transport Commission claimed that 'in the modernisation and equipment of British Railways the years 1955–7 were years of preparation; 1958–9 were years of development and 1960–1 and the years thereafter will be the years of achievement. From the present time onwards there will be a progressive increase in the rate of accomplishment and in the measure of public benefit which will be obtained.'

There is no doubt that in all the estimates which the Commission had been making as to the yield of investment in modernisation, there has been an undue strain of optimism. It had not allowed adequately for increasing competition from road and air transport; also it had not allowed adequately for the pressure of increased costs. But above all the estimates of the yield from the improvements had been unreliable. The valuable investigation carried out by the Select Committee on Nationalised Industries showed that no adequate satisfactory financial test had been made to show how far a completed project was really profitable. This is so important, in view of the huge sums lent to the Commission for modernisation, that part of the Select Committee's Report should be quoted.

384. Both in view of the importance of deciding for the future what should be the size and shape of the railways and because of the very large sums of money involved, it might have been expected that, in the first place, fairly precise calculations would have been made by the Commission –

(1) of the additional net return to be secured by each proposal and
(2) of the overall profitability – after that proposal had been carried out – of the service affected by it;

and that, secondly, these calculations would have been critically examined by the Ministry of Transport and the Treasury before approval was given to the necessary borrowing.

385. The evidence shows that the Commission duly calculated the additional net return on each scheme ((1) above) but they did not and, under their existing accounting arrangements, could not make the other calculation – that is the estimate of profitability that would result. As to critical examination by departments, that has only recently been undertaken – that is more than five years after the Modernisation Plan began.

A simple example illustrates this important point. A diesel passenger service is introduced, and the improvement attracts double the number of previous passengers and doubles the revenue. But even after this additional net return is allowed for, the service may be running at a deficit, especially when allowance is made for the service of the additional capital required for the change-over to diesel traction.

The report of the Special Advisory Group has never been published. We can only assume that the Government felt that the Group's criticisms would have made a difficult task almost hopeless. We know, however, some of the work it did from remarks made by Mr Marples, Minister of Transport, in a debate on British Railways on 20 October 1960. 'The Group had worked for six months and made recommendations to the Government on finance, statutory restrictions, modernisation and reorganisation. These recommendations were being carefully considered and as soon as the Government had formulated their proposals, they would lay them before the House in a comprehensive White Paper' (*Hansard*, vol. 627, col. 2358). Mr Marples also told the House that

the Special Advisory Group early on expressed doubts about the economic aspects of the London Midland electrification scheme, as it had been explained to it, and the Transport Commission had prepared a reassessment of the scheme in the light of its experience elsewhere as well as in the light of recent development, and this is under urgent examination by the Ministry. The Commission has agreed, pending the outcome of this examination, not to place new contracts (ibid. col. 2368).

In that debate Mr Marples also announced that he had

set up a committee – a compact study group as it were – under my own chairmanship to consider what sort of and how big a railway system we need in view of these factors [i.e. road transport, etc.]. The Commission is represented on this group and is co-operating in preparing a revised modernisation plan. We shall not only look at railway modernisation projects, but also try to satisfy ourselves about the modernisation programme as a whole. We cannot underwrite such a programme until the size and shape of the problem have been tackled in this way (ibid. col. 2366).

What a pity this was not done five years earlier.

In December 1960 accordingly the Government issued a White Paper (Cmnd. 1248) entitled Reorganisation of the Nationalised Transport Undertakings. This was the most important government pronouncement since the Transport Commission was created and therefore requires detailed scrutiny. We can assume that the conclusions in this White Paper are largely based on the advice given by the Special Advisory Group.

The Paper starts by enunciating the Government's aim 'that the nationalised transport undertakings shall be soundly based both in organisation and finance, providing efficient service to industry and the public, and giving a good livelihood and worth-while jobs to those who work in them' (para. 2).

The Government's main conclusions are:

(1) The activities of the Transport Commission are so largely diverse, that it is virtually impossible to run them as a single undertaking.
(2) In financial and commercial matters there has been a tendency for technical and operating factors to prevail over others. There has also been a confusion in judging what is economically right and what is socially desirable.

(3) The commercial capability of the railways is circumscribed by outmoded statutory obligations and restrictions on trading operations.

(4) Mounting deficits, the size of capital debt in relation to the earning capacity of the assets and the increasing burden of interest as modernisation proceeds, present a situation detrimental to the interest of workers, to financial control and to hopes of recovery.

In view of these considerations the Government decided to abolish the Transport Commission and replace it with a group of Boards. The finances of the Commission would be reorganised and the various units would be given 'the maximum practical freedom of operation in their commercial affairs'.

The Transport Commission would be replaced by five separate Boards, one each for the Railways, London Transport, Docks, Inland Waterways, and a Holding Company to own and run road haulage, provincial buses, hotels, Thomas Cook, etc. Docks and Waterways, which had been uneasy bedfellows, were separated at last.

Below the British Railways Board there would be several Regional Boards, which 'will be fully responsible for the management and operation of their regional railway system. Each will be autonomous in all matters which concern the Region alone.' The chairman of each Regional Railway Board will sit on the British Railways Board, which 'will be responsible for such matters as national staff and wage negotiations, overall control over finance and investment, policies for safety training and research, and the determination of the future size and shape of the railway system' (para. 14). The autonomy of the Regional Railway Boards, in view of this, would be of a limited nature.

The Minister of Transport will take over the 'coordination of policy between the new Boards, including allocation of funds for new investment' (para. 27). He will be assisted by a Nationalised Transport Advisory Council consisting of the chairmen of the Boards and others drawn from outside. This was a serious addition to the Minister's responsibilities, but in fact this Advisory Council has seldom met.

On finance the White Paper proposed that part of the Commission's capital was to be written off and part suspended; but, as we shall see, the proposals did not go far enough.

In the direction of commercial freedom, the railways were to be freed from statutory control except in the London area where

London Transport and British Railways have a monopoly of public passenger transport. This was a welcome reduction in the outmoded functions of the Transport Tribunal. Certain other restrictions, such as on the development of railway property, would be relaxed.

The White Paper was a useful step towards the realistic treatment of British Railways finances. It had been obvious for some years that all the calculations made by the Transport Commission of the ultimate viability of British Railways rested on very precarious foundations. The facts brought out by Mr Marples in his speech on 26 October 1960 show what a long distance from viability British Railways had travelled. On a gross turnover of £457 million in 1959, there was a deficit of £110 million. The gross takings per man per year on the railways was only about £880. About £200 per year of each railwayman's pay was found from the subsidy of £105 million.

Against these facts for 1959 can be set the Commission's anticipation in 1956 that the results of modernisation would put the railways into balance in 1961 or 1962.

The working deficit, including collection and delivery on the railways, continued to mount from year to year. From £42 million in 1959, it increased to £67·7 million in 1960, to £86·9 million in 1961 and £104 million in 1962 – the last year of the Transport Commission. Though the Commission earned a surplus on nearly all its other activities, such as London Transport, road services, buses and ships, that surplus was modest in contrast to the huge deficit on the railways. Interest and other central charges had to be debited both to the railways and the other activities; in 1962 the total deficit of the railways (including charges) rose to the high figure of £159 million.

In view of this declining viability, the arrangements of a Special Account for borrowing from the Minister of Transport sufficient to cover deficits, etc., as described earlier became more and more unreal. Instead, starting from 1960 the Minister made an outright grant to the Commission to cover the railways' deficit, which is not to be repaid and on which no interest is payable. That arrangement was continued after the winding up of the Commission in 1962 and the deficit on British Railways is now made good each year by a grant from the Minister out of his vote approved by Parliament. Thus for 1966 the grant amounted to £134·7 million. Section 22 of the Transport Act 1962 (amended by the Transport Finances Act

1966) provided that the aggregate of grants and loans from the Minister to meet deficits on revenue account should not exceed £800 million and should be restricted to the deficits in the six years from 1 January 1963, when the British Railways Board started functioning. By 28 February 1967 the total of the grants amounted to £517·8 million. Those amounts cover the period 1963–6 and the grants for the two remaining years 1967 and 1968 will almost certainly leave very little of the £800 million authorised.

The Transport Act 1962 implemented the decisions in the White Paper of December 1960. Section 39 of the Act provided that the Minister should divide the capital debt of the Commission between its five successors, and Section 40 provided that of that part allocated to the British Railways Board, a proportion should be suspended and should not carry interest and not be paid off at a fixed time, unless and until the Minister otherwise directs. By an Order on 20 March 1964 the Minister fixed the capital of the Railways Board at £1,562 million, of which £857 was to bear interest and £705 million was suspended. The rate of interest was fixed at 5·58 per cent and the £857 million was to be repaid by twenty-one annual instalments commencing in 1965. This arrangement for repayment of capital debt has already broken down. Repayments of the instalments for the years 1965, 1966 and 1967 have been postponed for twenty-five years; but the interest rates on the three instalments have been fixed at $6\frac{1}{8}$, $6\frac{1}{2}$ and 7 per cent respectively (1966 Railways Board Report, part ii, p. 9).

It might have been thought that the arrangements for capital reconstruction in the 1962 Act would have helped the railways by lightening the load of capital charges. Surprisingly it did not. In 1962, when the railways formed part of the Transport Commission, the interest charges and central administration charges debited to the railways amounted to £55 million. But the 1962 Act arrangements, described above, loaded the British Railways Board in 1963 with increased interest charges of £58·1 million. So far as capital is concerned, therefore, the reorganisation of the Transport Act 1962 was not helpful. Despite this, the requirement of the Act was that the Railways Board should 'pay its way' by the beginning of 1968 – a requirement we can now see has proved unattainable.

But the division of the Transport Commission's undertaking into five portions and the appointment of Dr (later Lord) Beeching to the chairmanship of the most important and difficult portion – the British Railways Board – was intended to and did effect a great change in British Railways; but as we shall see the success of the new regime was not as great as was hoped in 1961 and 1962, when it was being planned and put through Parliament.

Dr Beeching became Chairman of the Transport Commission on 1 June 1961 – nineteen months before its decease – in order to plan and put in hand the great changes which were proposed. At a press conference held immediately after his appointment the new Chairman referred to the 'deep-seated causes of the financial difficulties of the railways' and indicated his plan of action as follows: 'Doubts about the future of the railway system as a whole can only be resolved by a more thoroughgoing study of the present working and future prospects of the system than have been made so far. Such studies will take time.'

Dr Beeching had been a member of the Special Advisory Group whose report, as noted above, has never been published. He had some knowledge, therefore, of railway difficulties; but now that he was in a position of authority he was able to make the thorough survey necessary as a basis for reorganising the railways. The survey was completed in less than two years from his appointment and *The Reshaping of British Railways* was published on 26 March 1963. But some steps on the lines of the proposals in *Reshaping* had already been taken.

Reshaping is a massive report of sixty pages followed by eight detailed 'Traffic Studies' which provided the facts on which the Report was based. There was also attached a detailed report analysing in nine sections which passenger services should be modified or closed down.

The main difference between *Reshaping* and the modernisation proposals of the Transport Commission referred to earlier is that the latter did not envisage any basic changes in the scope of railway services or the general mode of working; they were based on the assumption that 'modernising' by itself would reduce costs, attract more traffic and so enable the railways to pay their way. *Reshaping*, on the other hand, proposed a drastic reconstruction of railways and a complete change of 'the whole pattern of the business'.

Very briefly *Reshaping* brought out the following main features of railway services.

Passenger

Stopping-services did not pay and suburban services in the London area nearly paid but outside London did not. Fast and semi-fast trains met their direct costs but only part of the indirect costs allocated to them.

Freight

Coal and coke, which brought in over 40 per cent of freight receipts, did pay their way; minerals met direct but not all indirect costs; general merchandise fell down badly and did not even meet direct costs. On the other hand, parcels and mails which went by passenger trains did meet all costs direct and indirect. This type of traffic and coal were the only two forms of traffic on the railways to make a net surplus over total cost. Every other form of traffic freight or passenger ran at a deficit. In 1961 general merchandise and stopping passenger trains were responsible for over three-quarters of the total deficit of the railways.

These facts led to fifteen proposals for reshaping the railways which are listed at the end of the Report. The most important may be briefly summarised as follows:

(1) discontinuance of many stopping passenger services and closure of many small stations to passenger traffic;
(2) improvement of inter-city passenger services;
(3) co-ordination of suburban train and bus services in collaboration with municipal authorities; alternatively fare increases and reduction of services;
(4) reduction in uneconomic freight traffic passing through small stations by closing them progressively;
(5) development of 'Liner Train' services to carry traffic composed of consignments too small in themselves to justify through trains;
(6) concentration of freight sundries traffic at about 100 main line depots – many of them associated with Liner Train depots;
(7) development of block trains for heavy freight such as coal, oil, cement, bricks, etc., which the railways are specially qualified to carry;
(8) continued replacement of steam by diesel or electric traction.

Dr Beeching took up his appointment in 1961 for five years and returned to Imperial Chemical Industries in 1966. What progress had been made by 1966 in reshaping the railway system as proposed in the Plan of 1963, and how far had that progress carried the railways towards viability?

Where the Railways Board could handle matters on its own responsibility, it could make progress; where it had to placate public opinion and secure the agreement of the Minister of

Transport, progress was much slower. It could close down a station to freight traffic by just deciding to do so; between 1962 and the end of 1966, it brought down the number of stations open to freight traffic from 5,200 to 1,500 – more than 900 a year on the average. But of 92 proposals submitted to the Minister in 1966 for withdrawing or modifying passenger services, only 25 were approved, and the Board complained it continued to incur losses on services it asked to have withdrawn.

British Railways became much more modern in the years 1962–6. The services to the Midlands and the North were electrified 'with an upsurge of 50 per cent in passenger receipts'. Freight liners made progress. Full train-load traffic developed, especially in coal. The railways made long-term agreements with important industries – particularly oil – whereby 'company' trains were run on a large scale; by 1966 there were over 1300 'company' trains a week, of which 400 were oil and 100 cement. The motor-car industry had special trains for carrying cars and components.

But nevertheless, as Table II shows, there was a decline between 1962 and 1966 in gross receipts, the number of passengers and the volume of freight traffic. Viability was still remote. Though the deficit had declined from the peak of 1962, and the Reports for 1963 and 1964 were cheerful about the reduction, it became clear by 1965 that the deficit would persist and even increase despite the great efforts of the Railways Board to modernise the railways, cut down losing traffic, attract more traffic and above all cut costs. After four years' hard work, costs had fallen from £569 million in 1962 to £542 million in 1966—an unsatisfactory result. The situation is summarised in paragrah 5 of the 1966 Report, which must be quoted:

Determined and continuous efforts to secure economies and to introduce improved operating methods have produced gross annual savings since 1962 of about £115 million, although these savings have had a relatively small impact on the financial results because a high proportion of them has been absorbed by higher wages and improved working conditions.

Railway staffs have declined from 476,000 at end 1962 to 339,000 at end 1966. But this very substantial decline is not reflected in the decline of costs referred to above, though over 60 per cent of railway expenses relate to staff. In fact in 1966 staff expenses were 63 per cent of total expenses; in 1948, the first year of nationalisation, the corresponding figure was 62 per cent. But, of course, in those eighteen years the number of staff had dropped almost to half.

In view of this dominating factor of staff costs and the almost continuous negotiations with the railway unions for improved pay and conditions, it is startling to read paragraph 25 of the 1966 Report. 'The appointment of a Board Member with special responsibility for industrial relations, announced towards the end of the year, is evidence of the importance which the Board attach to improving their relations with the staff.' This was a rather late appointment. The National Coal Board started in 1947 with such a Member, and it had possibly an easier problem because it had one industrial union. The railways, on the other hand, have always had three unions and many of the difficulties have been caused by inter-union rivalries.

The 1966 Report has moved far from the optimistic outlook of 1962, 1963 and even 1964. In paragraph 7 it explains that

the major sources of additional savings in working expenses, and in particular the conversion from steam to diesel traction, which have produced substantial benefits in recent years, are coming to an end and, while there is still much room for further savings from improved efficiency and for further traffic growth from the development of new means of movement such as the Freightliner and the large Container, it is apparent that under their financial remit British Railways results will continue to show a substantial deficit.

A hint of what the Board has in mind is contained in the remark that 'the continuance of a deficit on the railways, particularly when so large a part of it arises from the provision of social services, which should be a national or local rather than a railway responsibility, is bad for railway morale and the Board look forward to the development of a more sensible financial structure for the railways'.

On this last point, it can be agreed straightaway that the capital reconstruction in the Transport Act 1962 provided no real relief to the railways. As mentioned earlier in this chapter, interest charges on the railways were higher after than before the reconstruction, and they have, of course, increased steadily since 1962. In 1966 they stood at £64·2 million as compared with £55 million (before the capital reconstruction) and £58·1 million in 1963 (after the reconstruction). Considerable amounts of fresh capital had been spent on the railways during those four years. But the cardinal facts were that gross receipts in 1966 were £463·8 million as against £465·1 million in 1962, and that though operating expenses in 1966 at £542·1 million were down from £569·1 million in 1962, the railways were left with an operating deficit of over £70 million, which with the addition of interest charges became £134·7 million. Viability was still out of sight and it is clear from the above quotations from the 1966 Report that the Railways Board saw no hope without further – and drastic – financial reconstruction. On page 54 of the *Reshaping* Report, we find the following sentence: 'If the plan is implemented with vigour, much (though not necessarily all) of the Railways deficit should be eliminated by 1970.' That hope will clearly not be realised.

As it became obvious that the plans and hopes of the Transport Act 1962 would not be realised, the Ministry of Transport of the Labour Government set to work to plan once again the future of the railways and therewith the 'integration' of all transport – road and rail – which as we have seen from the beginning of this chapter was the policy underlying the Transport Act 1947. In July 1966 future policy was revealed in a White Paper on Transport Policy (Cmnd. 3057). This was a blue-print and the details were filled in by three White Papers issued towards the end of 1967: Railway Policy (Cmnd. 3439), Transport of Freight (Cmnd. 3470) and Public Transport and Traffic (Cmnd. 3481). Finally a Transport Bill was issued in December 1967, which is the most massive Bill ever laid before Parliament, running to 260 pages with 169 Sections, and 18 Schedules. The new policy – covering all forms of transport – has thus been spelled out in the most ample detail. This book has gone to the printer before this Bill has reached the Statute Book; but it is reasonable to assume that the Transport Act 1968 will only differ marginally from the Transport Bill 1967.

The main provisions in the Bill to ease the financial difficulties of the railways can be summarised as follows.

The 1962 Act was based on the assumptions that the railways could be cut down to a commercial size by elimination of unprofitable traffic, development of new profitable traffic and drastic reduction in operating costs. These assumptions were not realised. There was strong public resistance to the elimination of many unprofitable services. The Labour Government therefore rightly decided that they must squarely face the fact that non-paying passenger services would have to be retained which could not be cross-subsidised from profitable services. Therefore Section 36 of the Bill authorises the Ministry to pay a subsidy on these un-remunerative services, which it was estimated would initially be about £55 million per annum.

Section 37 of the Bill authorises the Minister to make tapering grants during the five years 1969–73 towards the cost of maintaining surplus track and signalling, pending its elimination. These grants were not to exceed £50 million in all.

As explained earlier, the Transport Act 1962 fixed the commencing capital of the Railways Board on 1 January 1963 at £1,562 million, of which £857 million was to bear interest and £705 million was suspended. Section 39 of the Bill provides that the £1,562 million should, on 1 January 1969, be reduced to £300 million. Loans contracted under the Transport Act 1962 were not affected by this arrangement; these were estimated to amount to about £70 million at the end of 1968.

These three arrangements for making life easier financially for British Railways can be described as realistic and unavoidable; it is useless to proceed further on the assumption that the railways can, as they are, be made viable. That is not to say that the new arrangements will automatically convert the railways into a well-managed and hard-thrusting undertaking. They will not in future be labouring under a crippling deficit, but they will be drawing substantial subsidies. The continuous procedure involved in identifying uneconomic services and calculating their losses could become as demoralising as labouring under a deficit. Searching for loss-making activities does not conduce to a profit-making outlook. The White Paper on Railway Policy (Cmnd. 3439, para. 15) expresses the hope that 'since the Board will be put in a position in which competent and dynamic management should enable the industry to break even, there should no longer be a need for any deficit grant from the Minister'. This hope may be realised: but it is somewhat unlikely.

This financial reorganisation of the railways is part of a much greater plan for 'integrating and co-ordinating' all road and rail traffic – whether freight or passenger – which the Minister described as 'practical Socialism' (*Hansard*, vol. 756, col. 1281). The most important part of this greater plan deals with freight.

In the second-reading debate on the Transport Bill the Minister described 'freight transport as an economic service to industry which must be organised on national lines, whereas passenger transport is much more closely linked to local community life and has important local social implications. This is one of the reasons why I have decided not to re-create a British Transport Commission with a responsibility over the whole publicly owned transport field.' This differentiation of freight and passenger traffic is borne out by the facts that the average passenger journey on rail is 22·1 miles but the average length of freight haul is 69·4 miles.

To deal with freight on a national basis the Transport Bill creates a National Freight Corporation, whose function it will be to integrate freight services by road and by rail. It will start by taking over the road freight and shipping services of the existing Transport Holding Company. This is one of the five organisations created by the Transport Act 1962 and has been successful in earning profits in running buses, road freight services, hotels, shipping services and Thomas Cook & Son. It will also take over from British Railways all the assets employed in the 'sundries' and 'freightliners' services, which might be defined as services handling traffic originating by road. These assets will be the depots, vehicles, warehouses and containers but not the trains which carry these goods. The Railways Board will be left responsible for marketing and operating the freight traffic originating by rail – such as full-train and wagon loads of coal and steel and company trains, i.e. trains booked by companies for full loads of oil, cement, chemicals and motor cars. 'In this way integration will be concentrated on the areas where it will be most productive – general merchandise, parcels and sundries' (Cmnd. 3470, para. 14). As the railways in 1966 lost £25 million on this miscellaneous freight traffic, they will be relieved of this loss, which will be transferred to the National Freight Corporation. Under Section 5 of the Transport Bill the Minister may make grants up to a total of £60 million to the Corporation during the years 1969–73 to make good their estimated losses on this traffic.

The N.F.C. will be a controlling and policy-making body and its operations will be carried out by subsidiary companies, two of which will be set up by the Railways Board for freightliners and sundries. In these companies the N.F.C. will hold 51 per cent of the stock and the Railways Board 49 per cent.

The key duty of the N.F.C. is laid down in Section 1 (1) (a) of the Transport Bill which enjoins the N.F.C.

(i) to provide, or secure or promote the provision of, properly integrated services for the carriage of goods within Great Britain by road and rail, and

(ii) to secure that, in the provision of those services, goods are carried by rail, whenever such carriage is efficient and economic.

The object under (ii) will be achieved largely by the provisions of the Bill for the licensing of goods traffic, to which the N.F.C. or the Railways Board will be able to raise objections. The hope is that the ton mileage of goods carried by rail will, by these means, increase by 30 per cent, which will be more than enough to offset the anticipated fall in the coal and steel traffic.

The difficulties in the working of these freight traffic arrangements are great. The N.F.C. and the railways are instructed in the Transport Bill to co-operate. This will be easy, when their interests coincide. But what happens if their interests conflict? After all, even if the N.F.C. secures the freight traffic, it is for the railways to carry it and to fit it into the schedules of their other traffics. To supervise this co-operation between railways and N.F.C., the Bill creates a Transport Integration Council which advises the Minister, who can then give directions to the appropriate Board. This Council replaces the Nationalised Transport Advisory Council set up in the Transport Act 1962 which has only met a few times and been useless.

The arrangements for favouring the railways by objections to licences for medium and heavy road vehicles are also going to create confusion. Obviously these arrangements for transferring traffic from private haulier to nationalised transport will take many months if not years, during which uncertainty will prevail. How is it possible to satisfy the criterion in Section 1 of the Bill, quoted above, that the carriage by rail is 'economic'? Railway costings are notoriously debatable and have been the subject of heated argument for many years. The White Paper on Railway Policy (Cmnd. 3439) has much to say on costing principles and methods for railways; Appendix E deals with a detailed and complex report by consultants called in to advise on this constantly controversial subject.

For passenger transport the Bill lays emphasis, as has been mentioned earlier, on its local character. Apart therefore from long-distance railway travel between cities, which will be left entirely to the Railways Board, local railway travel will come under the purview of new organisations known as Passenger Transport Authorities, which in turn will appoint Passenger Transport Executives. The members of these Authorities will be appointed by the local authorities in the areas designated by the Minister, except for one-seventh of the members, who will be appointed by the Ministers. The Authorities will have complete control of all forms of local traffic and will enter into agreements with the Railways Board as to the suburban rail services, fares, etc. The Authorities will also enter into agreements with the National Bus Company, which is being created by the Bill to take over from the existing Transport Holding Company the 25,000 buses and coaches which they own. Existing private bus operators will be allowed to continue their services, but the Authorities will have the power to revoke a licence for a particular service.

As suburban rail services lose money, the Government will give the P.T.A.s grants towards their costs on a tapering basis for a period of seven years (Section 20 of the Bill).

In the first instance the Minister will designate four major conurbations for Passenger Transport Authorities: Greater Manchester, Merseyside, the West Midlands and Tyneside. In these areas, the P.T.A.s will acquire compulsorily all municipal bus systems operating inside them.

The P.T.A.s will not do the detailed work, which will be carried out by Passenger Transport Executives, of not less than three nor more than seven persons. In Section 10 (1) of the Bill the Executives are equipped with no less than thirty-two powers, some of which are very wide-ranging. There is a queer provision in Section 15 (6) that if the Executive does anything without the approval of the Authority, even if the Act requires that approval, it shall not 'be held to be unlawful'. One can see serious friction between a masterful Executive and its Authority.

The P.T.A.s are similar to the Massachusetts Bay Transportation Authority set up in 1964 to serve a population of $2\frac{3}{4}$ million in Boston and its surroundings. That Authority has incurred increasing criticism for its extravagant financial behaviour.

Also the Minister of Transport and the Greater London Council have been discussing the possibility of the Council taking over London Transport. The Council has expressed its willingness to do so but no detailed agreement has yet been worked out. As London Transport has been losing money in recent years and has been subsidised by the Ministry of Transport, the Council will no doubt press for further financial help; it is not likely to agree that the rates should carry the deficit, which the Ministry of Transport would no doubt wish to transfer to them.

Though the P.T.A.s and the railways are enjoined to come to

agreement on the suburban railway services to be run in the areas, one can foresee considerable friction between the staff of the railways and the staff of the Passenger Transport Executives, which will be responsible for operating these complicated schemes. From the Minister's point of view these schemes have advantages. The P.T.A.s and not the Government will compulsorily acquire local buses; the Government have therefore avoided paying compensation. If losses are incurred in excess of estimates the P.T.A.s will have to issue rate precepts on the local authorities, which are their members.

The railways will thus be left in full control of only a part of their present activities. They will be responsible for only a section of their freight traffic, largely provided by two other Public Corporations – the National Coal Board and the British Steel Corporation. In passenger transport their important suburban traffics will be operated by agreement with the P.T.A.s, which will put them under the control of the Passenger Transport Executives. This slicing away of substantial parts of the railway system to outside bodies may well be regarded by railway staffs and railway trade unions as deplorable steps which reduce still further the importance of their industry, in which they have spent their working life. There has been much trouble on the railways from rivalry between the railway trade unions and their nervous fears at the steady decline in the number of railway staffs. The measures envisaged in the Transport Bill – particularly for the part to be played by the National Freight Corporation – are not likely to go through without serious difficulties from the railway unions. Can all these changes, which will go on for years, do anything but lower their morale still further?

There are many other important provisions in the Transport Bill, such as the revised arrangements for licensing road haulage vehicles and in particular for limiting the activities of the heavier vehicles. These will be bitterly resisted as they were twenty years ago when the Transport Commission was busy in acquiring them compulsorily.

In rejecting a monolothic structure such as the Transport Commission of 1947, the Minister of Transport has created a complicated group of interlocking corporations, which will have to co-operate in working a decentralised system of public transport. It will be mainly the responsibility of the Minister of Transport himself to secure this co-operation; it will be a tremendous and

D

thankless task. Serious trouble may arise if the corporations in their disputes with each other are backed by different unions; for instance, the National Freight Corporation and the Transport Workers may find themselves in opposition to the Railway Board and the Railway Unions. Meanwhile industry and commerce requiring efficient and reliable transport will suffer. It will be a miracle if the complicated and delicately balanced structure of the Transport Bill 1967 works smoothly and successfully.

TABLE III. ELECTRICITY SUPPLY (GREAT BRITAIN)

	1950	1955	1960	1962	1963	1964	1965	1966	1967
Value of total sales of electricity (£ million)	224·7	388·7	634	799·5	895·9	957·4	1074	1152	1194
Total sales (thousand million units)	45·5	67·4	102·4	122·4	133·8	140·3	151·1	156·9	161·7
Sales to industry (thousand million units)	22·9	34·6	50	53·5	56·1	61·6	65	66·7	67·4
Domestic sales (thousand million units)	14·4	20	33·3	45·2	51·7	51·7	56·5	58·9	61·3
Sales per domestic consumer (units)	1245	1459	2157	2827	3187	3127	3353	3442	3520
Average net selling value per unit (pence)									
1. All consumers	1·186	1·384	1·487	1·568	1·607	1·637	1·706	1·761	1·773
2. Industrial consumers	0·948	1·182	1·255	1·349	1·372	1·365	1·429	1·478	1·514
3. Domestic consumers	1·352	1·506	1·626	1·665	1·705	1·783	1·852	1·909	1·890
Capital Expenditure (£ million)	136·3	243·3	337·2	404·7	507·7	598·9	651·2 (1965/6)	710·7 (1966/7)	631 (1967/8 for England and Wales)
Average thermal efficiency of steam stations (per cent)	21·6	24·2	26·7	27·5	27·5	27·6	27·4	27·4	27·9
System load factor (per cent)	42·8	43·5	48·4	44	50·4	50·2	47·4	51·1	50·6

Source: Ministry of Power Statistical Digests.

4 Electricity

IN 1945 it was clear that some measure of reorganisation of the electricity supply industry was necessary; this was carried out by the Electricity Act 1947.

As explained in Chapter 1, Parliament had first attempted in 1882 to regulate this industry. At first electricity was only a new method of lighting and as such was in close competition with gas, which at that date was also a lighting medium. Consequently the early power stations were tiny affairs in some back street, providing direct current to the premises in neighbouring streets. In London, where the London County Council was not created till 1889, and the Metropolitan Boroughs not till 1899, many of the electricity undertakings were companies which naturally obtained franchises in the wealthier districts. In time some of the outer Metropolitan Boroughs, neglected by the companies, adopted the Electricity Acts and started their own undertakings. Outside London most municipalities in the 1890s started their own electricity undertakings; the country districts were, on the whole, left without supplies.

From the beginning Parliament had no doubt that ultimately electricity supply undertakings should be publicly owned. This did not spring from Marxian dogma but from the Victorians' inherent dislike of any form of statutory monopoly. The 1882 Act, therefore, gave the companies a franchise for twenty-one years, at the end of which the local authority could buy them out on favourable terms. Twenty-one years proved too short a period and the 1889 Act lengthened it to forty-two years.

From about 1900 it was apparent that electricity had a great role to play as a form of power, and larger power stations became necessary. This is not the place for a detailed history of the industry, but suffice it to say that the First World War made clear the urgent need for reorganising the industry. In 1919 the Electricity Commissioners were appointed and were made responsible to the Minister of Transport; it was thought that railway electrification would be a major development in the 1920s and that he, therefore, was the appropriate Minister to supervise development of electricity supply. At first it had been proposed to endow the Commissioners with powers to compel undertakings to be reorganised and amalgamated, but the House of Lords struck out the compulsory powers and the Commissioners were left as a supervising body with advisory powers; they could check and control but not initiate.

This grave deficiency had to be remedied if industry were to obtain the power it required. Each power station was a law unto itself and supplied its own neighbourhood. Generation of electricity had to be remodelled and standardised on a national system. For this purpose stations had to be interconnected and the supply generated at a standard frequency. There was nobody charged with this responsibility and so in 1926 the Baldwin Government passed the Electricity (Supply) Act, which set up a Central Electricity Board. Under the supervision of the Electricity Commissioners, this Board prepared schemes for selecting certain power stations and connecting them with a high-tension grid of 132,000 volts. The Board would construct and own the grid. The power stations were left in the ownership of the undertakers but put under the control of the C.E.B., which could give directions on their working. Relations between Board and undertakers were complicated and sometimes not harmonious. Technically the Board bought the whole supply generated by a selected power station and sold back to the owner of that station his requirements at a specially favourable rate. The determination of that rate was an involved affair and, if not settled by agreement, was carried out by the Electricity Commissioners.

Between 1926 and the outbreak of the Second World War this work of integration was completed by the C.E.B. In 1926 there were 491 generating stations; in 1938 there were 171 stations interconnected by the grid. Under C.E.B. control these stations were operated in such a way that only thirty (base-load) stations ran the full year and fourteen of the most economical stations supplied 50 per cent of the electricity generated (*British Fuel and Power Industries* (P.E.P., 1947), p. 158). The country thus started the Second World War with an integrated system of electricity generation.

But electricity distribution had not been touched and a committee was set up in 1935 under Sir Harry McGowan (later Lord

McGowan) to review this field. There were 562 supply undertakings of all sizes and degrees of efficiency. Though A.C. had
become general, D.C. was still supplied by some undertakings;
methods of charge varied and distribution voltages were not
standardised.

Two-thirds of the undertakings were under public ownership,
and the great municipalities were proud of their electricity undertakings. Electricity was profitable and many municipal undertakings made useful contributions in relief of rates. But in between
the boroughs and around the boroughs there were company
electricity undertakings of varying status – some merely distribution companies with limited franchises and some power companies
with no limit to their franchises. These power companies were
forerunners of the Central Electricity Board: they were pioneers
who set up fair-sized power stations and thus overcame the
difficulties arising from the small units, which were the results of
early legislation and which had rapidly become out of date.
Relations between local authority undertakings and company
undertakings were not good. The former regarded themselves as
the vessels chosen by Parliament and those local authorities whose
areas were served by company undertakings were waiting to take
them over at the end of their forty-two years' franchise. Consequently companies which covered both urban and rural areas
resented the possibility of ultimate fragmentation of their undertakings as the urban areas bought themselves out, leaving them
with small uneconomic fragments between the areas of local
authorities. Technically this was indefensible and retrograde. The
obvious solution was integration of all the undertakings in an area,
but this was bedevilled by politics; on what basis would one
combine privately owned and publicly owned undertakings?

The McGowan Committee of 1936 could find no better solution
than area schemes centred on a well-organised undertaking:
sometimes that would be a company, sometimes a local authority.
The Chamberlain Government lacked the courage to stir up this
nest of hornets and so nothing was done between the McGowan
Report and the Second World War. The field was therefore left
clear for the Labour Government in 1945.

They accordingly produced their Electricity Bill early in 1947
and their remedy was, of course, nationalisation. A British
Electricity Authority (later renamed the Central Electricity
Authority) was to be set up to take over all the generating stations

and the high-voltage grid. Distribution was to be dealt with by twelve Electricity Boards in England and Wales: two such Boards were to cover the South of Scotland. The North of Scotland was already catered for by the Hydro-Electric Board which had been created in 1943 as a result of the efforts of Mr Thomas Johnston, then Secretary of State for Scotland.

This set-up was modified in 1955 when the two Area Boards in the South of Scotland were detached and united into one South of Scotland Electricity Board which was made responsible for generation as well as distribution in its own territory. The responsibility for this Board was transferred from the Ministry of Fuel and Power to the Scottish Office. Scotland was thus endowed with two electricity boards, each autonomous in its own area and responsible for its own supplies. The Mackenzie Committee in 1962 recommended that they should be amalgamated into one Electricity Board for Scotland, but this recommendation was not accepted by the Government, who decided that close consultation and co-operation between the two Boards were enough.

The nationalised electricity supply industry started operations on 1 April 1948. In July 1954 the Ministry of Fuel and Power set up a Committee 'to inquire into the organisation and efficiency of the electricity supply industry etc.' which reported in January 1956. The chairman of the Committee was Sir Edwin Herbert (later Lord Tangley) and the Report is therefore usually referred to as the Herbert Report.

As a result of this Report the Electricity Act 1957 was passed, revising the Electricity Act 1947 and setting up a new structure for the industry. As from 1 January 1958 the Central Electricity Authority was abolished. It was replaced by an Electricity Council and a Central Electricity Generating Board. These will be described later.

The history of nationalised electricity supply falls therefore into two periods. The first lasted from 1 April 1948 to 31 December 1957 when there were the Central Authority and the Area Boards; the second from 1 January 1958 when there have been three organisations: Electricity Council, Central Electricity Generating Board and Area Boards.

In the set-up created by the Electricity Act 1947 the dominating body was the Central Electricity Authority. It alone was responsible for raising finance for the industry. All the financial requirements of the fourteen (later twelve) Area Boards were submitted to the Authority, which scrutinised them and, after approval, incorporated them with its own requirements into one whole, which was then presented to the Government. The Authority was the only producer and wholesaler of electricity; the area boards were retail distributors. Further, the Authority had a general power of supervision over the Boards which is set out in detail in Section 6 of the Electricity Act 1947. For instance Section 6 (1) lays it down that:

The Central Authority may give such directions to Area Boards as appears to the Central Authority to be necessary or expedient for this purpose of co-ordinating the distribution of electricity by Area Boards and exercising a general control over the policy of those Boards, and every Area Board shall give effect to any such directions given to them by the Central Authority.

The latter part of this section gives the Central Authority full power of control.

The history of electricity supply in the ten years 1948 to 1957 is therefore mainly the history of the Central Electricity Authority.

Chapter 10 of the Herbert Report examines in detail the relation between the Central Electricity Authority and the Area Boards and shows that these powers of the Authority were exercised to the full – to the extent of causing resentment among the Area Boards. The Committee was particularly disturbed by the fact that the Authority as the producer and wholesaler insisted on controlling the retail price at which the Area Boards sold to the consumer. There was no arbitrator between Authority and Area Board.

Why, it may be asked, was the Authority put into such a strong position? The answer is simple. The Labour Government worked to the policy of setting up strong national Public Corporations to administer the industries taken into public ownership. They were very centralised. The National Coal Board, set up in 1946, stood by itself; its subsidiary bodies were devised and appointed by itself. The Central Electricity Authority and the Transport Commission – both created in 1947 – had subsidiary bodies appointed by the respective ministers, but in both cases ministers had to consult with the central organisation, whose views on appointments were not likely to be disregarded. Another important factor was that the Treasury, faced with indefinite financial commitments in uncharted territory, naturally preferred to deal with one large central organisation.

The problems before the new organisation on vesting day, 1 April

1948, were many and serious. There was an acute shortage of coal and the domestic consumer was rationed in his use of that fuel. He therefore turned to fuels under his control – gas and electricity – and used them hard to remedy his shortage of solid fuel. The year before, in February 1947, the shortage of coal had led to a breakdown in electricity supplies; there was not enough coal for the power stations. So there was a strong and increasing demand for electricity, limited only by shortage of appliances, which were in short supply.

But the industry was in poor shape to meet increasing or even existing demands. In the earlier years of the war several power stations were completed, but the Government would not sanction plans to build further stations. These could not start working for several years and therefore were of lower priority than the immediate demands of the war. Not only was generating plant short, but transmission and distribution networks were in poor condition and breakdowns due to overload a frequent occurrence.

It is not surprising, therefore, that in its first few years electricity supply during the winters was often seriously inadequate. The fundamental problems of electrical supply are twofold: electricity cannot be stored and it must be supplied on demand from the switch. So if too much is demanded, the engineer must by technical devices slow down the supply to the consumer by reducing voltage and/or frequency; but if demand still keeps on rising, a stage is reached where the slowing down will materially affect the working of the power station plant and he has then no alternative but to cut off supply to some consumers. All these devices had to be used repeatedly.

It is a slow business to build a power station, and to speed matters up it was decided to standardise the design of a generating set at 30 megawatts.* This was necessary but unfortunate in that it delayed the development of more powerful sets.

The Central Authority and the Area Boards struggled hard to improve the supply of electricity and their efforts began to tell. They had advantages. For the first time electricity supply was under unified control and planning ahead became much simpler than hitherto. Shortage of electricity was painful and therefore the plans of the industry to improve supplies were given high priority and capital was made available. Between 1947 and 1957 the capacity of generating plants doubled as did the sales of electricity. Doubling

* A megawatt (MW.) equals 1000 kilowatts (kW.).

D 2

its size every ten years has been the dominating characteristic of electricity supply almost from the beginning. As we shall see later in this chapter a fascinating and difficult question to answer is how much longer this relentless and unvarying growth in demand will continue.

The two main consumers of electricity are industry and the home. Many large firms in industry generate their own electricity – in amount about one-ninth of the public supply. Nevertheless industry rapidly increased its consumption as it reorganised itself after the war and the country began its post-war era of full employment. As industry expanded, it turned out the electrical appliances which, in the absence of domestic help, moved from luxury to necessity; with the increasing number of new homes – which use far more electricity than old houses – the domestic user consumed more and more, though it was not till the late fifties and early sixties that the increase in consumption became a problem. For the great convenience and cleanliness of electricity led to a vast expansion of what is termed 'direct space heating', that is, the use of electric fires during any hour of the day at the convenience of the consumer. It will be remembered that coal was rationed until 1958.

During the early fifties the rate of installation of generating plant exceeded the rate of growth of the basic demand for electricity. But unfortunately the basic demand is not all; there is also peak demand. On a cold winter day the peak demand might be double that of a summer day. There is therefore a difference in the seasonal demands; but there is also a difference between days in one season – according to the weather and between different hours on the same day. If there were a really cold spell in the winter, electricity supply would become inadequate. The station engineers would resort to the various technical devices referred to above.

The cause of this was mainly the increase in domestic consumption and in this electricity tariffs play a part. The industrial consumer pays first of all a charge for his maximum demand which is varied by the 'coal clause'; that is, when the price of coal changes – it has always been an increase since the war – the maximum demand charge is adjusted accordingly. The industrialist uses his electricity for a fixed number of hours a day and unless it is a continuous process, does not use it at the weekend. Secondly, the industrialist pays a follow-on charge for the number of kilowatt hours ('units') which he takes. The domestic consumer, on the other hand, uses it seven days a week for about sixteen hours a day and often uses more at the weekend – especially in space heating – than during the week. It has therefore been an established belief among electrical engineers that the domestic consumer practises 'diversity' and they therefore encouraged this consumer by 'promotional tariffs' to increase his offtake. These tariffs were in two parts. The first part was either a standing charge based on floor space, number of rooms or some similar measure or a high charge for a block of units; the second part was a follow-on charge for each unit.

It is obvious that both the industrial and domestic tariffs were 'promotional', in the sense that the more units which were consumed the lower was the 'average' price per unit because the standing charge forming the first part of the tariff was spread over a large number of units. Thus between 1948–9 and 1955–6 the average price per unit sold to industry increased from 0·947 to 1·194 pence; and the average price to the domestic consumer from 1·339 to 1·533 pence. These were modest increases over seven years of inflation. The electricity supply industry has always made much of the fact that its product was relatively cheap. But this cheapness cannot be regarded as an unalloyed benefit, as the industry has now come to appreciate.

For by emphasising the cheapness of electricity, the industry in its belief of 'diversity' encouraged the indiscriminate use of its product which in turn created difficulties in meeting the full demand. The industry distinguishes between 'simultaneous maximum load met during the year' and 'simultaneous maximum potential demand during the year'. In the nineteen years from 1948 to 1966, the two figures coincided only for the five years 1956–60 (*Ministry of Power Statistical Abstract*, 1966, table 81).

It is not surprising therefore that the programme of capital development increased rapidly. In 1948–9 the amount of new generating plant commissioned by the Central Authority was 423 MW. which increased nearly fourfold to 1,632 MW. in 1955–6. This represented a very great achievement, but, as the Authority itself pointed out, 'there is still, however, a shortage of plant' (1955–6 Report, para. 83).

Mr Herbert Morrison, as the senior Minister on nationalisation policy, had felt that it would be an advantage if at suitable inter-vals – say seven to ten years – an outside body could examine the working of the great organisations set up after 1946. As we have seen in Chapter 2, the National Coal Board set up its own Com-mittee of Inquiry under Dr (afterwards Lord) Fleck. As mentioned earlier in this chapter, in the case of electricity we have the Report of the Herbert Committee (Cmd. 9672). This is a most valuable report because it is the only case of a full and thorough enquiry into the workings of a nationalised industry by an outside committee; the Herbert Report, running to 508 paragraphs and 125 recommendations, is far fuller than the Fleck Report. These are the only two reports by outside bodies on nationalised industries after more than twenty years of nationalisation. There was the hush-hush Working Party on the Transport Commission to Mr Marples, whose report was not published. Apart from these there are the Reports of the Select Committee on the Nationalised Industries which are described in Chapter 7 and which have a limited value.

Because many of the recommendations of the Herbert Committee were adopted in the Electricity Act 1957, which remodelled the structure of the industry, the Herbert Report has now become to some extent an historical document. But no student of the nationalised industries should fail to read it most carefully because of the light it threw on the inner working of a great and rapidly expanding nationalised industry. Here it is only possible to summarise briefly some of the main recommendations of the Committee. The sketch of the considerable achievements of the industry in the years 1948 to 1957 given above will help to provide a background to these recommendations.

The main recommendations of the Committee are as follows:

We believe, firstly, that the formal structure of the industry is not conducive to the highest efficiency. So far it has been made to work. But it contains unnecessary complications and weaknesses. . . . Nowhere in the industry is there any critical and fully effective appraisal of the huge sums in the capital and revenue programmes and budgets. The Minister himself in approving such programmes, and advising Parliament to approve them, has perforce to rely in the main upon the industry's own assessment of its legitimate requirements. We are satisfied that there is a real and valuable job to be done within the industry by an independent supervisory body (para. 501).

We believe, secondly, that the industry has not yet solved the problem of the right degree of delegation within the formal framework. Partly, no doubt, as a result of anxiety over public accountability, there is a tendency to do work in whole or part several times over at different levels (para. 502).

We believe, thirdly, that the industry has a long way to go in the introduction of modern aids to good management. In budgeting, in work study, in operational research, in incentive wage systems, it is not in the van. Indeed in some respects it would not be unfair to say it is lagging (para. 503).

We believe, fourthly, that the industry must take very energetic steps to ensure that it attracts and retains an adequate supply of first-rate talent for both technical and managerial posts. Part of the trouble lies in the low level of salaries, part in the limited number of independent commands (para. 504).

The four points we have made above are all inter-linked. Up to the present the *esprit de corps* in the industry remains good. There were and are inevitable personal difficulties and problems but the zeal and loyalty of staff taken over in 1948 still remains. The very size of the industry and the remoteness of authority lead to loss of morale unless positive steps are taken to build it up. We feel that too many purely management decisions are taken at the centre (para. 505).

Our fifth general impression is that the industry has not done as much hard thinking as it should about the economics of electricity supply. The whole field of public utility economics bristles with difficulties that emerge in terms of investment problems and pricing problems. The avoidance of waste and efficiency of the industry depend on the right answers being given to these problems (para. 506).

Electricity supply is a monopoly with a constantly growing demand for its product. These facts expose it to two serious risks, either of which could, in our view, sap its efficiency. The industry could, without financial embarrassment, jog along comfortably without much effort; and it could be used as a device for implementing national policies and for transferring income from one section of the community to another without the burden of these policies being properly weighed in Parliament or by the Minister. We attach great importance therefore to the industry being run on business lines. It should have one duty and one duty alone: to supply electricity to those who will meet the costs of it and to do so at the lowest possible expenditure of resources consistent with the maintenance of employment standards at the level of the best private firms (para. 507).

To back up these forceful views the Committee proposed a reorganisation of the industry's structure, the main feature of which was the creation of a Central Electricity Generation Board to carry out the functions of generating and transmitting electricity in bulk for supply to the Area Boards. The Central Authority would be reconstituted and would have a small but expert staff which would supervise and approve the plans and functions both of the Generation Board and of Area Boards. This Central Authority would consist of persons from outside the electricity supply industry. 'Serving members of the Statutory Area and Generation

Boards would not be eligible for membership of the Authority' (para. 253).

This raised a serious issue for the Government – the most serious in the whole Report. The new Authority clearly resembled the Electricity Commissioners, who had been abolished by the 1947 Electricity Act. Those Commissioners were necessary because in those days electricity supply was in the hands of 560 undertakings, the majority of which were small; supervision and guidance were required. But it was very difficult controlling a few large undertakings which, by definition, would be run by the most capable and experienced men in electricity supply; if they were not, the Minister was failing in his duty of selecting the best-qualified men for these responsible posts.

There were two further difficulties in this proposal. How would the industry react to supervision from a body outside its own ranks? 'Serving members' were not to be appointed. Retired members would not be able to undertake such a formidable task as was proposed for the new Central Authority. If they came from outside the industry, they would have to recruit staff with expert knowledge of electricity supply, who presumably would come from inside the industry.

The second difficulty was even more serious: the proposed Central Authority would be so strong that, in effect, it would take over the responsibilities of the Minister of Power. If he could find a small group of first-class men to supervise the industry, he would be quite unable to challenge their decisions; he would have to accept them. But the responsibility to Parliament is his and he has to convince the Treasury to put up the vast and increasing sums for this huge capital-intensive industry. This very important question – how far can a Minister and his department supervise a nationalised industry – is dealt with in Chapter 8, 'Government and the Nationalised Industries'.

So it is not surprising that the Government did not accept the new model Central Authority. Instead the Electricity Act 1957 set up an Electricity Council – modelled on the Gas Council set up by the Gas Act 1948. The huge monolithic organisations created by the post-war Labour Government after ten years' experience were out of favour; the decentralised Gas Industry was regarded as an example to follow. The members of the new Electricity Council were the twelve chairmen of the Area Boards, three representatives of the Central Generating Board and six independent members appointed by the Minister. Of these six, only one came from outside the industry, who was appointed part-time deputy chairman. Professor Edwards, who had been a member of the Herbert Committee, was, after four years as deputy chairman, appointed chairman of the Electricity Council.

The working of this rather large 'federal' Council of twenty-one members is described in the evidence given in 1962 to the Select Committee on the Nationalised Industries. As might have been expected, a vote is seldom taken – and then on unimportant issues. There are twelve Area Board chairmen on the Council and only three representatives of the Generating Board. But the decision on the most important issue – the bulk supply tariff of the Generating Board – on which there might be serious differences, is not for the Council but for the Generating Board itself, which nevertheless consults the Council and has regards to its views. Clearly the views of the independent members and above all the chairmen of the Council are of great importance.

The Council will advise the Minister and will assist the Generating and Area Boards in their plans for maintaining and developing the industry. It will be the body for conducting labour relations for the industry – which are, of course, on a national scale. Finally, it will be responsible for research.

On finance, the 1957 Act departs from the 1947 Act. That provided that the Central Electricity Authority should be the only body authorised to issue electricity stock. When, in 1956, issues of stock were replaced by Exchequer advances, the Authority was, of course, the only body to which these advances could be made.

The 1957 Act makes all the Boards – Generating and Area – financially autonomous. Each Board has to ensure 'that the revenues of the Board are not less than sufficient to meet the outgoings of the Board properly chargeable to revenue account, taking one year with another' (Section 13). The 1947 Act, on the other hand, provided for the lumping together of all the revenues of Authority and Boards. Naturally, therefore, the 1957 Act allows each Board to raise its own stock or to borrow on its own account from the banks; otherwise there would be little meaning in the financial autonomy. Nevertheless Section 15 (3) of the Act provides that Exchequer advances shall only be made to the Electricity Council; that fact, to some extent, weakens the formal financial autonomy of the Area Boards, because it is the Council which advises the Minister, who approves capital programmes and provides the necessary finance.

In 1964 the Electricity Council negotiated with the trade unions a scheme for changing, by stages, the status of the industrial employees of the industry. The main features of the first stage were that hourly rates of pay were replaced by annual salaries with the same sick pay scheme as technical and administrative employees. The second stage provided for revised shift workings and for the five-day week to be staggered over the seven days of the week, coupled with a reduction in the working week from 42 to 40 hours. The third stage provided for increments for continued service. It will be interesting to see how this scheme works out. Electricity supply, being a huge and expanding public utility industry, can and should afford to strike out into new and imaginative lines in industrial relations.

As regards recruitment of first-rate talent for both technical and managerial posts, there has been a great change. With the advent of nuclear power it has become all the more necessary. The Herbert Committee was satisfied that the policy of the Central Electricity Authority in recruiting, training and finding responsible posts for graduates was unsatisfactory. Too few graduates were recruited and after training had to compete for higher posts with older men, who had more experience but who were not likely to be suitable for top management. As competition for recruiting graduates into industry became more and more intense in the fifties, the intake of graduates by the Central Authority dropped to very low figures – eight in 1954–5, seven in 1955–6, nine in 1956–7 and eleven in 1957–8. The Herbert Committee concluded (para. 328): 'we do not consider the industry will be able to provide a top management of the requisite calibre from its own ranks.'

The advent of the Electricity Council had early results. In 1959–60 forty-one graduates were recruited. The industry started a university scholarship scheme, which is now supplying the industry with a steady stream of mechanical and electrical engineering graduates. Unlike some other nationalised industries electricity supply is expanding and has a great future before it. Also it does not stand alone but is closely connected with a strong electrical manufacturing industry where there are great firms of repute. In a sense, therefore, electricity supply has to compete for staff with those firms which supply it with plant and machinery and for which it is often the principal, if not the only, customer.

Would it not be to the advantage of both sides of the electrical industry if they arranged a scheme for the interchange of some staff – say for a period of two years?

The fifth point which the Herbert Committee makes about the economics of electricity supply is perhaps the most crucial of all. It is more than twelve years since the Report appeared and we cannot yet say that the 'difficulties that emerge in terms of investment problems and pricing problems in public utility economics' have been overcome.

Progress in dealing with these difficulties was bound to be slow. There was first the personnel in the industry with their natural and praiseworthy utility outlook. Supplies to consumers must be maintained at all costs and in all conditions; this was a great tradition well honoured. To refuse marginal supplies because they were fantastically expensive was unthinkable. Secondly, the problem of determining the costs of differing loads in a highly complex and integrated system of supply is most difficult and cannot yet be said to have been solved. It can only be solved by the Electricity Council processing by the most modern methods the statistics and information which they alone possess. Anyone outside the industry can do nothing on this. It is possible to see something of this refining process in tariffs in the bulk tariff fixed by the Generating Board for supplies to Area Boards. For instance that tariff has day- and night-running rates. But the large quantities involved and the limited number of offtake points make metering easy and inexpensive. It is a very different matter with $17\frac{1}{2}$ million consumers.

In the last ten years there has been only one significant change in retail tariffs – the general adoption of an off-peak tariff for taking electricity at night at about half the price of the charge during the day. This was first used for under-floor heating, which had limited appeal; but in recent years it has been developed for night storage heaters, which have proved popular for domestic use. The Electricity Council reports that in 1966–7 6,675 million units were sold on off-peak tariffs out of a total of 141,500 million. It is a modest contribution improving the system load factor by $2\frac{1}{2}$ per cent.

But certain general features of the retail electricity tariff are noticeable. In the sixteen years between 1950 and 1966 the average net price per unit to the industrial consumer increased from 0·948 to 1·478 pence – an increase of 56 per cent. The corresponding increase to the domestic consumer was from 1·352 to 1·909 pence – an increase of only 41 per cent (*Ministry of Power Statistical Abstract*, 1966, table 95).

These figures show that the domestic consumer has been receiving his electricity on favourable terms as compared with the industrial consumer. The substantial increase in domestic tariffs of September 1967 should go some distance in correcting this disparity, which has been a serious factor in the domestic contribution, especially by direct space heating, to peak loads in the winter.

The severe winter of 1962–3 gave the supply industry a shock. In the extreme weather of that winter the maximum demand met fell short of the maximum potential demand by about 2,600 MW. – achieved, of course, by slowing down frequency and voltage and shedding load. This crisis forced them to review their operations and to revise their estimates of future demand and of capital expenditure required to meet it.

As power stations and high-tension grids take about six years to produce, the load met in 1962 had been planned in 1956. The estimates of 1956 show 'that certain assumptions have been falsified by subsequent developments, especially in the domestic sector of demand'. In the three years preceding 1962 'the demand for electricity from industry has grown by only an average of 4·8 per cent per annum but domestic sales have grown by 17·4 per cent' (1962–3 Report, paras. 15 & 18). So the Council set to work in 1963 to prepare a revised capital programme. The following Table gives the original estimates of demand for the years 1963–4 to 1968–9 and the revision made in May 1963 (Electricity Council Report, 1962–3, para. 24):

	National simultaneous maximum demand			Total units required		
	Original estimate	Revised estimate	Actual	Original estimate	Revised estimate	Actual
	Thousand MW.			*Thousand million kwH.*		
1963–4	31·9	32·1	29·9	136·2	136·9	132
1964–5	34·3	35·1	31·3	146·8	150·5	141
1965–6	37·0	38·3	33·35	158·5	165	148·8
1966–7	39·9	41·8	33·97	171·2	181	152·8
1967–8	43·0	45·7	35·81	185	199	162·7
1968–9	46·4	46·4	—	199·8	219	—

'Total units required' is the quantity generated and is about 8 per cent greater than the quantity sold. This 8 per cent is used by the supply system.

What is clear from these figures is that both the rate of growth in electricity consumption and in maximum demand have in recent years declined considerably. Over the four years 1 April 1963 to 31 March 1967 output increased by 16 per cent – an average of 4 per cent per annum (not compound) as against the estimate quoted above of 10·1 per cent per annum compound.

A good commentary on the above table is contained in paragraph 28 of the 1968 Report of the Prices and Incomes Board on the Bulk Supply Tariff of the C.E.G.B. (Cmnd. 3575):

28. The forecast made in 1963 for five years ahead was highly important for the planning of the programme of construction of generating plant and of the transmission system to meet the peak demand expected in the winter of 1968-69. The level of demand forecast was 31 per cent greater than is now expected. This means that if the construction of new stations and the deliveries of plant had not been subject to any delays and if the scrapping of old plant were not accelerated, the plant margin would have been up to a hypothetical 49 per cent rather than the earlier planned margin of 14 per cent.

The construction delays referred to in the preceding paragraph are very costly. Capital charges arise on plant not yet commissioned. At the end of 1967 there was a backlog of unfinished plant amounting to 7,546 MW. (ibid. para. 32). Not only was this costly, but the delay prevented the replacing of old plant with low thermal efficiency by up-to-date more efficient plant,. The result is that the overall thermal efficiency of conventional steam stations has hardly progressed over the last five years.

In September 1965 the Labour Government published the National Plan. The electricity industry, taking account of the assumptions of economic growth in the Plan and of recent figures of electricity demand, rather quickly produced in January 1966 a forecast for 1971–2 of a maximum demand of 55,000 MW. and of energy requirements of 246·7 thousand million units.

These figures have been steadily reduced year by year as a result of the unfortunate economic developments from 1966 onwards.

The question whether electricity supply will continue to double every ten years – as it has done hitherto – is of national importance. This most capital-intensive of all industries is spending over £600 million a year, of which a substantial amount has to be borrowed from the Government. Since April 1963 the rate of growth has been below expectations. In September 1967 domestic electricity charges were increased by about one-sixth. The growth of off-peak space- and water-heating and the competition of gas should reduce the frightening winter peaks that have caused trouble.

The capital development programmes spelled out above look too large for the next decade. If sales do not rise as forecast, the capital charges will become crippling on the lower turnover, which in turn will put charges up further. The industry will have to slow down its capital development programme, which, of course, can only be done very gently, as contracts are placed five and six years ahead. At the same time it should tackle with more energy one of the main causes of the high winter peaks in bad weather, which provide a great stimulus for high capital expenditure. The industry is well aware of this problem as the following paragraphs show.

The shock of the severe winter of 1962–3 had another effect besides leading to a drastic increase in the capital programmes. It persuaded the industry that the time had come to grapple with the promotional domestic tariff, which was obviously an important cause of the difficulties in meeting maximum demand. This was such a significant decision that the relevant paragraph 76 of 1962–3 Report must be quoted in full:

Electric space heating is so simple, effective and clean that it is bound to develop further. The Electricity Council have set up a working party from the Area Boards, the Generating Board and the Council to review the problem urgently. This working party is concurrently investigating the characteristics of the domestic load, particularly the space heating aspects, and considering possible alternative tariffs. Existing tariffs in all boards include off-peak rates, which encourage the use of electricity at times of low cost. The question is whether there is a tariff it would be practicable to apply to domestic and possibly small commercial and industrial consumers, which would present a system of prices, guiding them even more effectively to use electricity when it is cheap rather than when it is expensive. The working party are also endeavouring to assess the extent to which such a tariff might influence consumers' usage, provide protection for the system and how far the resultant savings would be worthwhile in relation to the additional metering costs. In short, whether a change from the present forms of tariff would be worthwhile.

This is followed by paragraph 77, which lists six alternative tariff systems to the one type in force.

A reader of these paragraphs might conclude that at long last the industry was starting the 'hard thinking about the economics of electricity supply' which the Herbert Committee had suggested in paragraph 506 of its Report quoted earlier. The nettle of the promotional domestic tariff, which was obviously worrying the industry, was being grasped.

The Working Party set to work in 1962. The year after we read in paragraph 153 of the 1963–4 Report as follows:

Concern was expressed in the winter of 1962–63 regarding the effects of the growing space-heating load on the pattern of demand and hence the costs which were being incurred by the industry in meeting this load. The establishment of a Working Party to examine this problem was mentioned in the Council's Report for 1962–63, and they have studied the long-run marginal costs likely to arise from meeting current trends of growth in demand for space heating. Their results are being considered in relation to pricing policy and the development of retail tariffs.

We move on to 1964. In the 1964–5 Report we are told of various pieces of research into the characteristics of the domestic load. But no reference is made to the Working Party so urgently set up two years before.

We now come to 1965. After further references into research into the domestic load, the Council announces an experiment into three types of alternative domestic tariff. As this is important and will be discussed for years to come, paragraph 213 of the 1965–6 Report deserves quotation:

To frame acceptable domestic tariffs, knowledge is required not only of the costs of supply which can be inferred from load characteristics data, but also of the ownership of appliances and the practical aspects of metering. The industry has decided to arrange experiments in which samples of domestic consumers will buy their electricity under special tariffs. Three tariff forms are being tried:
(1) A simple seasonal tariff with a higher rate during the three winter months.
(2) A seasonal time-of-day tariff which has a high rate for peak hours on winter week-days, a low night rate and an intermediate rate for the rest of the year. This tariff in particular requires complex metering.
(3) A load/rate tariff in which the price varies with the level of electricity demand, being low when the consumer's demand is below a certain predetermined level. This type of tariff is widely used in Norway for domestic consumers.

These experiments involve 3400 consumers in six Area Boards and are likely to last for at least five years.

It may be noted that the first of these experimental tariffs – a seasonal tariff with a higher rate in the winter months – was tried out by the industry on a nationwide scale in the winter of 1948–9. It was done at the request of the Minister of Fuel and Power following the Report of the Clow Committee. The industry tried the experiment with great reluctance and persuaded the Minister not to repeat it.

To sum up. In 1962 the industry was sufficiently worried by the effect of domestic demand on the peak winter load to set up a Working Party to consider six possible alternative tariffs or combinations of them. We do not know what happened to that Working Party.

Three years later the industry decided to carry out a small-scale experiment – involving 3,400 out of fifteen million domestic consumers on whom three alternative tariffs would be tried out. We are told that these experiments are 'likely to last at least five years'.

At the earliest, then, these experiments will be concluded in 1971; with the cautionary 'at least' the date might be 1972 or 1973. But even when the experiments are concluded, the results will have to be scrutinised and decisions made on them. If it should be decided that one or more alternative tariffs should be introduced to replace the present domestic tariff, one or two years at least might be necessary for the change-over–particularly if new types of meter were involved; these would have to be manufactured.

We were told in 1963 (1962–3 Report, para. 74) that

the supply industry has for some time been concerned about its vulnerability to direct methods of space heating by electricity, which can be switched on at any time without restriction, particularly in very cold weather. Any one of its sixteen million or so consumers can at any time buy an electric fire and add to the risk, to which the system is exposed in such weather. In total there is probably more than 250,000 Mw of equipment of all kinds connected to the system, of which more than 130,000 Mw is estimated to be installed in domestic premises, and of this about 28,000 Mw is attributable to direct domestic space heating. On the other hand, the total generating capacity of the system is only some 30,000 Mw.

The supply industry is taking about ten years to devise a policy to cope with the threat described in the preceding paragraph.

Meanwhile, stimulated by this threat, the huge capital investment programme of the industry was expanded further, at a time when demand for electricity began to slacken. The result is that the industry is now more than amply equipped with generating and transmitting equipment. The capital requirements have risen from £326·5 million in 1961–2 to £616·4 million in 1966–7; in 1961–2 the industry borrowed from the Government £173·7 million; this had increased to £379·3 million in 1966–7.

The Herbert Committee reported in January 1956. Is it not time now that a powerful committee be appointed to examine the great capital expenditure of the electricity supply industry and the effects of that expenditure on the national economy?

TABLE IV: GAS (GREAT BRITAIN)

	1950/1	1955/6	1960/1	1962/3	1963/4	1964/5	1965/6	1966/7	1967/8
Value of total sales of gas (£ million)	126.3	185	234.1	270.8	277.8	298.6	324.9	354.5	391
Total sales (million therms)	2337	2583	2612	2867	2924	3169	3486	3755	4199
Sales to industry (million therms)	580	742	852	852	861	915	928	908	914
Domestic sales (million therms)	1357	1364	1291	1493	1554	1727	2005	2267	2652
Average sales per domestic consumer (therms)	121	113.2	106.7	124.1	128.9	142.3	163.7	182.8	211
Average net selling price per therm (pence)									
1. All consumers	12.98	17.2	21.51	22.86	22.96	22.77	22.52	22.79	22.47
2. Domestic consumers	14.6	19.7	25.8	26.88	26.9	26.36	25.56	25.49	24.69
3. Industrial consumers	9.49	12.89	15.45	16.05	16.07	16.05	15.87	16.02	15.94
Capital Expenditure (£ million)	33.39	57.9	42	57.4	89	88.3	119	207.8	282

Source: Gas Council Annual Reports.

5 Gas

THE history of the nationalised gas industry falls into two distinct periods. In the first, from May 1949 to about 1960, the industry was making little headway. Since 1960 it has undergone a revolution and is rapidly changing its outlook and character; indeed the shape of the gas industry in the 1970s is perhaps the most fascinating problem in the whole field of energy in Britain. This chapter therefore will start by describing the first twelve years. The second part will deal with the revolutionary changes in the sixties.

Apart from the abortive nationalisation of iron and steel, gas was the last industry to be taken over by the Labour Government of 1945–50. In the case of gas there was an up-to-date Report by the Committee presided over by Mr Geoffrey Heyworth (now Lord Heyworth), which probed the weaknesses of the industry and suggested that the industry be reorganised under public ownership.

Gas was an old industry by 1948, with nearly a century and a half of history; it had clearly been fashioned in the Victorian era. Its organisation at the end of the war left much to be desired, as the Heyworth Committee pointed out. About 64 per cent of the gas was supplied by nearly 700 companies, but these ranged in size from the great Gas, Light and Coke Company to tiny companies in small country towns, and even villages. Of these companies, 334 had a capital of less than £20,000 and 194 a capital between £20,000 and £100,000. Many of the small companies were grossly inefficient. They operated on too minute a scale to afford competent staff and up-to-date plant, their service was often inadequate and the gas they supplied left much to be desired in its quality. In the inter-war years holding companies had sprung up which had bought up many small companies, reorganised them and given them the advantage of competent technical guidance. But except in few cases these purchased companies were not contiguous and physical amalgamation was not possible.

The remaining 36 per cent of the gas was supplied by public authorities, mostly municipal undertakings. They were common in the Midlands, Lancashire, Yorkshire and Scotland. They also varied greatly both in size and efficiency. They ranged from large and efficient undertakings such as Birmingham, to municipal undertakings so small they could hardly afford to pay a qualified gas engineer. In many cases the plant and distribution network were old and worn out.

Unlike the colliery and electricity companies, the gas companies did not embark on a campaign of opposition to nationalisation. Perhaps they felt it would be hopeless – having seen several more powerful industries taken over. After the Heyworth Report they could not really put up much of a case.

In fact one may surmise that the gas industry was even anxious to be nationalised. What was its future otherwise? The coal industry, on which it depended for its raw materials, had been organised into a monolithic statutory monopoly. How were they to bargain with it unless they themselves were organised on a national basis? Their formidable rival, electricity, was also organised under a powerful central authority. Both these giants had state backing and both had access to cheap state-guaranteed capital. How could the gas industry hope to survive unless it were similarly organised and similarly financed? There was little attraction in the splendid isolation of private enterprise, and little reluctance in mounting the band wagon, even though for decency's sake it might be described as a tumbril.

The industry therefore put up no opposition. On the other hand, opposition in Parliament was fiercer. The first flush of enthusiasm for nationalisation was waning and the Conservative Opposition put up a tough fight. The committee stage of the Gas Bill was marked for its prolonged sittings, the final session lasting without a break for the record period of fifty-one hours. But the fury in Parliament found no echoes outside; it was difficult for the country to become excited or disturbed.

The new organisation provided in the Bill seemed a great improvement on its three predecessors – coal, transport and electricity. There was no powerful central body dominating the industry. The supply of gas, unlike the supply of electricity, was at the time a local and not a national responsibility. So the twelve Area Boards set up under the Bill were autonomous. They supplied themselves with their gas and were responsible for their own finance. But the Government required some national body to deal with national issues. Industrial relations were handled nationally, and the financing of the industry had to be arranged through some central organisation. So the Bill provided for a Gas Council. This was an exceptional body among the nationalised industries. It consists of the twelve chairmen of the Gas Boards, together with an independent chairman and deputy chairman. It had a small organisation and except on questions of general policy, which were decided at Council meetings, the Gas Boards could proceed independently. The measure of decentralisation was, therefore, great, and as few of the general issues affecting gas roused popular interest, the gas industry was seldom in the lime-light. The Gas Council might be described as a federal body – somewhat like the Senate of the United States – where each unit, however large or small, is equally represented. One can only conjecture on the course of its deliberations. But it is safe to assume that, as in all federal bodies, the constituent units show a prickly independence which at times make the chairman's task difficult.

Gas was nationalised in 1949 and may be said to have been *felix opportunitate*. In the preceding years the industry had expanded and when taken over looked with confidence to still greater expansion. Before the war the prospects of the gas industry had seemed uncertain. Its young competitor, electricity, was making great strides and doubling its output every few years. Between 1929 and 1939 sales of gas increased by only 10 per cent; in the same period electricity increased two and a half times. Clearly gas was finding it difficult to hold its own. Then came the war. In the ten years 1939 to 1949 gas sales increased by nearly 50 per cent and the rate of increase in electricity slackened. Both industries suffered from shortages of plant and fuel, but the gas industry had greater reserves of plant, because before the war it had been working well below capacity. During these ten years any supplier of fuel found a ready market. Gas and electricity, unlike coal or oil, were not rationed during this period; all attempts to devise a rationing scheme for the two metered fuels broke down before the administrative difficulties.

Consequently both gas and electricity during this period were faced with large unsatisfied demands for supplies – unsatisfied because there was not always the plant or raw material available. Much obviously had to be done and much capital invested to reconstruct the power stations and gas works to enable them to cope with future demands.

In electricity, as we have seen, a vast capital programme

followed nationalisation. But in the case of gas, it was soon apparent that the leeway of unsatisfied demands has been made up and that the industry's growth has slackened down to a snail's pace, comparable with the pre-war period. In the ten years between April 1950 and March 1960 sales of gas per annum increased from 2,402 to 2,540 million therms, or about 6 per cent; this gave an annual rate of increase of less than 1 per cent. Fluctuations in sales were on a very minute scale and less gas was sold in 1959–60 than in each of the preceding five years. In other words, the industry's sales were static, and such slight expansion as there had been took place in the early years following nationalisation; this in a prosperous period, with overfull employment and with a rationing of coal which lasted till 1958.

The slow growth during the ten pre-war years might be attributed to poor economic conditions and unemployment, though as we have seen these had no relevance for electricity. In the years after nationalisation the gas industry had all the help it could ever have hoped for – and more.

The slight increase in the 1950s in the sale of gas was the result of enhanced industrial activity. Sales to the domestic consumer, on the other hand, which are rather more than half the total, steadily declined year by year. The figures are given in Table IV. Here again the gas industry had great opportunities. Millions of new and reconstructed dwellings have been equipped with modern fuel appliances. For example, during the five years from April 1951 to March 1956 the Gas Boards sold 3,153,000 gas cookers, and cooking is the base domestic load for the gas industry. These modern cookers, more efficient than their predecessors, required less gas to do the same work. But there are a million new domestic consumers. In other words, domestic consumers were using less and less gas per head. In 1950–1 the average annual consumption per domestic consumer was almost 125 therms; in 1959–60 it had fallen to 104. Cooking habits have changed; the modern housewife cooks less than her mother. Some forms of cooking – such as boiling water for our national beverage, tea – have more and more been taken over by the electric kettle.

Though sales of industrial gas have been increasing at a moderate rate, the number of industrial gas consumers had fallen every year since nationalisation. In 1950–1 they numbered 114,300 but in 1959–60 they had declined to 89,700. Total sales of gas to industry, however, had been increasing.

Meanwhile the gas industry had been modernising itself. The Victorian pattern disappeared. In the 1950s it embarked on a considerable capital programme which was modest compared with electricity's programme, but which, nevertheless, was heavy for an industry whose sales had become static. The net value of fixed assets (after allowing for displacements and depreciation) added to the industry in the eleven years from 1 May 1949 to 31 March 1960 was £401,489,645 (1959–60 Report of Gas Council, p. 147), or just about £36½ million per annum. This was a considerable investment by an industry whose future looked more and more doubtful.

Nationalisation came at a most convenient time for the industry. After the war much of the manufacturing plant and even of the distribution system of the old undertakings was scrap. The gas industry had played a most useful part in the war and had successfully coped with great difficulties. In 1948 there were, or so it appeared, large and unsatisfied demands for gas. The State took over the industry, and handed control to the most successful managers of the larger undertakings. In the first Gas Council, nine out of the fourteen members had been associated with the management of company undertakings; it is interesting to note that not one member of the Council had been connected with a municipal undertaking. The remaining five chairmen of the Area Boards were newcomers.

Each Board was autonomous and each could prepare its own capital programme. They would be tied in a bundle and presented to the Government as the programme of the industry. But they were in fact twelve different programmes, worked out in the light of local conditions and dealing with local problems. Compared with electricity the whole twelve were modest enough; they therefore attracted little attention.

For the new managers of the gas industry, nationalisation meant a wonderful freedom. Gas was an old industry and the Victorians had displayed much ingenuity in devising controls over local monopolies. Devices such as maximum dividends and sliding scales, close control on the raising of capital, parliamentary scrutiny over every development – that was the world in which the manager of a gas undertaking moved. During the war further controls had been imposed; all price increases required authorisation by Government, and any project for capital expenditure underwent the closest scrutiny. All these controls were removed by the Gas Act 1948.

The men in control were, with one or two exceptions, in charge of much greater units than they had ever contemplated. Before nationalisation they might have thought of raising ten or twenty thousand pounds of capital for a project; a hundred-thousand-pound project would have meant long deliberation. Now they were contemplating millions of pounds of expenditure. Before the war they would have had to convince the Council of their local authority or their Board of Directors and then take their case to the Board of Trade. After overcoming these obstacles they would have had to promote a Private Bill and face a House of Commons Committee who would cross-examine them closely on the merits of the case. Now they merely had to prepare the schemes and take them to London where the Gas Council would automatically submit them once a year for Government approval. How could a Government be seriously critical of such a collection of schemes?

So the gas industry modernised itself. Hundreds of old and inefficient works were closed; they were reduced from 1,050 at vesting day to 428 in March 1960. The larger works were extended and linked together; 21,200 miles of mains were laid in the eleven years from nationalisation.

During the 1950s, therefore, the gas industry spent considerable sums on rebuilding its plants and mains. But it found itself in increasing difficulties in justifying this expenditure at a time when the market for gas remained static. For instance in May 1954 the Gas Council published a programme of development, *Fuel for the Nation*, for the seven years from 1 April 1953 to 31 March 1960. During that period it was estimated that the gas industry would require £366 million additional capital, of which £92 million would come from their own resources and £274 million would have to be borrowed. To back up this programme of development estimates were put forward of the increase in gas consumption up to 1960. Domestic consumption would increase from 1,366 million therms in 1952–3 to 1,536 million therms in 1959–60 – an increase over the period of 12½ per cent. Industrial consumption would increase from 639 million therms in 1952–3 to 794 million therms in 1959–1960.

These estimates were badly out. Domestic consumption, instead of rising from 1,366 to 1,536 million therms, declined to 1,268 million therms. The forecast for industrial consumption was more than successful. Instead of increasing from 639 to 794 million therms, it actually increased to 819 million therms.

What were the underlying difficulties facing the gas industry in the 1950s? First and foremost came their dependence on coking coal as the raw material for gas-making. It is well known that relations between the National Coal Board and the gas industry in the fifties were not good. The former was struggling to increase coal supplies by mechanising the mines. In doing so, it produced large quantities of small coal which found a ready market in the expanding electricity industry. Coal with coking properties, however, was more difficult to produce and was required both by the gas industry and the steel industry for their coke ovens. This type of coal came largely from older coal fields such as Durham, which together with Yorkshire supplied over three-fifths of the industry's requirements. The unscreened smalls burned under power-station boilers were of no use to the gas industry, which required mostly graded coal (that is, coal roughly half an inch to two inches) from which coke could be produced. This type of coal was more expensive to produce than the ever-increasing quantities of smalls; therefore when coal prices increased the gas industry usually paid a larger increase than its electricity rival. What was more, as the older coal fields such as Durham became worked out, there would be difficulty in maintaining supplies of coking coal. By the mid-fifties it was clear to the gas industry that if they were to expand they could not depend on coking coal; they had to find alternative raw materials for making gas.

In 1950–1 the gas industry paid £86 million for its coal supplies; six years later the cost had risen to £151 million. This substantial increase in raw material costs was a basic factor in increasing the price of gas. In the ten years from 1950 to 1960 the average price of gas to the domestic consumer had risen from 14·8 pence to 24·91 pence per therm – an increase of 68 per cent. In the same ten years the average price of electricity to the domestic consumer had risen from 1·346 pence to 1·687 per unit or 25 per cent. The average price of gas had therefore in the 1950s increased nearly three times as much as the average price of electricity. The domestic consumer, who provided almost 60 per cent of the revenue for gas, was naturally taking less and less gas. In gas there are two types of domestic consumer – credit and prepayment. Between 1950 and 1960 the former reduced his annual consumption from 141 to 113 therms; the latter from 116 to 99½ therms.

The prepayment consumer is peculiar to gas. He is in fact a very stubborn Victorian survival. In electricity he is insignificant. As he pays for his gas in advance, he is far more price conscious, especially as he is usually a less affluent consumer. His reaction to a price increase is to reduce consumption, over which he has more control through prepayment. Extensive rebuilding of older urban areas is gradually bringing his number down, though even now he outnumbers the credit consumer. But as we shall see later in this chapter, his importance is diminishing.

There was another cogent reason for loosening dependence on coal as a raw material. Carbonisation of coal produced by-products as well as gas, and the most important of these was coke. As the fifties wore on it became more and more difficult to sell all the coke. For instance at the end of the winter of 1959–60 the industry was left with $2\frac{1}{2}$ million tons of coke in stock. Solid smokeless fuel was not selling as fast as anticipated. The gas industry was a two-fuel industry, producing gas and coke. In view of the increasing difficulties in selling coke, would it not be possible to become a one-fuel industry – producing gas only?

So from the mid-fifties the industry turned its attention earnestly to finding alternative processes to the carbonisation of coal. Ever since the industry was nationalised it had financed a search in Britain for natural gas, but the results of considerable expenditure on exploration have been meagre.

One alternative to the carbonisation of coking coal was the total gasification of lower-grade coals by the Lurgi process. This produces a low-grade gas which requires enriching to reach the calorific value of town gas. Two Lurgi plants were built in Scotland and the Midlands. But after much discussion between Coal Board and Gas Council, it became clear that the Lurgi process was not as cheap or as satisfactory as other processes which were being developed.

To meet peak loads in winter the gas industry had a quick process in the production of water gas from coke. As this gas is of low calorific value, it is then carburetted with oil. As stocks of coke were large, the making of carburetted water gas was useful in reducing unwanted coke.

So a technical revolution in the production of gas was started which has proceeded apace in the sixties. It is likely that the changes resulting from the substantial discoveries of North Sea Gas will take about ten years to be fully effective, and therefore the shape of the new gas industry will not be fully apparent till well into the seventies. Meanwhile, it is possible to see what has happened in the sixties from the following table.

SOURCES OF GAS SUPPLIES

	1958/9	*1966/7*
	Percentages	
1. Coal gas	65·1	28
2. Carburetted water gas	14	6
3. Oil gas and other gas	2·3	30
4. Bought from coke ovens	16·4	10
5. Bought from oil refineries	2·2	7·5
6. Liquefied petroleum gas	—	11
7. Imported and other methane	—	7·5
	100	100

Items 3, 5 and 6, all of which depend on the production of gas from some form of oil, amounted to 4½ per cent in 1958–9, but were 48·5 per cent in 1966–7. The percentage derived from coal had decreased by more than half.

At first, recourse to oil took the form of placing a gas works near an oil refinery, buying the refinery's 'tail gas' and reforming it into town gas. But in the early sixties a series of petrochemical processes were developed by Shell, I.C.I. and the Gas Council itself for transforming oil into gas. These processes had enormous advantages. This oil gas is much cheaper than coal gas because the oil gas plant costs only about £10 per therm against £60 per therm with carbonisation plant. Oil gas plants are small and compact compared with the conventional gas works. They were much less of a nuisance to their surroundings and the gas they make is non-toxic.

The case for abandoning coal as a raw material for gas-making and switching over to oil was abundantly clear, even to a Labour Government anxious, by all means possible, to keep open the markets for coal. In a White Paper on Fuel Policy issued in 1965 (Cmnd. 2798) the Government admits the superiority of oil in this respect. 'The Government is satisfied that the trend of the gas industry towards petroleum should be accepted. Measures to influence coal consumption by the gas industry (other than strictly limited adjustments from year to year) would involve a heavy economic penalty, and would not be in the interests of the economy as a whole.'

But these oil gas plants had some disadvantages. Though new in design they were ordered in fairly large numbers because of their

E

obvious advantages. They involved new and elaborate petro-chemical processes with plant of special steels working at high pressures and temperatures. The 'commissioning' of a carbonisation plant was a smooth and well-known process – perfected over a century. The commissioning of an oil gas plant was a headache. Delays were frequent because of teething troubles; and from time to time serious breakdowns occurred when the plants were working flat out at a time of great demand.

The type of oil used in these plants was naphtha – a light fraction which was available in abundance with the great expansion of oil refineries. The oil companies could be relied upon to fulfil their contracts to supply; it was obviously of great importance to a public utility to be sure of obtaining its raw materials. But the Suez crisis of 1967 showed that even the international oil companies sometimes encounter difficulties which take time to overcome.

But these oil gas processes were barely under way when the whole future of the gas industry was changed by the discoveries of natural gas under the North Sea.

As mentioned earlier in this chapter, the gas industry had spent considerable sums in exploring for natural gas in this country – with disappointing results. By 1960 it was clear little help could be hoped for from this source. But between 1957 and 1960 the Gas Council had participated in an experiment for bringing in natural gas from Algeria, in liquid form. In November 1961 after the experiment had been successfully concluded, the Government authorised the Council to enter into a contract to purchase annually for fifteen years 350 million therms of natural gas to be delivered at Canvey Island on the Thames. The first delivery was in October 1964.

The purchase of this gas was made by the Gas Council on behalf of eight Area Boards. The liquid natural gas is discharged at Canvey Island, where it is regasified and then pumped through a high-pressure grid from Canvey Island to the North of England where it has two terminals, at Manchester and Leeds. Each of the eight Area Boards would use the imported methane as it wished. This grid foreshadowed a great change in the structure of the gas industry. Instead of twelve areas, each autonomous because it was entirely responsible for producing its own supplies of gas and then selling them, we now had a co-operative scheme whereby eight Boards took from one pipe supplies of imported gas under a scheme prepared by the Gas Council. This was the first important change in the set-up of the gas industry; further changes have quickly followed.

But the greatest development in natural gas, which was revolutionary, came from the North Sea.

Early in the sixties it was confirmed that there was a huge deposit of natural gas in the north-east district of Holland – near the North Sea. This strengthened the belief of geophysicists, which had been held for some time, that natural gas was to be found under the bed of the North Sea. Groups of oil companies were formed to carry out surveys of the North Sea and the Gas Council joined one of the groups, which in May 1963 started a survey of 20,000 square miles of the North Sea off the coasts of Yorkshire, Lincolnshire and Norfolk.

But exploration of the North Sea had to be controlled and regulated and therefore an international agreement was concluded dividing the bed of the North Sea between the States which bordered on it. The North Sea is shallow and does not reach 200 metres in depth except in limited areas; consequently it was divided along a median line and the British portion was the western half reaching from the Shetlands to the Strait of Dover. The Continental Shelf Act 1964 vested in the Crown all the rights in this part of the North Sea and the Crown, through the Ministry of Power, could grant licences to explore the bed and take the natural gas.

The group of which the Gas Council formed part was granted licences in September 1964 to explore thirty-six blocks of the North Sea bed, and the group entered into a contract with an off-shore drilling company to carry out the necessary drilling. The first find of natural gas in the North Sea was made by British Petroleum in September 1965 and throughout 1966 and 1967 discoveries were reported by various groups. The group of which the Gas Council formed part was fortunate in making several discoveries. Drilling is still going on and it will be several years before the full riches of the North Sea bed are revealed.

But the gas industry cannot wait till then. There is enough evidence of ample supplies available to justify urgent action in making use of them. In February 1966 a contract was made by the Gas Council with British Petroleum for a supply of not less than 50 million cubic feet a day, increasing, if possible, up to an average of 200 million.

The Gas Council was enabled to do this because it had received increased powers under the Gas Act 1965 which supplemented the Gas Act 1948. The Act imposed on the Council a new duty 'to promote and assist the co-ordinated development of efficient and economical gas supplies in Great Britain'. The Council was given new powers 'to manufacture gas, to get or acquire gas in or from Great Britain or elsewhere and to supply gas in bulk to any Area Board'. It was also empowered 'to manufacture, treat, render saleable, supply or sell solid fuels by-products and products' on the same basis as Area Boards. In all respects therefore the Gas Council is now on the same footing as Area Boards; even more, it can supply the Boards with bulk supplies – a power which will become more and more significant as time goes on. Thus the original loose and decentralised structure of the gas industry, which has often been described as the most satisfactory of all which were created between 1946 and 1949, has largely been modified.

The discovery of substantial quantities of natural gas in the North Sea will create serious problems for the industry, of which organisation is probably the least. It is obviously necessary to strengthen the central organisation because technical developments are on such a scale that no one Area Board can afford to carry on by itself. In fact it is disappointing that for sixteen years the Area Boards have not co-operated more in helping each other. It was not till 1966 that a major link was established between two Boards – East and West Midlands – to help each other in time of need.

The improvements in the sixties in sales of gas have been largely in the form of space heating, which has intensified the winter peak and will pass on to gas some of the troubles of electricity described in Chapter 4. To cope with such troubles, it is obviously preferable to store large quantities of gas to be brought out in the winter. These can only be held by a central organisation and should preferably be underground. The Gas Act 1965 lays down procedure for creating such underground storage. In connection with the methane imported from Algeria, frozen ground storage for 42,000 tons of the liquefied methane have been provided at Canvey Island where the methane comes ashore. To cope with all these developments the Gas Council has had to increase its staff considerably.

A serious problem created by substantial quantities of North Sea gas will be financial. In the fifties the industry equipped itself with new carbonising plant, shutting down hundreds of old works.

Most of these new plants will have a useful life through the 1970s. Then came the various oil gas processes, and from the early sixties the industry started equipping itself with these new oil plants, which can produce gas so much more cheaply that it would pay to shut down carbonising plants which have still much useful life but which have become obsolescent. The prime cost of making gas in a carbonising plant could be higher than the total cost in an oil gas plant. Hardly have these oil gas plants started production when natural gas from the North Sea began to be available. Not until an adequate supply of this natural gas is assured and distributed can the Area Boards risk a slackening of their programme of oil gas plant construction. If there is a very rapid increase in the demand for gas the problem of paying for this rapid obsolescence will be eased. But the quantities of natural gas coming forward may be so great that it may be difficult for demand to increase fast enough to absorb them. Expenditure on depreciation and additional provision for obsolescence are therefore likely to increase considerably and may for some years be a serious burden.

It will take some time to get this natural gas to the consumer. Pipelines are already being built from the wells to the coast and then from the coast to points inside the Area Boards' territories. These pipes will be linked up with the trunk grid for imported methane. That grid will have to be extended to the four outlying Boards which do not participate in the imports – South-Western, Wales, Northern and Scotland. Thirty-six-inch pipes with working pressure of 1000 pounds to the square inch will require special steels not usually supplied by the steel industry.

There is also the heavy task of converting consumers' appliances to take natural gas, which has twice the calorific value of town gas. An estimated expenditure of £400 million has been suggested for this work. This is a once-for-all task which will be spread over several years. The difficulty will be in training sufficient men to carry out the change speedily.

The gas industry claims, quite naturally, that all the North Sea gas should be sold to itself for distribution through its pipes. Under the Gas Act 1948 the industry has only a monopoly of distributing gas, because it alone can break up roads to lay mains. Anyone can manufacture gas for his own use just as anyone can generate electricity for his own use. The Continental Shelf Act 1964 has a provision enabling the Minister of Power to authorise a supply of piped natural gas to be given to industrial premises. There might obviously be cases where this is desirable; as for instance in a chemical plant requiring large quantities where the length of pipe is quite short and where perhaps the gas is supplied by an affiliate of the chemical company.

The prospects for the gas industry in the 1970s are very bright. In the twenty years since nationalisation it has undergone several rapid technological changes, which have revolutionised its part in the national economy. It may well develop into a major supplier of energy, whose competitive strength may have an effect on the three other major fuels, coal, oil and electricity.

But – and this is important – this bright prospect depends on a settlement of the price of North Sea gas with the oil companies, particularly the major companies such as Shell and Esso. When this book went to press no settlement had been reached except with two minor oil companies. The major companies with their far-flung interests – including the sale of oil products in the U.K. and the price for Dutch natural gas exported to France, Belgium and Germany – may possibly decide to quit North Sea exploration rather than give way on a price which, taking all factors into account, may not be remunerative.

6 Steel

THE nationalisation of the iron and steel industry in 1949 was a highly exceptional measure. It was pushed through Parliament with great vigour and determination. The fact that the Labour Government was so persistent with a measure which can fairly be described as in no way popular, is important as it sheds light on the policy of nationalisation. For the following reasons this measure stood in a class by itself.

When the Iron and Steel Bill came before Parliament in November 1948 it was the last of a series. Coal, transport, electricity and gas (and of course the Bank of England), had all been brought under public ownership. Then came iron and steel, which differed from all these. The case for this last measure seemed difficult to put across. It was not so convincing and more difficult to understand. Yet the Labour Government gave much of its time and energy to this project. The whole 1948–9 session of Parliament was dominated by the Iron and Steel Bill. The House of Lords insisted on delaying the coming into force of the measure, and, though it received the Royal Assent on 24 November 1949, the vesting date was postponed from 1 May 1950 to 1 January 1951, 'or to such later date, not more than twelve months later, as the Minister of Supply may by Order substitute'. Furthermore, the Government had proposed an amendment, deferring until 1 October 1950 the appointments to the proposed Iron and Steel Corporation which was to own all the shares of the Iron and Steel Companies to be taken into public ownership. As a General Election was bound to be held at the latest in the summer of 1950, these government amendments meant the acceptance of the House of Lords' view that the coming into force of the Bill should be delayed until after that.

In the event the Labour Government was returned with a minute majority. The Iron and Steel Act 1949 came into force on 15 February 1951.

The Labour Government was clearly determined to force

through, at all costs, the nationalisation of the iron and steel indus-try. Many of the criteria adopted for the previous Nationalisation Acts were missing in the case of iron and steel; so there must have been other considerations which took their place.

The subject deserves close scrutiny because iron and steel is in fact the classic Socialist case for public ownership. Why was the Labour Government so determined and persistent with iron and steel? Its case for it had to be carefully made. To begin with, it could not, as in the case of other industries already national-ised, claim that the industry was inefficient and required drastic reorganisation under public ownership. There was no Reid Report as in coal, nor Heyworth Report as in gas. Admittedly there were old and inefficient units in the steel industry, but what industry in 1949 was completely modern and efficient? In any case, after the difficult inter-war years and the great effort of the war, one would expect that the iron and steel industry would require bringing up to date. But the industry was developing rapidly, even though it had been threatened with nationalisation since the General Election of 1945. The output of crude steel in 1945 was 11·8 million ingot tons, in 1948 14·9 million, in 1949 15·55 million, and in 1950 16·3 million. Considering the great difficulties of the post-war period and the length of time required for developing steel production, this was a good record.

When the Opposition pressed the Government to indicate how it would reorganise the iron and steel industry once it had been taken over, Mr Morrison became indignant at the thought that the Government should do some planning in advance of nationalisa-tion. His outburst was so revealing that it is worth quoting in full:

It is next argued that we ought to have embodied in the Bill specific and detailed plans for the future organisation of the industry. This seems to me a preposterous suggestion. It comes from the academic mind of the right honourable Member for Warwick and Leamington. It really is a preposterous suggestion that before the industry has been socialised, before the Act of Parliament has been brought in, and before any powers have been obtained at all, my right honourable Friend [Mr Strauss], a politician, should work out in detail the specific technical future of the industry down to considerable detail, embody it in the Bill, and thereby deprive the scheme of all fluidity. It really does illustrate the lack of practical minds among the members opposite and the unreal world in which they live. Surely the wise thing, if the industry is to be socialised, is to provide for it to be taken over, to let the shares vest in the Iron and Steel Corporation and then let the Corporation, composed of competent business people, be responsible for the management of the industry, subject to such general directions as the Minister of Supply may give them. That is surely the sensible and rational way to proceed in this matter (*Hansard*, vol. 458, col. 492).

The good record of the industry in the years 1945–50 is borne out by the second Annual Report of the Iron and Steel Corporation, which covers the period October 1951 to September 1952. 'Capital development continues at a high level and the general programme of development which outlines the pattern of reconstruction and new building for the next five years has been largely settled' (para. 6). The use of the word 'continues' is significant; the Corporation, as the public owner of the industry, does not claim that this state of affairs is due to its advent. 'The Corporation and the Companies have been able to finance the operation of the Companies and the heavy capital investment without recourse to new loans or to the issue of more iron and steel stock during the year' (para. 8). In other words, despite living for six years under the threat of nationalisation, the industry had not slackened its efforts and had ploughed back large sums as if its future were free from doubt.

But the Corporation goes further in its praise.

The Corporation record with satisfaction the present state of the industry. Production of steel is now running at a higher rate than ever before in the history of the industry (para. 9).

In recording the marked progress and results which the Companies have achieved, the Corporation express their pleasure and appreciation of the manner in which the directors, managements, technicians and work people in the Companies have devoted their energy and skill to improving the efficiency of the industry and promoting increased production (para. 11).

Finally, the Corporation pays a tribute to the excellent industrial relations in the industry. 'Labour relations in the industry continue to be cordial and co-operative. The provision of amenities, continued modernisation of plant and new construction, are making a progressive contribution to the improvement of working conditions' (para. 10). The iron and steel industry has never had a major industrial dispute. Labour has always alleged that the workers are enthusiastic for nationalisation. Of course the Iron and Steel Trades Confederation has passed resolutions in favour; one would not expect a trade union to do anything else. But the good industrial relations since 1945 show that the workers were not excited by public ownership nor depressed when thrust back into private capitalism.

During the many debates in Parliament it was suggested by Labour members that public ownership was necessary because much of the industry was obsolete and could not be replaced, except when the industry was replanned in a far-seeing national development plan. This was refuted by the evidence of the Iron and Steel Corporation.

The way in which development has been shaped for the next five years has meant that the fundamental problems of the location of the steel industry have not been raised in an acute form, since the work will consist mainly of balancing existing units. When this process is completed and the time comes to carry out the third review of development for the five years or so beyond 1957 or 1958, it will be necessary to consider afresh the question whether to provide increasing production of steel from new works in the traditional areas or break entirely new ground. This question will raise many difficult problems concerning, for instance, labour supply, housing, the relative advantages of using home or imported ore, strategical considerations, shipping, the provision of port facilities and the extent to which it is desirable to have direct control over ore fields overseas, the sources of supply of coking coal, transport costs and the location of established and new markets for steel at home and abroad (Second Annual Report, para. 86).

When Labour members spoke glibly of starting brand-new works and scrapping obsolete plants, one wonders how many of the considerations listed above were present in their minds. The slow decease of the hand tinplate mills in South Wales, which everyone had known for years were obsolete in face of the continuous strip mill, showed how difficult a transfer of industry could be, even when the case for the transfer was overwhelming.

In the above passage the Iron and Steel Corporation referred to 'the third review of development for the five years beyond 1957 or 1958'. We now have that third review published by the Iron and Steel Board in July 1957. In chapter II of that review the Board considers the problem of old and obsolete works. It points out that 'there is some difficulty in defining the term "obsolete" when applied to steelworks plant' (para. 187). 'Some old plants have been well maintained or replaced piecemeal through the years, and too little would be gained from a new plant to justify the cost of their replacement' (ibid.). Sometimes the location is obsolete because the original ore field is worked out. The Board estimated that the amount of obsolete plant in 1955 was very small. In the case of pig iron it was 4 per cent, in crude steel $6\frac{1}{2}$ per cent and in billets 4 per cent. In steel plate and in heavy steel it was negligible. Iron and steel, unlike transport, was not a 'poor bag of assets'.

So there was very little support for the case that the iron and steel industry was too inefficient to be allowed to carry on in its existing state, and that the only cure was public ownership with its attendant reorganisation.

Another argument frequently advanced by the Labour Government was that public ownership was necessary to enable the nation to compel the industry to follow a policy in the national interest. Any form of control short of public ownership was inadequate. This is a key argument and requires the closest scrutiny. We have suggested elsewhere in this book that there is confusion in the Labour mind between ownership and control; the public ownership is sought as an end in itself, without realising that the concept of public ownership was fashioned in the day of the *laissez-faire* State, when government control of industry was unknown. On the other hand, in the second half of the twentieth century when the State has armed itself with vast powers over all forms of economic activity, there is no necessity to own an industry in order to control it. In fact the State can exercise a more flexible and powerful control over an industry by not owning it. The State, in that case, is not closely identified with the industry; its prestige is not bound up with its success; the political element does not dominate relations with the industry; and finally the industry is not financially spoon-fed.

This argument for the necessity of public ownership in order to exercise control was forcibly put by Sir Stafford Cripps in the second-reading debate on 16 November 1948 (*Hansard*, vol. 458, col. 321):

Now we are seeking to have some measure of foresight in our economic activities, we must be able to plan ahead for production. The whole of our capital investment programme . . . depends upon supplies of suitable qualities of steel, and we must be able to plan this most important of our economic activities ahead; and that we certainly cannot do if we are to be driven to rely upon the reactions of uncontrolled private enterprise to a changing world situation in which they may demand again the restriction of markets, high prices, international cartel agreements, tariffs and import restrictions as a condition of making the necessary supplies available to the country.

We cannot allow the steel industry to determine, from the point of view of its own profitability, the limits of its own expansion. The only entity that can take the risk, in the present highly speculative circumstances of world economy, as to the future size and form of the steel industry that we can build up, is the Nation as a whole.

However that is to be done it means we must have a form of general control or nationalised ownership of the industry. . . . I have already explained that the present private monopoly control that now exists cannot be carried on, so that we are left with the one solution of nationalisation.

This is a sad picture of a helpless nation and Government cowering before an all-powerful industry, which demands tariffs and import restrictions; otherwise it will not make available to the country the steel it requires. How domineering an industry must be to behave in this way, and how feeble the Government which gives way to these blackmailing demands. It is not surprising that Sir Winston Churchill's comment was, 'What nonsense'.

All this is predicated of an industry which for the sixteen years previous – since 1932 – had leaned heavily on the Government, and for the greater part of the time had been under government control. There is something mysterious about the fascination exercised on the Labour mind by the word 'steel'. 'Steel is power': the leaders of the steel industry are 'steel barons'. The steel industries, not only in Britain but in countries such as Germany or France, have been frequently described as the powers behind Governments, which danced obediently to their command. The Ruhr had also its 'steel barons'; in France the Comité des Forges was a great force behind the scenes, particularly in the 1920s.

It would be absurd to suggest that the constant propaganda among Socialists about the hidden power of the 'steel barons' was a decisive influence in bringing nationalisation about; but it would be equally absurd to deny that it provided a background, particularly for the rank and file.

Two other main arguments were employed by Sir Stafford Cripps in his speech in the second-reading debate referred to above. The first was that there was a strong element of monopoly in the iron and steel industry and in an industry of such great importance monopoly must be public and not private. There was force in this argument. But Sir Stafford Cripps spoke as if the industry was a single unit activated by one mind, whereas it consisted of a large number of firms of varying capacity and efficiency, and in competition with each other. It is true that 'Steel House', the headquarters of the British Iron and Steel Federation, had great influence and spoke for the industry as a whole. But that was also true of many other trade associations.

But what was really peculiar about this argument on monopoly was that no one, however Tory, suggested this vital industry should go its own way free from government control. As we shall see later, the de-nationalisation carried out by the Conservative Government in 1952–3 did not mean handing back the iron and steel industry to its previous owners, free and untrammelled from government control. There were no two opinions about the importance of the iron and steel industry, and the necessity of controlling this important industry so that its operations matched the national interest. But such control did not involve public ownership; it could quite well be achieved without any transfer of ownership.

The second argument of Sir Stafford Cripps was minor, though described by him as major. Steel was the basis of defence and the requirements of steel for defence must be safeguarded. This was only a special instance of the general Labour argument that the nation must, in the national interest, control an industry so vital and monopolistic as iron and steel.

It is well known that there was a strong division of views in the Attlee Cabinet on the desirability of nationalising steel. The Left, with definite Socialist views on public ownership, won. Spokesmen for the Government had therefore to make the best case they could. We have seen this happening again in 1965–7.

There was a serious problem in defining 'iron and steel' for the purpose of nationalisation. All the Acts had difficulties of definition, and marginal problems arose. Railways might run hotels and docks; colliery companies might own coke ovens and brickworks; gas companies might own water undertakings. But such problems of definition at the margin were trivial compared with the problem of defining iron and steel. No two iron and steel companies were alike. Mr Strauss, the Minister of Supply responsible for the Iron and Steel Bill, explained the difficulty (*Hansard*, vol. 458, col. 60):

It is clear, however, that the pattern of national ownership appropriate to coal, gas, electricity and transport, would not suit the iron and steel industry. The units that comprise this industry vary enormously, not only in the type of product they make, but to the degree that they are engaged, directly or through subsidiaries, in ancillary activities, from mining ore to the manufacture of finished products. Moreover, many of these firms bear names which are known and respected throughout the world, and a source of justifiable pride to their managements and all their employees. To destroy the individuality of all these concerns would be regrettable, and to break up abruptly and wholesale the industrial combinations of which they form a part would cause a serious dislocation over a wide field of industry.

For these reasons the Government decided that the wise course was to depart entirely from precedent; to preserve the entity of the companies which come within the scheme, and to effect our purpose simply by transferring their securities from the present holders to a public corporation. By this means it will be possible to combine all that is best in private enterprise with public ownership.

We, therefore, propose in the Bill that there shall be an Iron and Steel Corporation of Great Britain, owning all the securities of the major concerns at the core of the industry – that is the sections of the industry responsible for the production of iron ore, pig iron, ingot steel or the hot rolling of steel.

Later on he says (col. 62):

In considering how to attain our objective of public ownership we were faced with many problems none greater than that of demarcation. Which firms should be taken over and which left outside? The leaders of the industry thought that this problem was insoluble and asserted that we should be forced to break up a vast number of closely-knit industrial structures, with chaotic effect over a wide area of industry. They anticipated that we would take over the large steel-making concerns and sever them from all their subsidiary and ancillary activities to which they were firmly linked.

But we, too, appreciated the folly of such wholesale dismemberment. Apparently it never dawned on these prophets of woe that we might be intelligent enough and bold enough to avoid this difficulty by the simple expedient of taking over in the first instance not only the steel-making plants, but also their subsidiaries, lock, stock and barrel.

These remarks of Mr Strauss are revealing. The tribute to the iron and steel companies is hardly consonant with the abuse showered upon them. The concern about destroying the individuality of the companies to be taken over might have occurred to Labour ministers at an earlier stage when at a stroke they swept away the higher managements of the industries taken into public ownership.

To that extent a holding company as public owner is preferable to a Public Corporation, which is also responsible for management. But Mr Strauss is going too far when he suggests that 'their personnel and internal organisation, and such *esprit de corps* as they may have achieved will be unaffected'. While on the one hand Mr Strauss asserts that the change in ownership can make no difference, on the other hand he sees that the changes made by a vigorous Iron and Steel Corporation might have a disturbing effect. 'We do not anticipate, nor do we think it would be wise, that sudden or drastic changes should be made in the early days of the Corporation's life. No man who pulls his weight need fear for his position at any time.' But he might pull his weight in a manner objectionable to the Corporation and then, as the Corporation was master, he would have to knuckle under or go. The individuality and initiative referred to in such glowing terms by Mr Strauss would be endangered in proportion to the activities of the Corporation.

In the upshot the Iron and Steel Corporation had too short a life to leave any mark on the industry. It took over on 15 February 1951, and on 26 October in the same year a General Election took place which resulted in a Conservative Government. It immediately made known its intentions in the King's Speech to introduce a Bill 'to annul the Iron and Steel Act with a view to the reorganisation of the industry under free enterprise, but with an adequate measure of public supervision'. The Corporation had, therefore, little more than eight months of effective life, and during that time the activities of the 298 concerns over which it had acquired control could hardly have been affected by nationalisation.

The Conservative Government proceeded with its plans for denationalising the iron and steel industry and the new Iron and Steel Act received the Royal Assent on 14 May 1953. On 13 July 1953 the new Iron and Steel Board charged with the control of the industry took up its duties.

Under Section 3 (1) of the Act the duty of the Board is to exercise a general supervision over the iron and steel industry, with a view to promoting the efficient, economic and adequate supply of iron and steel products under competitive conditions. It was to keep under review the productive capacity of the industry with its necessary fuel and raw materials. It was also to supervise research arrangements and all matters affecting the personnel employed, with the great exception of 'terms and conditions of employment'; in other words these were not to be in any way involved in negotiations with trade unions on wages, hours of employment, etc.

As regards development, the Board could insist, after formal notice, that schemes of a certain kind could not be embarked upon except with its consent. The Board decided that schemes costing more than £100,000 must be submitted to it for approval. The Act provided that, if the Board decided that additional capacity for production were required in the national interest, and that capacity would not be provided by the industry, the Minister himself could provide it. Much was made of this by the Labour Party in the debates on the Bill. The intention behind the clause was to have some reserve power to make some unusual provision of capacity which was definitely unremunerative but which was necessary in the national interest – e.g. a plant to produce some special steels in an emergency. The Labour Party suggested that the purpose was to leave the unremunerative activities to the State, while the steel companies confined themselves to the profitable lines. In fact the powers in this clause have never been invoked.

As regards the supply of raw materials for the iron and steel industry, the Board had powers under Section 11 of the Act to make arrangements for the importation of any raw materials required, if it was satisfied that existing arrangements were inadequate and could not be improved by consultation. If the Board so desired, it could arrange for the importation to be carried out as a common service for the industry.

In fact, soon after the end of the war, the British Iron and Steel Federation had formed a special company, B.I.S.C. (Ore) Ltd, which had the responsibility of purchasing, importing and distributing all imported ores. In 1951 this company embarked on the building of ore carriers to be used for bringing imported ores into Britain. Since then the fleet of ore carriers has been steadily expanded.

Clause 24 of the Iron and Steel Act 1967 (which is described later in this chapter) provided that the Iron and Steel Board should be dissolved at a date to be fixed by the Minister of Power and its assets and liabilities transferred to the British Steel Corporation set up under the Act. The Board was accordingly dissolved on 28 July 1967. As it started functioning in July 1953, it has had altogether a life of fourteen years and we are now in a position to assess its achievements as supervisor of the steel industry during that period.

As background to what happened during these years we should remember that the Act of 1953 provided that the nationalised steel industry should be sold back to private enterprise. The individual companies had been, as mentioned earlier, left intact by the Act of 1949 – all their shares being held by the Iron and Steel Corporation. The difficult task of selling these shares back to the public was placed on the Iron and Steel Holding and Realisation Agency, the greater part of the task being completed in about five years. The task was difficult because the public was reluctant to invest in shares of steel companies, as the Labour Party had definitely stated when the Act of 1953 was passed that it would, when it came to power, renationalise the industry. This threat, duly carried out in 1967, made investors nervous as, of course, they were quite unaware what terms of compensation would be offered by a Labour Government. One consequence of this was that I.S.H.R.A. had to choose very carefully the time to offer the steel shares to the public and were forced to tempt investors by making the terms of the offer attractive. Even so, the poor financial record of Richard Thomas & Baldwins precluded any chance of selling that company to the public and it has accordingly remained throughout in public ownership.

A second and serious consequence of the threat to renationalise was that the steel industry could not, in the normal manner of private industry, look to the market to provide finance for development. They had to provide it all from their own resources – depreciation funds, etc. Accordingly when it became necessary to promote a major capital project – such as a strip mill for producing sheet costing £150 million – the industry could not find the finance. When it was finally agreed that the construction of a strip mill could not be delayed, the Government had to step in and the Macmillan Government made the political decision to construct two strip mills – one by Richard Thomas & Baldwins at Newport and the second by Colvilles in Scotland. As the former was publicly owned, the finance was provided in the usual form of an advance to a nationalised undertaking. Colvilles, on the other hand, received a loan of £50 million on commercial terms.

Despite these financial difficulties the industry during the period of Iron and Steel Board supervision went ahead with developing and modernising itself. In its Reports the Board gives the following figures of capital expenditure on development schemes costing more than £100,000 each during the years 1953 to 1966. (See table on p. 146.)

These figures do not include expenditure on schemes of capital development costing less than £100,000 for which the Board's consent was not required. The Board estimated the annual expenditure on these smaller schemes as ranging between £10 and £20 million. The British Iron and Steel Federation has calculated that the steel industry since 1946 has spent over £2100 million on its development. Even allowing for the injection of government money for the strip mills at Newport and Ravenscraig, the amount spent by the steel industry from its own resources is impressive. It certainly does not bear out the statement of the Minister of Power on 6 May 1965 in the House of Commons: 'Experience since denationalisation suggests that the necessary expansion of capacity is unlikely to take place without huge injections of public money' (*Hansard*, vol. 711, col. 1579). By the end of 1965 the plant capacity of the industry had been increased to 32 million ingot tons which was more than adequate to meet all requirements. It had not been adequate in the 1950s when there were shortages of steel. But these shortages were made good in the later fifties and the early sixties; in 1965 production of steel reached its peak at 27 million tons of which 4¾ million tons were exported.

	£ million
1953	49
1954	52
1955	58
1956	75
1957	95
1958	105
1959	99
1960	146
1961	199
1962	170
1963	77
1964	55
1965	50
1966	42
	1272

The supervision of the Board can be said therefore to have produced an adequate expansion of capacity. But its powers were in some respects not adequate or satisfactory and the feeling that this was so was reinforced by major changes in the steel industries on the Continent. The Board itself was prepared to admit that the Act of 1953 had been passed at a time of very different conditions and that serious changes were required. In paragraphs 12 and 13 of its 1965 Report the Board made admissions which were so important that they justify quotation:

As the Board have previously stated, the provisions of the 1953 Act are in many respects out-of-date. The powers comprise a weak veto on company development schemes, the right to move the Government to arrange additional capacity in certain circumstances, and the right to fix maximum prices. All these powers are of a negative and passive character and reflect the conditions of scarcity and shortage which prevailed when the Board were set up in 1953. They have sufficed to bring about the necessary expansion of capacity and they have kept prices at very reasonable levels, but they have not proved as effective as was hoped in stimulating efficiency nor can they be used to force the industry to adapt itself to present-day requirements.

The problem falls under two heads, namely (1) the more economic use of manpower and (2) the structure of the industry. As far as the former is concerned, much is dependent on the utmost co-operation between management and trades unions in reviewing and modernising the manning practices in the industry. As regards the second, the Board have for long been of the opinion that the industry needs to be reorganised into fewer but individually larger units equipped with plant of a greater size than is generally the case at the moment. Technical studies undertaken in the Board's organisation certainly support the view that great advantages are to be derived from the concentration and reorganisation of production.

Overmanning and larger units of production – these are the cries heard on all sides. The industry itself admits them. But in considering them it is necessary to have regard to the outlook of British industry as a whole and not to the steel industry in isolation. With all respect to the Iron and Steel Board, it is difficult to believe that even if, in 1953, it had been endowed with far greater powers than it was then given, it would have been able to slim the steel industry of its excess manpower. The industry itself, in part 1 of the Benson Report, estimates its excess manpower at 100,000 and asks for ten years in which to reduce its labour force by that amount.

Up to 1961, the steel industry was operating in a sellers' market. In boom conditions, where prices were easily maintained at a profitable level, both management and the unions would have resisted reductions in manpower.

For overmanning is to be found in most British industries, whether publicly or privately owned. International comparisons on this point usually show Britain in a poor light. It requires great determination on the part of the management and great co-operation on the part of the trade unions to achieve any worth-while reduction of manpower. Even if there is some success in achieving such a reduction, it is bought at such a high cost that the main purpose of the effort is largely or wholly nullified – as we have seen in the case of the railways. It is improbable that an Iron and Steel Board would have been so powerful that it could have forced both sides of the industry to undertake unpleasant reforms which so few of British industries have been able to carry out. The national climate was unpropitious.

It could have had more success in creating larger units if it had possessed positive instead of negative powers on capital development. But even on this point some caution is necessary. The industry today has adequate plant capacity which has grown naturally by development or replacement of existing plants. Very large new units mean that other units must be shut down, with great upheaval of labour and creation of redundancy. The economy of large plants is derived from lower costs – including reduced costs of labour. To achieve such economy requires the utmost determination not only in planning – which is easy – but in carrying through to its conclusion a project which creates great upheavals.

In the quotation above from the 1954 Report the Iron and Steel Board suggests that though it has 'kept prices at a reasonable level' these prices have not stimulated efficiency or forced 'the industry to adapt itself to present day requirements'. Throughout the Board has operated a system of maximum prices, which have been used by the industry as standard prices. As there was a sellers' market in steel up to 1961, maximum prices were a protection to the consumer. The prices were fixed on the basis that they should be high enough to encourage investment and low enough to compel producers to modernise and replace expensive methods and plant by modern ones. Also they should be low enough to give the engineering industries as steel consumers a chance to sell their exports. In fact these industries benefited greatly from these maximum prices.

Because steel is such a highly capitalised industry and suffers severe cyclical fluctuations, the steel industry in most countries develops a price leadership of some kind; in this country this leadership had been exercised by the Iron and Steel Board. The industry had a collective agreement whereby all producers kept to the maximum prices, but the Restrictive Practices Court in June 1964 decided that this agreement was contrary to the public interest, though it did not question the propriety of the fixing of these prices by the Board nor did it question the reasonableness of the prices themselves.

It has been suggested that this collective agreement showed that there was no competition between the steel companies. There is obviously some truth in this but lack of competition in price does not rule out competition in delivery dates, quality, etc. Of course some steel companies make such specialised products that there is no competition against them, except from imports.

The newly-formed British Steel Corporation endorsed this view in paragraph 64 of its Report on Organisation of August 1967 (Cmnd. 3362): 'True price competition has never operated successfully in the iron and steel industry in this or in any other country.'

In 1965 the Iron and Steel Board concluded that changed conditions, and in particular the 1964 judgment of the Restrictive Practices Court, had made inappropriate the central control of maximum steel prices. The industry now had adequate capacity, demand was fluctuating and there was severe international competition. So the Board and the industry collaborated in devising a less rigid system which was analogous to but not identical with the system in force in the European Coal and Steel Community. Prices would be free to move according to market conditions and would be settled by individual producers within a framework of rules similar to those in the Community. Public accountability would not be weakened. The Board would supervise the arrangements and would reimpose maximum prices in cases where market prices became excessive. The rules would help to guard against a recurrence of the disastrous fall in prices which had happened in pre-war years when competition had been completely unregulated.

The Board thought that such a system would provide flexibility and a new commercial element which would help to bring about a more efficient use of the industry's resources. It therefore asked the Government in September 1965 if it would authorise the use of the new system in lieu of the maximum prices, which it proposed to discontinue. The reply to this request is described as follows in paragraph 8 of the Board's Report for 1965:

The Government replied that, in the light of the various considerations, they could not accept a change in the method of fixing maximum steel prices at the time, and would, if necessary, take statutory action to prevent it. The Board are, in consequence, continuing for the time being to determine maximum steel prices.

We now come to the renationalisation of the Iron and Steel Industry, which was carried out by the Labour Government in the years 1964–7.

The Queen's Speech of 3 November 1964 declared that, in accordance with the pledges at the recent General Election, the Government would initiate early action to re-establish the public ownership and control of the iron and steel industry. But as the Government had only a majority of about three, it was not in a position to force through such a highly contentious measure. To keep its intentions before the public, therefore, the Government in April 1965 issued a White Paper on Steel Nationalisation (Cmnd. 2651). Every student of public ownership should read the White Paper most carefully because it contains the considered case of the Labour Government for its resort to the device of whole-sale nationalisation. In this chapter only the salient points can be mentioned.

After stressing the importance of the steel industry (para. 4) and describing the arrangements for its public supervision since 1932 (described earlier in this chapter), the White Paper comes to its main arguments for nationalisation in paragraphs 10 to 12 which are entitled 'The Defects of the Present System'. Those arguments briefly are as follows:

(1) Private enterprise in steel cannot, with any form of supervision, be reconciled with the national interest. In its present form the industry would not provide the necessary capacity and quotes the arguments about the new steel mill. The White Paper does admit that present capacity is adequate but suggests that will not necessarily be the case in the future (para. 10).

(2) The Government would have to provide finance for the expansion of the industry. 'Over the past 10 to 15 years public money totalling over £400 million in aggregate has been provided to the steel companies.' This rather vague statement relating to an indefinite period has been dealt with earlier in this chapter (para. 11).

(3) Competitive conditions in the industry are missing. 'In the Government's view, these monopoly characteristics in this basic industry point to the need for public ownership under which price policy would be determined and prices fixed with regard only to the public interest (para. 12).

It would be most interesting to know what kind of prices these would be.

The policy enshrined in the White Paper was debated in the House of Commons on 6 May 1965. The Government secured a majority of four. Clearly a Bill to nationalise steel was out of the question with such a majority and the Government did not resume action till after the General Election of March 1966 which gave it an ample majority.

During this interval the steel industry put forward two proposals to the Government. One was for the replacement of the Iron and Steel Board by an Authority with stronger and more positive powers of control. The other was for government participation in steel shareholding up to a possible 50 per cent. Both proposals were rejected by the Government.

The industry also pressed the Government to promote a speedy and authoritative review of its organisation before legislation to nationalise was passed. This was also refused.

The industry thereupon set up its own 'Development Co-ordinating Committee' under Sir Henry Benson, which produced part 1 of its Report in July 1966. This dealt with the common steelmaking section of the industry and proposed the formation of larger units.

These belated efforts of the industry did not deflect the Government from the course it had set out on, and the Iron and Steel Bill was produced in June 1966. The second reading took place on 25 July and the Bill reached the Statute Book on 22 March 1967. Vesting day was fixed for 28 July 1967.

The Iron and Steel Act 1967 is a faithful copy of the Iron and Steel Act 1949 in very many respects; no less than forty-nine pages – exactly half of the ninety-eight pages of the Bill – are revived provisions of the defunct Act of 1949. This showed how similar in concept were the two Nationalisation Acts.

But there was a major change in the definition of the industry to be taken over. The Act of 1949 took over about 100 companies; the Act of 1967 took over 13 (Richard Thomas & Baldwins being already under public ownership). These companies with their subsidiaries operate 22 integrated works, and 42 other iron and steel works, employed about 220,000 persons – about 70 per cent of the total manpower of the industry. These companies account for over 90 per cent of the production of iron ore, pig iron, oxide carbon steel, heavy steel products, sheet and tin plate. In addition, they have a strong position in producing most of the other main steel products.

This Act therefore, unlike the 1949 Act, leaves a small but sizeable private sector. As the Iron and Steel Board disappears when the Act comes into force, these firms – many of them

producing specialised steels – would have been left without supervision. So the Act brings them under the Minister's supervision.

Prior to vesting day – 28 July 1967 – the British Steel Corporation had been appointed on 27 April. In fact as an organising
committee it had been working since 30 September 1966. The Iron
and Steel Act had set out no plan for the organisation of the
industry after it was taken over. Following the precedent of 1949
(referred to earlier) this task was left to the B.S.C., which is
required to review the 'organisation of the activities under its
control' and submit a report to the Minister of Power within a year
of vesting date. As the B.S.C. had, in fact, been working on this
problem since September 1966 the first Report was produced in
August 1967 and published as a White Paper (Cmnd. 3632).

The main feature of this Report, which is to be followed by
another, is the grouping of the steel companies into four groups,
each controlled by a group managing director who is a member of
the Corporation. Though the Report is an interesting effort it does
not deal with the really difficult problems – in particular the balance
of power between the Corporation and the groups and in turn
between the groups and the companies which compose them. How
far are the companies to be allowed any autonomy? Formally the
companies are remaining in existence. It will be most interesting to
see how this problem of balance of power is tackled. We have seen
in the other industries dealt with in this book how the issue of
centralisation or delegation has repeatedly appeared. In the case of
steel with only fourteen companies – each with its own traditions
and outlook – the problem will be exceptionally difficult.

The Iron and Steel Act 1967 is a purely political effort; it is in
no way relevant to the economic needs of Britain in 1967. *The
Economist* (8 May 1965) put it succinctly: 'The Government has
hardly bothered to argue for its ritual nationalisation of steel – nor,
certainly, to hint what changes it has in mind to make in the
industry.'

PART THREE

Aspects of the Nationalised Industries

7 Parliament and the Nationalised Industries

IN this chapter 'Parliament' means the backbenchers in the House of Commons and, to some extent, in the House of Lords: the members of the Government are not, in this chapter, included in the term 'Parliament'. They are dealt with in the next chapter.

The creation of the nationalised industries was a political act, and while there was a Labour Government the attitude of the majority of the House of Commons towards them was one of unqualified support. When the Labour Government was replaced in 1951 by a Conservative, the backbenchers on the Government side began to be restive and critical of these industries. Generally, the attitude of the Government itself was Laodicean, but in two of the industries – transport, and iron and steel – it took definite measures to revise the Acts passed during the Labour regime.

But from 1947 Parliament had begun to raise the general and very difficult question 'what should be the relations between Parliament and these industries?' Members complained that they did not know what was going on in the nationalised industries. When they put parliamentary questions, many were disallowed as dealing with subjects for which no Minister was responsible. They could, and did, write to the Boards of the industries, and received replies – usually signed by the chairman; but that did not satisfy. Occasionally they could move a motion on the adjournment at the end of a day's debate. That only gave half an hour for discussion, which was too fragmentary. Once a year there could be a debate on the Annual Report of a nationalised industry. Sometimes one of the Boards promoted a Private Bill, which gave members a chance of airing their views on the industry, and obtaining some information.

But the total of all this was not much, and there was a feeling of dissatisfaction that somehow or other these industries were removed from the scrutiny of Parliament, so that inadequate information about them was obtainable. There were suggestions that industries were 'accountable to Parliament'. It is interesting to look for the sources of this dissatisfaction. Most members reasoned as follows: by Acts of Parliament certain industries had been taken into public ownership. The finances of those industries were provided either directly by the Treasury, or indirectly by Treasury guarantee. The Acts laid down that the industries were to conform to national policy. Many members found constituents seriously affected by the actions of these Boards, but obtained little satisfaction when they raised the matter with the Boards. If ministers were approached they pointed to the terms of the Nationalisation Acts and refused to discuss these matters because they were not within their own responsibility, but fell within the scope of 'day-to-day' administration. Surely, members argued, there must be some piece of parliamentary machinery which could be devised to overcome these difficulties and give the House of Commons an opportunity of informing itself about what was going on in the nationalised industries. It may be objected that the Reports of the Boards, presented each year to Parliament by the responsible Minister, gave members all they wanted, and as there was usually a debate on the Reports, members could obtain all information they wanted in the course of those debates. But the Annual Reports were not regarded as satisfactory. As the Report from the Select Committee on the Nationalised Industries puts it (H.C. 235 (1953) p. 4): 'the nationalised industries publish voluminous reports, but these do not completely meet the needs of Parliament or the Public, partly owing to their sheer volume and complexity, and partly because information is not necessarily available on matters on which it is required, or when it is required.'

These Reports are published several months after the year to which they relate, and a debate on the report may take place some months after publication; the debate may, therefore, be nearly a year later than the events which are reported. Furthermore, in the early days, the Reports were difficult to read and grasp. Some of the Boards made little pretence of catering for the uninitiated and their Reports contain too many technical terms. Many Reports told too much and, at the same time, too little. There was a great mass of facts and yet not enough editing.

One must admit that there has been gradual improvement in some Reports. There is, for instance, considerable difference between the Reports of the Transport Commission up to 1952 and those after 1952. The earlier Reports are a mass of facts and figures with an occasional generalisation; the later ones are the work of a competent editor, whose purpose it is to educate the public in the affairs of the Transport Commission. The later reports are pleasantly shorter than the earlier ones – about eighty pages compared with anything up to two hundred pages. This difference in length is not accounted for by the shrinkage in functions of the Commission. They are shorter because they are more concise. The Reports of the National Coal Board have also become more concise and readable, and the Reports of the Electricity Council show a welcome improvement over those of the Central Electricity Authority.

These Reports are made to the appropriate Minister and laid by him before Parliament. The Reports vary considerably. No one has prescribed to the Boards the form of Report which they should adopt. Such prescription would be difficult and might well be out of date very quickly because of a rapid change in conditions. Presumably the important student of the Report is the Member of Parliament anxious to investigate the nationalised industry. But when the Report is debated in Parliament, there is little evidence that many members have read through it. Though the formal motion before the House may be concerned with approval of the Annual Report and Accounts of a Board, nevertheless many speeches will raise topics unconnected with the Report and will range far and wide, often bringing in political issues.

This is inevitable. It is to be expected that Labour members naturally and instinctively set out to prove that the Boards can do no wrong and resent criticism as a form of attack. In the eyes of the Conservative members, on the other hand, it is doubtful whether they can do anything right, and most probably anything they do is wrong. The Reports of the nationalised industries therefore never receive the impartial, careful and thoughtful scrutiny they require. Members on the whole have not devoted the necessary effort to acquainting themselves with the contents of the Report and that is to be expected, as members are very busy. As we shall see the Select Committee has helped in this respect.

The whole purpose of the Annual Report submitted to the Minister, and presented by him to Parliament, was to provide the opportunity for an annual scrutiny. But members themselves complained that the debates on the Annual Reports tended to degenerate into discussions on points of local or constituency significance.

Many of the speeches in these debates fall into one of two

categories. One is by the trade union official who was once a miner or railwayman, and indulges in reminiscences which are hardly relevant, and which draw the contrast between the bad old days and the wonders of the new dispensation. Then there is the constituency speech where the member discusses the industry purely in a local context – the closing of a branch railway line, or local dissatisfaction with dirty coal, or inadequate electricity supply. The Acton Society Trust Report, referred to later, contained the following analysis of parliamentary speeches on the nationalised industries:

An analysis of speeches shows that the content of each can generally be divided into four parts. Speakers tend to open with a number of miscellaneous formalities – congratulating or decrying previous speakers etc. Next they usually consider it necessary to establish that the troubles now besetting the industry derive from the past errors of the opposing party. After this the member comes to his own knowledge of the subject, recounting the experiences and reminiscences. Finally in the time left, the member addresses himself to the particular subject of the debate – the railway deficit, the man-power shortage in the coal mines, etc. This account is unjust to the best speeches; in the worst, the final and relevant part of the speech is omitted altogether (p. 20).

As ministers refused to answer parliamentary questions on subjects for which they had no responsibility, a great part of the activities of the nationalised industries was outside the scope of the questions. Mr Morrison, speaking on 4 December 1947 on behalf of the Labour Government, had made it clear that ministers would refuse to answer questions on 'matters of day-to-day administration' of the nationalised industries; they had no responsibility for such matters. This was strongly opposed by Captain (later Viscount) Crookshank on behalf of the Opposition, and the Speaker found his position embarrassing in being constantly compelled to turn down questions. Finally, on 7 June 1948, the Speaker announced that this refusal of ministers to answer brought into operation Rule 26 of Erskine May's *Handbook on Parliamentary Procedure*. Despite the operation of the Rule, the Speaker had decided that when he thought the subject of the parliamentary question was 'of sufficient public importance', he would direct the question to be accepted, and it was then for the Minister to decide whether or not he was prepared to answer.

Both Government and members felt that this problem was of some importance, and finally a motion was passed on 4 December

1951 appointing a Select Committee 'to consider the present methods by which the House of Commons is informed of the affairs of the nationalised industries and to report what changes, having regard to the provisions laid down by Parliament in the relevant Statutes, may be desirable in these methods.'

This Committee produced its first Report on 29 October 1952, and its final Report on 23 July 1953. The final Report begins by examining the various ways in which Parliament can be informed about these industries and comes to the conclusion that these ways, e.g. motions, parliamentary questions and debates on the Annual Reports, are inadequate. It lays down a doctrine – which is very questionable – that in a general way the nationalised industries are accountable to Parliament. It then makes the startling statement that 'the nationalised industries had insufficient opportunity of presenting their case to Parliament and to the Public, and were exposed to public pressure in various ways, and much irresponsible criticism' (para. 5).

No indication is given of the source of the irresponsible criticism. If it comes from the public, then surely it is the fault of the nationalised industries in not equipping themselves with competent public relations departments. It was hardly the task of Parliament to look after them in this respect. If, on the other hand, the irresponsible criticism came from members themselves, surely it was a reflection on the members concerned. All the nationalised industries treated M.P.s with courtesy and respect. In some cases, e.g. with Area Gas and Electricity Boards, the chairman often took care to contact the M.P.s throughout his Area and offered to supply them with information as and when required. When an M.P. wrote to a Board, it was usually the chairman who replied. The problem was not the difficulty of obtaining information from the nationalised industries; any M.P. who took the trouble could get as much information as he wished. The problem rather was that the information thus obtained could not be discussed publicly in the House of Commons, or could not be obtained through normal channels in the House of Commons. Where the member's constituents were annoyed or infuriated by the action of a nationalised industry, the M.P. wished naturally to take up their cause publicly, and show his constituents how active he was on their behalf. This was only natural; it was his duty, and his constituents expected it of him. A letter from a chairman of a Board – sometimes not very forthcoming – was a poor substitute for a public discussion. The

M.P., even if he disagreed violently with the Board, could not take the matter further. Though they were under public ownership, the nationalised industries were independent corporations and had statutory responsibilities, and they often could not agree with the views of the member. There were instances of strong local resentment led by local M.P.s which had brought about some change in policy, but these were very infrequent.

A paper published by the Acton Society Trust, *Accountability to Parliament*, contained the following report on an analysis of parliamentary questions on the nationalised industries (p. 7): 'Analysis has shown that many questions, including both those answered (or evaded) and those refused, reflect a preoccupation on the part of members with local problems of management, as opposed to overall efficiency.' Questions on particular products or services have received far more attention than, for example, capital projects, training and promotion policies or research. The problem of the balance of nationalised industries in the economy as a whole and the amount of their share of the nation's capital resources has received scarcely any considerations.

Having therefore postulated, on inadequate grounds, (*a*) that Parliament required more information and (*b*) that the nationalised industries were anxious to supply that information, the Select Committee concluded in its Report of July 1953 that the best course would be for Parliament to set up a Special Committee which would 'offer the additional means of informing Parliament of the affairs of these industries, compatible with their statutory position, and with constitutional propriety'. The proviso contained in the last nine words was to prove a stumbling block and was to show how inadequate had been the premises on which their conclusion was shaped, and how they had failed to realise that their newly-found doctrine of 'accountability to Parliament' did not, unfortunately, square with the provisions of the Nationalisation Acts. The nationalised industries were statutory bodies and had to work within the framework of the Acts which created them; without amending legislation, not even Parliament could enunciate doctrines not to be found in those Acts. In fact 'accountability to Parliament', as we shall see, cuts clean across the tenor of those Acts.

In paragraphs 7 to 13 of the Report, the Committee reviews the arguments for and against a Special Committee; to any impartial eye the arguments against are overwhelming. Lord Reith, in his evidence to the Committee, put clearly the main constitutional point of view. 'A Select Committee on a nationalised industry was, in effect, a negation of what Parliament deliberately did in setting it up. Parliament passed a sort of self-denying ordinance, taking from itself the right to direct interference, as with Government Departments.' A further important point made by Lord Reith was that a committee might start with the best intentions as a friendly body, merely seeking information, but 'might end by investigating and controlling'.

The Committee does not attempt to counter these arguments. In paragraph 15 of its Report it faces the dilemma – should it 'accept the objections and abandon all possibility of dealing with the situation; or, despite the difficulties, make – with due safeguards – provision for such an enlargement of the field of parliamentary accountability as would provide the House of Commons with the information which it rightly requires, without, in obtaining that information, interfering with, or jeopardising the efficiency of the nationalised industries'. The members plumped for a Committee and considered its possible field of work.

In the first place the 'proposed new Committee should consider all the published accounts and auditors' reports of the public corporations and make representations about such matters as seem to require consideration by the Boards, or debate in the House of Commons'. Secondly, it was to have regard to 'not merely to present and past financial probity and stability, but to future plans and programmes'. Thirdly, the Committee would ask for any 'information as to the policy of the corporations', except where they had acted on a direction from a responsible Minister, or where collective bargaining arrangements were involved, i.e. negotiations with trade unions, etc. (Report, paras. 18 to 21).

The Committee would deal with the chairmen and the Boards of the industries and concentrate on general lines of policy, avoiding all matters of detail and administration. It then makes the extraordinary suggestion (para. 24) that, with its Annual Report 'each corporation should publish the best estimate it can make of the percentage increase or decrease since the date of its establishment, in the average cost to the consumer of its products or services, taken as a whole. . . . This figure [which was to be presumably a single percentage figure] would enable the Committee to form some opinion, though not a conclusive one, on the efficiency of the industry, as it could be compared with the general cost of living index.

This suggestion can only be described as astounding. How

F

would it be possible to prepare such a figure for the Transport Commission, or for the National Coal Board? And when it was prepared, would it have any meaning? Was it possible by some single percentage to assess the efficiency of vast and complex industries?

Finally, the Committee recommends that the new Select Committee should be assisted by a senior officer of the rank of the Comptroller and Auditor-General, who would in turn be helped by at least one professional accountant. His task would be to examine the Reports and Accounts of the industries and draw the Committee's attention to matters requiring investigation.

This Report must have caused the Government serious embarrassment, as can be seen from the line taken by Captain (later Viscount) Crookshank when it was debated on 8 February 1954. On the one hand, Parliament was clearly restless at the lack of direct contact with the nationalised industries and felt a sense of frustration. On the other hand, any parliamentary contact in the form of a committee, as suggested, would cut right across the structure of the Nationalisation Acts, which laid the responsibility for supervising these industries in the national interest on Government and not on Parliament. The embarrassment, therefore, arose from the fact that no Select Committee could function on the lines suggested, without seriously prejudicing the responsibility of ministers.

Captain Crookshank's statement, therefore, was, on the one hand, placatory in its generalities. On the other hand, when it came to detail it laid down restrictions and conditions on the operations of the proposed Select Committee. His speech showed that the Government had decided that it dare not attempt to persuade the House of Commons to abandon its ambition for a direct contact with the nationalised industries. But, on the other hand, it would take care that the contact led to very little results. So Captain Crookshank admitted that in the Nationalisation Acts Parliament had hardly been mentioned and that the accountability of the nationalised industries to Parliament was 'left too much in the air'. Of course a Select Committee on the nationalised industries was not a constitutional innovation and could not be objected to as such. After these preliminary generalities came the conditions. The Committee was not to enquire into detailed administration, nor into future plans and programmes. Nor into negotiating machinery for wages and conditions. The rights of ministers were not to be touched; the evidence submitted to the Committee was not to be published; the Committee would have no sub-committee and would investigate only one industry at a time. Nor would it be provided with the senior official proposed by the Select Committee.

Having thus apparently deprived the Committee of all work of any significance, Captain Crookshank ended with the soothing suggestion that it would enquire into current affairs and the immediate past, and on all matters of finance.

The House authorised the appointment of a Select Committee on the lines proposed by the Government, after grave doubts had been expressed on all sides.

During the debate Mr J. Maclay suggested that ministers will always defend and support the Boards for which they are responsible. He spoke from experience as a former Minister of Transport and his words are worth quoting:

> The minister comes along, and it does not matter what his political party is, he will almost inevitably find himself wanting to defend that industry. That attitude is probably a weakness of this Nation, but it is so. A minister is almost certainly going to defend something for which he has a certain responsibility and it is highly unlikely that the minister will stand up in the House and make a savage attack on a body, with which he has come into daily contact (*Hansard*, vol. 523, col. 888).

Though the debate took place on 8 February 1954, it was not until 16 March 1955 that the Select Committee was appointed. This delay of thirteen months showed the difficulty of deciding on the terms of reference of the Select Committee. These excluded four fields of enquiry:

(1) Matters decided by or which already engage the responsibility of ministers;
(2) wages and conditions of employment and other questions normally decided by collective bargaining arrangements;
(3) questions which fail to be considered through formal machinery established by relevant Statutes;
(4) matters of day-to-day administration.

(1), (2) and (4) are clear. (3) refers to such questions as railway charges, which are determined by the Transport Tribunal set up under the 1947 Transport Act.

Thus carefully shackled, the Select Committee which was constituted on 7 July 1955, after the General Election, set out to explore its field of activity. It found it so stony and the prospect so uninviting that on 14 November 1955 the Committee reported that the terms of reference with their four prohibitions left it 'insufficient scope to make inquiries or to obtain further information regarding the nationalised industries which would be of any real use to the House' (H.C. 120 (1955–6)).

Thus the problem was handed back to the Government, and Parliament was still devoid of machinery for investigating the nationalised industries.

The Government was obviously nonplussed because it was not until a year later, on 29 November 1956, that it brought the subject back to the House. Then Mr Butler moved the appointment of a Select Committee with the original terms of reference with the four prohibitions omitted (*Hansard*, vol. 561, cols. 395 et seq.).

Mr Butler's tone was apologetic and guarded. It was clear that the demand for some kind of Select Committee was too strong to be abandoned without a second attempt. But he had grave doubts and described the appointment of the Committee as an 'act of faith'. If it didn't work, some other method must be devised. He instanced several fields of enquiry where he thought the proposed Select Committee might do useful work and which did not fall within the direct responsibility of ministers. There was an imposing list of seven subjects for investigation, but some of them were extremely vague and, as members pointed out, the Select Committee would not get far without entering the prohibited areas of the earlier terms of reference.

Mr Butler made it clear that though the four prohibitions in the earlier terms of reference were not to be included in the later, nevertheless the four banned groups of subjects were still banned; their boundaries, however, were to be discovered by trial and error and the exercise of tact by the chairman. *Solvitur ambulando* was the policy of the Government. The Select Committee was to start by scrutinising the Reports and the Accounts of the Boards and was to proceed by asking questions based on those Reports and Accounts. It would therefore be dealing with the past and would have to work forward from the past. It was not clear whether the Committee was barred from investigating matters not referred to in the Reports and Accounts or whether it could ask questions about activities not dealt with in those Reports and Accounts.

The Labour Party opposed the appointment of this new Select Committee, and, though invited by Mr Butler to offer constructive suggestions, admitted that it could not. Apparently the Labour Party was conducting its own private review 'of these problems of accountability and efficiency in the nationalised industries' and would, in due course, produce its own proposals. Mr Callaghan, the Labour spokesman, made two minor suggestions. As ministers have the statutory power to demand any information whatever from the Boards, they should accept all parliamentary questions asking for information, obtain it under their statutory powers, and give publicity to this information by incorporating it in an answer. Sir Patrick Spens, the chairman of the Select Committee, pointed out that this proposal had already been considered and turned down, because such questions would flood the Order Paper. In any case, as an M.P. could usually obtain such information by writing to the chairman of a Board, why clutter up the parliamentary machine with questions usually dealing with minor or local matters?

His second suggestion was more publicity for the Consultative or Consumers' Councils. The malaise of these consumer organisations is dealt with in Chapter 12, and a little more publicity would have made no difference. It was clear from the Labour speeches that that Party was as devoid as the Government of ideas on how to bring Parliament into closer touch with the nationalised industries.

In their pamphlet *Public Enterprise*, published in July 1957, the Labour Party view is that 'the problem of Parliamentary responsibility is not an easy one to solve' and that 'on the whole we think that, as the Select Committee now exists, it should be given a fair trial' (p. 47).

The whole debate was on a high level. Clearly this intractable problem of providing closer contacts between Parliament and the Boards had set members thinking. Mr Champion (col. 642) pointed out that, when Parliament debated the affairs of a nationalised industry, much of the time was wasted. 'One is always struck by the fact that so much of the time Parliament devotes to the examination or supposed examination, of these industries, is devoted to trifling questions, often to minor unimportant constituency points.' In other words – Parliament reform thyself.

Mr Watkinson, in his reply for the Government, made the startling statement (col. 641) that 'everyone in the House wants to have proper parliamentary control of the nationalised industries'. Presumably in that case both sides of the House will set about revising the Nationalisation Acts. For where, in those Acts, is there provision for 'proper parliamentary control'? What do these three words mean? The fact is that the procedure of Parliament cannot cope with the problem of 'public accountability' of a group of vital and complex industries, unless these industries were converted into

Departments of State. If such conversion took place, parliamentary business would be hopelessly overloaded.

The Select Committee thus approved in November 1956, made its first Report in October 1957 (H.C. 304 (1956–7)). The Report falls into three parts. The first deals with 'Ministerial Control of Nationalised Industries'. The remainder deals with two minor nationalised Boards – the North of Scotland Hydro-Electric Board and the South of Scotland Electricity Board. The affairs of these two Boards are not an adequate basis for a Report on the important subject of 'Ministerial Control of Nationalised Industries'.

The Committee produced a second Report on the National Coal Board dated 29 April 1958. That Report deals with leading issues in the coal-mining industry such as investment, manpower, prices and the problem of the balance between the output of large coal and small coal. The investigation began in July 1957 and finished in April 1958; there was a long interval during the parliamentary recess. The Committee received 30 memoranda, of which 24 were submitted by the National Coal Board. What did the investigation achieve?

To begin with, there is no doubt that the information contained in the Minutes of Evidence is of great value. Much of it can be extracted from the Annual Report of the N.C.B. but much of it cannot. There are expressions of opinion which are valuable in providing a background for policy. The enquiry started with a long statement by Sir James Bowman, the chairman of the Board, in which he put up a strong defence of the Board's policy and suggested that the Committee

might consider the kind of half world in which we live as the National Coal Board. What are we? We are not flesh, fish or good red herring. We are not a commercial undertaking; we are not a public service; we are a bit of each. It is all right. We are prepared, as the National Coal Board, to accept all the responsibilities which Her Majesty's Government seek to place upon us and play our part in the national economy, but what we do object to is that, having done this, there is such a complete misrepresentation of the facts.

When he made this statement to the Select Committee he had been with the National Coal Board for seven years, but he still found it difficult to realise that the post-war nationalised industries were an entirely new form of enterprise which fell outside the usual categories and in dealing with which we all find ourselves somewhat at a loss. It is not 'misrepresentation' that is the difficulty, as Sir

James suggests: the difficulty is that, with the best will in the world, we cannot find the right method for classifying the facts of the nationalised industries.

What did the Select Committee set out to achieve with all this labour? What was the purpose of it all? Its function (Report on National Coal Board, para. 5) was 'to acquaint the House with the activities and problems of the nationalised industries, to question those industries on the matters about which members are most perplexed, and to report to the House with such comments as are appropriate'. The Committee did not 'refrain from criticism when they think that, on the evidence, it is called for; but they have tried not to become involved as critics with the day-to-day administration of the Board on the one hand and with matters of Government policy on the other'.

At the end of its Report, the Committee felt it necessary to justify itself against possible accusations that the work involved was a trial to a harassed National Coal Board:

It gave the Board the chance to state their case fully and clearly. The witnesses seized their opportunity and in the Committee's opinion made full use of it. In the early stages of the enquiry, perhaps due to their inexperience of the procedure the witnesses appeared to be unduly on the defensive, but in later sittings a better understanding developed. The Committee consider that the substantial amount of time spent in giving evidence and preparing memoranda will prove of value to the Board and that this kind of enquiry is not prejudicial to the good administration and direction of the affairs of the nationalised industries (para. 141).

As the Committee itself says, 'A large part of the Committee's Report is purely factual' (para. 139). This statement is followed by a summary of eleven conclusions and recommendations. Many of them are obvious and some of very little value – either to the Government, Parliament or the National Coal Board. What are we to make of the recommendation on uneconomic pits which reads as follows:

It would be foolish to refuse to invest money in the pits simply because, under an artificial average-price system, they are not showing a profit at any given moment. Nevertheless some closing of uneconomic pits may be essential to withstand competition from oil, and, in the future, nuclear energy.

One important recommendation dealt with the 'Gentleman's agreement' under which the Minister of Power has the final word

on the fixing of coal prices. The Committee approved the purpose of
the agreement but disliked its informality. It rightly proposed that,
when this power was used, it should be disclosed to Parliament. The
Board should 'consult the Minister as to the public interest and,
having done so, should then take full responsibility for their price
determination'. If the Minister didn't like the decision he should
give the Board a direction in writing. The Government refused to
accept this recommendation (*Hansard*, vol. 591, col. 847).

This refusal was made on 14 July 1958, in the course of a debate
in the House of Commons on the Coal Board's Report for 1957 and
on this Report of the Select Committee. In the twelve months
before the debate, a change had come over the fortunes of the coal-
mining industry. After many years of shortage, coal had become
surplus, unsold stocks were mounting and a new kind of anxiety
was affecting the industry. The debate was quite tense. Tributes
were paid to the work of the Select Committee, whose Report had
shed some light in dark places and thereby helped members to
make more purposeful contributions to the debate. But it would be
an exaggeration to say that the Report seriously affected the debate,
which followed the traditional lines of all coal debates since 1947;
the Government tried to prove that they were doing everything to
help the coal industry, while the Opposition tried to prove that all
the industry's difficulties were due to government policy. The
tributes to the Select Committee's Report from both sides were
due to the cautious character of the Report, which did not come to
grips with the major problems of the industry.

This Report of the Select Committee on the National Coal
Board was followed by a third Report in May 1959 on the Air
Corporations. This is a massive document of over fifty pages and
the minutes of evidence reveal over 2,500 questions and 46
appendices – just double the number of questions in the Report on
the Coal Board. The Air Corporations are not dealt with in this
book, so we need not go into the Report in detail. But there is one
part of the Report which must be mentioned – the relationship
between the Minister of Transport and the Air Corporations. The
Committee was clearly surprised at the close and extensive co-
operation between Government and airlines. 'The strongest
evidence of the co-operation is given by the extent to which the
Corporations tacitly allow powers to the Minister which the
statutes do not.' The conclusion at which the Committee arrives
is that 'they consider it essential to the efficient running on com-

mercial lines of the Air Corporations that there should be a clear-cut division of responsibility between the chairman on the one hand and the minister on the other. When the minister wishes, on grounds of national interest, to override the commercial judgement of a chairman, he should do so by a directive which should be published' (Report on Air Corporations, para. 218).

Air Corporations operate from government-owned airports over routes regulated by international and inter-governmental agreements at fares agreed on internationally. Their competitors are largely state-owned airlines. They require, at times, large amounts of foreign exchange for purchase of aircraft, etc. It is inevitable that co-operation between Government and Air Corporations should be of the closest character.

The fourth Report of the Select Committee was published in July 1959 (H.C. 276 (1958–9)) and is a special Report which raises the whole question of the future activities of the Committee. Knowing that a General Election was coming, the Committee was rightly anxious to draw conclusions from its $2\frac{1}{2}$ years' work for the guidance of any successors the new Parliament might appoint.

The great problem had been the lack of competent help to enable it to tackle the problem of investigating the nationalised industries. A mass of reports and documents relating to an industry would be put before the Committee; how was it to select for investigation the important issues which lay buried in that mass? The Committee thought of two ways:

First, an accountant with experience of industrial and commercial accounts would have been very helpful in analysing the formidable tables of figures laid before the Committee, and in pointing out their significance. Secondly, a research worker with training in economics could have informed the Committee about what had been written on the subject. He might have helped them to decide which lines of enquiry would prove productive and might have helped them to investigate important questions (Special Report, para. 8).

Select Committees are assisted by a Clerk of the House and in the past that was adequate help because such Committees investigated matters mainly of procedure. But the training and competence of a House of Commons Clerk were not suited for the type of work referred to in the preceding paragraph. The Select Committee accordingly consulted some very important people about this additional help; these included Mr Butler, as Leader of the House, Mr Gaitskell as Leader of the Opposition, the Second

Secretary of the Treasury and the Clerk of the House of Commons. The evidence of all these witnesses is of great constitutional interest.

Some definite conclusions emerge from the evidence. Staff to assist a Select Committee must owe allegiance to the House of Commons. A civil servant borrowed from the Treasury might be put into an embarrassing position, as the Committee might wish to criticise his department. It would be undesirable (and Mr Butler stresses this point) for the Select Committee to acquire a skilled accountant/economist staff; it might 'give the nationalised industries a false impression of what the relationships of Parliament with them really are', and might suggest that the staff 'were going to pry into them in a way which might do more harm in the end to the constructive work the Committee wish to do' (Question 241). In any case a Select Committee is only appointed for a session; so it could not offer employment for more than a session. A possible way out would be for the Select Committee to appoint an assessor. He would be an expert on the industry under investigation, who would attend meetings and on whose behalf the chairman would put questions to witnesses. A precedent existed for such an appointment in an investigation into the telephone service in 1921, and precedents count for much in the House of Commons; Mr Butler supported this proposal.

The Select Committee left it to the House elected in October 1959 to consider the problems in the Special Report with a view to giving the new Select Committee some additional help.

Naturally enough the Select Committee does not examine the fundamental question whether it is worth while continuing its labours. It believes 'that the need to provide an effective link between Parliament and the nationalised industries is of great importance' (para. 2) though 'the relationship of Parliament to the nationalised industries presents a new and special problem'.

The new Parliament elected in October 1959 reappointed the Select Committee on Nationalised Industries on 30 November. It got down to work immediately and held its first meeting on 4 December, finishing on 11 July 1960, after meeting twenty-eight times. The subject was British Railways, on which it produced the fifth Report of 93 pages after putting over 2,000 questions and receiving 56 documents which form the appendices to the Report (H.C. 254-1 (1959–60)). This was on a much greater scale than the comparable investigation into the National Coal Board, which resulted in a Report of 60 pages, after 1200 questions and 30 documents.

This enquiry imposed a great strain on the British Transport Commission. Sir Brian Robertson and his senior colleagues had to cope with over 1700 questions. His staff submitted no less than forty-eight documents, some of which are quite massive. One paper, for instance, on the financial inter-relation of the regions of British Railways includes six annexes which fill twelve pages with statistics.

In paragraph 354 of the Report the Committee reminds the House of Commons of its function. 'Your Committee do not attempt to solve the problem of British Railways, nor is it their function to try to do so. Their task is to present the facts to the House and to make such comments as seem appropriate.' The difficulty was that a group of members of Parliament had not the necessary time or expertise to unravel the very tangled affairs of British Railways. The Committee made a very determined effort to discover how serious deficits arose in the operations of the railways. It reports the fact (para. 137) 'that the Commission cannot say with any precision where this £42 million [of deficit] is lost' and as 'the Commission cannot say', the Committee cannot report on this vital issue.

The Select Committee, however, makes some comments which are of value. It is worried by the fact that in the organisation of the Commission 'there should have been no one authority whose only duty in the field of transport was to ensure an efficient system of railways' (para. 358). It is not satisfied that the Commission have treated the recruitment of technical staff with the urgency it deserves (para. 370). It deplores 'the imprecise methods of costing' employed by the Commission (para. 374). It is surprised 'that large expenditures have been undertaken on modernising parts of the undertaking, without any precise calculation of what the profitability of those parts will be on completion'.

The amazing fact is that while the work of the Commission was under detailed scrutiny by the Select Committee, the Government were carrying out their own investigations by means of the Special Advisory Group under Sir Ivan Stedeford. Furthermore, having received the Reports of this group and of the Select Committee, the Government set up a committee under the chairmanship of the Minister of Transport 'to consider what sort of and how big a railway system we need' (*Hansard*, vol. 627, col. 2165). In a debate on 26 October 1960 the House of Commons considered the Annual Report for 1959 of the B.T.C. as well as the Report of the Select Committee. Though Mr Marples made several complimentary references to the Committee's Report, his description of it was that 'it made a searching examination of the fundamental questions but it left me and the Commission – and understandably left us – with more questions than answers.' On the other hand he refers to the 'recommendations' and 'advice' of the Special Advisory Group. In particular he mentioned (col. 2368) that the Group had 'early on, expressed doubts about the economic aspects of the London Midland electrification scheme' and that 'the Transport Commission had prepared a reassessment of the scheme'. This had all been going on while the Select Committee had also been considering the scheme and had come to the conclusion that 'the right policy now seems to your Committee to be to complete the scheme as soon as possible' (Report of the Select Committee, para. 393).

We can conclude that the Select Committee is a useful piece of machinery for delving into facts. It is not equipped to make a competent survey on which the Government can act, as was the case, for instance, with the Herbert Committee on Electricity Supply. It would be a pity if the existence of the Committee – and it is now well established – were regarded as making it unnecessary to appoint an investigating Committee from time to time. The Committee's Reports neither produce 'accountability to Parliament' nor do they give ministers a basis for policy decisions.

But against the advantages of the discovery of facts by the Select Committee must be set the disadvantage of the work it entails for the Boards of the nationalised industries. Appearance before the Select Committee must be regarded as an occupational hazard of a chairman.

As mentioned above, the Select Committee on Nationalised Industries is sessional and is therefore reappointed each session after a motion has been duly passed. This is an advantage in one way as it allows fresh members to join. On the other hand there is the disadvantage of a changing composition mitigated by the fact that there are a few stalwarts with a permanent interest in these industries who provide the element of continuity and expertise carried forward from one investigation to another.

The Select Committee works hard. Its Reports tend to become longer and longer and the completed Reports with ancillary volumes have become a formidable collection of reading matter.

The Report of the Gas Industry published in July 1961 is longer than that on British Railways published in July 1960; 34 meetings were held on gas and 28 on railways. At the former 2,000 questions were put by the Committee; at the latter 3,000. The greater length of the Gas Report was largely due to the fact that all the twelve autonomous Gas Boards had to be seen. This factor also affected the Report on Electricity at which over 4,000 questions were asked: this investigation (with the permission of the House) straddled over two parliamentary sessions.

During the latter part of the investigation the Committee was faced with the difficulties in electricity supply which took place in the winter of 1962–3, which brought a note of urgency into its deliberations. But this could only be dealt with indirectly as the Committee's terms of reference cover the reports and accounts of the electricity Boards which were published before the Committee set to work.

By now the Select Committee is a well-established feature of the parliamentary scene. Most years it settles down to an investigation of one of the nationalised industries and produces a Report which contains much useful and even valuable information.

Ministers, of course, do not appear before the Committee though they are regularly criticised for their 'extra-statutory interferences' in the running of these industries. This is a subject which will be fully dealt with in Chapter 8. The Committee, consisting of back-bench members, does not seem to appreciate the strength of the forces which are compelling Government after Government – whatever its political complexion – to influence and even to control the policy of these industries because it conceives it to be in the national interest to do so. This, of course, was not foreseen or spelled out in the Nationalisation Acts, which were passed twenty years ago in conditions very different from those of the sixties.

The Select Committee is a typically British institution. Despite all the pangs of its birth and the constitutional difficulties of playing its part in the nationalisation set-up, which are described earlier in this chapter, the Committee and the curious compromise which it represents have come to stay. Ministers and their departments, on the whole, welcome it as a safety valve for the House of Commons. The Committee's criticisms of their conduct are answered in papers which are laid before the House; and except occasionally on minor issues ministers pursue their familiar ways.

Though the senior members of the industries find it a burden to be investigated by the Select Committee, they also seem to welcome its activities. At any rate they say so. The Committee represents parliamentary opinion and is accordingly treated with deference. It gives chairmen opportunity of speaking frankly and ventilating their views in a way which is not otherwise possible.

The Reports, and even more the minutes of evidence and memoranda submitted to the Select Committee, are valuable to the student of the nationalised industries. They are no doubt also studied in the industries and the relevant government departments. But their circulation is limited and most of all in the House of Commons to which they are addressed.

The steady flow of reports from the Select Committee has made much more remote the possibility of a critical investigation by a competent outside committee on the lines of the Herbert Committee on Electricity Supply. That is a pity. The Herbert Committee led to a necessary reorganisation of the industry in the Electricity Act 1957. For reasons explained earlier, the Select Committee cannot probe deeply or range widely over an industry; it has not the staff to do the work. Recently it has secured the services of an advisory economist, who must be helpful to the Committee in selecting problems for investigation.

There are other facets of 'parliamentary accountability'. Despite the work of the Select Committee, the House is still worried about parliamentary questions on the nationalised industries, controversy on which started, as we have seen, as far back as 1947. On 25 February 1960 Mr Butler made a statement which is so important that it requires quotation in full.

Hon. members have recently inquired about the scope for Questions in the nationalised industries.

With your permission, Sir, may I say that we must adhere to the view that ministers can answer Questions for which they have a recognised responsibility. Otherwise, they would inevitably find themselves encroaching upon the managerial functions entrusted to the nationalised boards.

Ministers would, of course, answer for the matters which the industries are required by Statute to lay before them, and for appointments, finance and matters on which they themselves have statutory powers or duties. In addition, they may from time to time be concerned with other questions of broad policy affecting the industries.

There is no hard and fast formula by which these matters could be identified and opened to Questions in the House, but provided Questions on the Paper relate to ministers' responsibilities for matters of general policy, they will consider sympathetically the extent to which they can properly apply.

This statement led to supplementary questions which occupy several columns of *Hansard*. In the course of these exchanges, Mr Butler informed the House that the ministers concerned had had a meeting among themselves and that 'the only new point in my statement relates to ministers' responsibility for matters of general policy'; he agreed that 'there is no very great extension. We shall try to interpret general policy in as broad a manner as we can.'

This 'new point' can only relate to government policy in matters where there is no definite statutory responsibility; e.g. the 'gentleman's agreement' on coal prices. Mr Butler did not attempt to give examples of 'general policy'. Presumably members will find out by trial and error where ministers are prepared to answer; the Table, in doubtful cases, will presumably enquire from the Department whether the Minister concerned is prepared to answer and in view of Mr Butler's assurance of 'sympathetic consideration', the Minister will be prepared to reply if he has any responsibility at all.

A new and important aspect of 'parliamentary accountability' developed from 1956 onwards. As will be explained in Chapter 9, the Finance Act 1956 substituted advances from the Treasury for issue of stock by the nationalised industries, backed by government guarantee. Only the Coal Board before 1956 had been financed by such advances.

It has been the normal practice to grant by statute to each nationalised industry borrowing powers up to a certain amount, which enabled them to borrow for some time ahead. The Coal Industry Nationalisation Act 1946, for example, authorised the Minister of Fuel and Power to advance to the Coal Board within five years up to £150 million; any further advances after that were to be settled by Parliament. The Electricity Act 1947 authorised the electricity supply industry to borrow up to £700 million. As time went on these sums, of course, proved inadequate. A series of Acts has therefore been passed increasing the limits from time.

For example in 1956 a Bill was introduced to increase the borrowpowers of the Coal Board from £350 to £650 million. There were objections from some members, who pressed for an annual review of the investment plans of the Coal Board. The Government was not prepared to agree but compromised by including a provision that where the sum to be borrowed in any one year exceeded by £75 million the sum outstanding in the preceding year, a Statutory Instrument would be laid before the House for its approval; the first such instrument was debated and approved on 3 December 1958. There have been a number of such Statutory Instruments which have been laid before the House of Commons. These give members an opportunity to raise issues on the operations of the relevant Boards and to that extent, Parliament receives information and can make comments. But as in other financial matters, Government gets its way and 'accountability to Parliament' is nominal.

To sum up, we can say there are roughly four methods in which members of Parliament can show their interests in the nationalised industries.

These are:

(1) Parliamentary Questions;
(2) debates on Annual Reports, motions on the adjournment, and debates on odd occasions such as private bills;
(3) the Select Committee on nationalised industries;
(4) financial debates on Bills for borrowing powers, Statutory Instruments authorising increased advances etc.

As regards questions, members have become more resigned in recent years to the unpalatable fact that the Acts which created the nationalised industries severely limited the scope of their powers. When anything serious happens in those industries in which the Government is concerned, ministers will usually make a statement which can become the subject of questions; but the frontier of 'day-to-day' working has on the whole been maintained.

In the last ten years there has been a fair increase in the work of the Select Committee which has been useful in providing a safety valve. With the great expansion in the nationalised industries and their increasing importance in the economy, their capital development has gone ahead. So there have been more financial Bills, and Statutory Instruments arising therefrom which give more opportunities for debate.

But when all is said and done, the twenty years' development of a group of large nationalised industries has shown that this addition to the public sector has resulted in an expansion in the already vast powers of the Executive. Parliament has been forced to look on, with a feeling of helpless indignation, at the fact that it has but little part to play in supervising this development. 'Parliamentary accountability' has proved a will-o'-the-wisp. The founding statutes of these industries gave Parliament a remote and fitful part to play, a fact which was not realised at the time those statutes were passed. Much has been written in recent years of the decline of parliamentary control over the Executive. An important contributory factor in that decline has been the great expansion of the public sector, a substantial part of which is now formed by the group of nationalised industries. These give the Government a massive power and a massive responsibility in the country's industrial set-up which did not exist before 1945.

It is ironical that Labour back-benchers who demand more nationalisation do not realise that if their wishes were met, their own status in Parliament would be diminished even more than at present. Public ownership and parliamentary procedure do not go well together.

8 Government and the Nationalised Industries

THE pattern of relations between Government and the nationalised industries was clearly laid down in the Nationalisation Acts. Public Corporations were established by the Acts to take over the assets and liabilities of the industries covered by the Acts. These corporations were to be commercial concerns and not government departments. They were charged with certain responsibilities and functions. They would make such charges as would enable their revenues to meet their outgoings. This was not expected to be the case in every year – that would have been too rigid and drastic. So there is always a proviso that this obligation was spread over a period.

But these great Public Corporations stood in special relations to a Minister, with whose department they were to co-operate. Thus the three nationalised fuel industries – coal, gas and electricity – had defined relations with the Minister of Fuel and Power – now the Minister of Power. Similarly the British Transport Commission had relations with the Minister of Transport and the Iron and Steel Corporation with the Minister of Supply. The new British Steel Corporation deals with the Minister of Power. What were these relations?

The Minister was the shareholder who had bought out the previous owners, or rather he represented the shareholders. For the previous owners were bought out by an issue of stock carrying a Treasury guarantee, or, in other words, by gilt-edged stocks.

As representative of the shareholders the Minister had to see that the finances of the industry were properly conducted. He prescribed, therefore, the form of accounts and appointed the auditors. As soon as the accounts were audited they had to be submitted to the Minister, together with a report on the year's working; he in turn laid these documents before Parliament.

The Boards had to lay before the ministers general programmes of capital development, of education, and of training and research. These programmes were only to be submitted 'from time to time';

some Acts (such as Coal and Transport) required the Minister's approval; others such as Electricity only required 'consultation' with the Minister. In fact financial stringency meant annual submissions, and the Annual Reports of the Boards have many complaints about the limitations on capital development.

But the most important functions of the Minister were two. The first was that he had power to give a Board 'directions of a general character as may appear to the Minister to be requisite in the national interest', and the Board was obliged to 'give effect to such directions'.

There has been much misunderstanding over this power to give a 'direction of a general character'. Time and again ministers have been pressed by irate or impatient members of Parliament to give the Boards 'a general direction' and ministers have always refused. The power was intended to be used in a narrow sphere in cases of 'national interest', and was clearly intended to deal with serious issues. All such directions were to be printed in the Annual Reports and therefore we know only two have been issued.

As explained in Chapter 6 a Conservative Government took office in October 1951 which was pledged to repeal the Iron and Steel Act 1949. Accordingly on 13 November 1951 the new Minister of Supply issued a general direction to the Iron and Steel Corporation, instructing it not to make any important change in the financial structure or management of the industry, without first receiving the Minister's consent in writing. The intention was clear: to avoid any change in the nationalised steel industry, while legislation for repeal was being prepared; this ultimately was the Iron and Steel Act 1953.

The second general direction was issued by the Minister of Transport to the Transport Commission in April 1952 directing it not to increase certain charges. Relations between Government and the Transport Commission were strained and the Government was determined that certain increases in charges were not to take place. It was well known at the time that the Prime Minister, Sir Winston Churchill, was taking a personal interest in the matter, as was shown by a statement issued from No. 10 Downing Street. Doubts were expressed whether this direction indeed complied with the requirements of Section 4 (1) of the Transport Act 1947, but even if it did not, what was the Transport Commission to do? It could not appeal to the Courts nor indeed would it have wished to do so. This example showed that a determined Government could have its way with a nationalised industry.

The Minister's second power is to appoint the members of the Board. These powers of appointment are very sweeping. None of the Acts lays down terms or conditions of appointment. The Minister can fix the period of appointment and determine the salary and emoluments. The usual practice has been to appoint full-time members of Boards for five years. No Board member has any security beyond the period for which he is appointed. He cannot be certain that he will be reappointed. There may be a change of government policy before the end of his period of office: his post may be changed or abolished and he might find himself unemployed. Ministers even have the power to dismiss a member if he 'is otherwise unable or unfit to discharge the duties of a member' and this power was employed in the case of the chairman of the Yorkshire Electricity Board, who had been sent to prison for an offence against the building licensing regulations. Circumstances might arise when cessation of employment takes place even during the period of appointment. For instance, when the National Coal Board was reorganised after the issue of the Report of the Committee under Sir Alexander Fleck, all the members of the Board, to facilitate that reorganisation, had placed their resignations in the hands of the Minister of Fuel and Power. Several of the members were not reappointed.

In these days employment without pension is becoming a rarity, but in the case of Board members it took some time before pension arrangements were sanctioned for members of Boards; these arrangements were made by regulations issued by the appropriate Minister. It is consequently important for the member to be allowed to hold his post for as long a period as possible so that he might earn maximum pension. All this gives the Minister considerable influence over his appointees.

Very little attention has been given to this question of patronage by ministers. The number of appointments is considerable, especially those in the hands of the Minister of Power, who appoints the personnel of the National Coal Board, the Electricity Council, the Electricity Generating Board, the twelve Area Electricity Boards, the Gas Council and the Twelve Area Gas Boards. Since 1967 the Minister is also responsible for appointing the members of the British Steel Corporation. In all the appointments number nearly 250, of which about 80 are full-time.

The great era of patronage was the eighteenth and early nineteenth centuries, and the corruption which it occasioned led to a public revolt. In the latter half of the nineteenth century public appointments were placed in the hands of impartial bodies, such as the Civil Service Commission, working on the results of public competitive examinations. Nationalisation on a substantial scale has reintroduced patronage in the sense that ministers have in their gift valuable appointments and are not accountable to anyone for the selection of their appointees. All they need say to Parliament is that they have appointed the best man they can find, and the qualifications laid down in the various Acts are so varied and extensive that there is no difficulty in bringing the appointee under one or other of them. Naturally ministers are very anxious that they should be above suspicion in making these appointments and they therefore welcome a clear code of rules which enables them to play safe. This is the main – though unspoken – argument against 'commercial' salaries, and it is this difficult and unsolved dilemma of nationalisation that makes nonsense of the claim that the Boards of the nationalised industries are commercial organisations. Appointees to these Boards soon realise – if they have not realised it before – that they are working within the framework of a statute, in close collaboration with a government department, subject to pressure from ministers which they cannot resist, and liable to constant attack from the public and public bodies. The glare of the limelight upon them is only less fierce than upon ministers themselves.

By the nature of his post a Minister of the Crown is someone rather aloof – segregated on a pedestal so to speak. He holds vast powers and is treated with great deference: for he is the personification of the Crown in the sphere of his department. Relations between the industrialists who man the Boards and the Minister who appoints them cannot be free and easy. The approach to the Minister must inevitably be through his senior officers, who, after all, are permanent and know the persons and problems of the industries with which they deal, and are not changing figures in the political scene, as are ministers.

The importance of the nationalised industries to the national economy has become such that ministers and Boards must often meet. Statements and questions in the House prove that. The influence of the Government on the policy of the nationalised industries is becoming stronger and more continuous. By this development ministers have come to exercise a great degree of power, for which they are responsible to no one. It is not the ministers who make the formal decisions but the Boards, and therefore there is no overt act for which a Minister can be held responsible by Parliament. The constitutional importance of this development over the last twenty years has been dealt with in the preceding chapter.

In the years since nationalisation relations between Government and nationalised industries have subtly and steadily changed. The original picture was of powerful Public Corporations going their independent way on a commercial basis. Occasionally some important issue would develop on which consultation with ministers might be desirable and in the last resort there might be, very rarely, a general direction from the Minister in some matter of national interest. Mr Herbert Morrison drew a picture of this kind in his speech on 8 February 1954, in the debate on the Report of the Select Committee on Nationalised Industries. He described in these terms his relations, as Minister of Transport, with the Central Electricity Board. But the analogy of the pre-war Public Corporations was a false one; they differed substantially from those created between 1946 and 1950.

For one thing they raised their own finance and secondly they were of limited scope. No great national issue arose on their policies. The nation was hardly conscious of their existence. How many of us before the war could have given a simple description of the work of the Central Electricity Board?

It has been suggested in some quarters, e.g. by Professor Keeton in *The Passing of Parliament*, that a Board of a nationalised industry is 'not a corporation at all, except that it has a legal personality so that it can sue or be sued as a unit. It is, in fact, an emanation of the Ministry which, by a pleasant trick of nomenclature well known to Government Departments, has been called something else to make it more palatable to the public at large' (p. 151). Professor Keeton develops the point further (p. 152): 'The Departments, having to an important and increasing degree emancipated themselves from the control of Parliament and the Courts, now enjoy a stranglehold upon the economic life of the country, operating through dummy monopolies, whose officials are appointed by them and are responsible to them, and whose activities are subject to control and supervision by the Departments on all questions of broad policy.'

This over-simplifies the picture. To begin with, the identification of Minister and Department is overdone; one proof is the change of policy inaugurated by the Conservative Government in 1951. The suggestion that the Boards of the nationalised industries are merely the puppets of the officials of their 'parent' department, or even of the Minister of the Department, and have no views of their own on matters of major policy, ignores the vast and complex activities of these Boards. They are responsible for controlling industries with long traditions and highly developed personalities; they are in constant relations with large numbers of senior officials who have spent their lives in the industry; they have to deal with the trade unions which represent the workers in the industry and which have formulated their own policies. Most of the Board members have themselves spent their lives in the industry and are closely identified with its outlook.

It is therefore unrealistic to suggest that these varied and numerous activities of the Boards are controlled by a handful of government officials who have no technical competence in the industries concerned. The evidence produced in this book has been all to the contrary – that no Government has been able, effectively, to control the working of the nationalised industries. A crucial example has been schemes of capital development, which have been formulated by the industries and have willynilly been adopted and financed by Government.

There is, of course, as explained earlier in this chapter, frequent discussion between Boards and their officials with the Minister and his officials, on general questions of policy. That is inevitable, but such discussions cannot be described as simply one group giving instructions to another group. There is, of course, co-operation and continuous give and take.

Though Conservative ministers never displayed the warm partisanship of Labour ministers, nevertheless the natural role for a Minister was to support the nationalised industry for which he was responsible. As Mr Maclay pointed out in the debate on the Report of the Select Committee in February 1954, referred to in Chapter 7, the broad policy of these very important industries is always under discussion between Minister and Boards. The Annual Reports make frequent references to such consultations and so do ministers' speeches in the House. It is natural, therefore, for ministers to feel that both they and their Departments are closely identified with the policies and actions of the Boards, and publicly they try to put the best interpretation on them. If ministers became openly critical of the Boards, the Government would naturally be asked, why do they not get the Boards to change their policy. They cannot publicly disagree with the Boards to any material extent because such public difference of opinion would cause alarm and despondency among the Boards and their staffs, and would be gleefully seized upon both by opponents of the Board and opponents of the Government. It is only in serious crises, such as 1952, when the Government and the Transport Commission differed on fundamental policy, that differences can be ventilated. It is interesting to note that in the debate on the 21 October 1953, on the Commission's Annual Report for 1952, the government spokesman reverted to form, welcomed the Report and was conciliatory in his attitude towards the Commission. By October 1953 a new Commission had been appointed and the Government wished bygones to be bygones.

In view of this close co-operation between Minister and industry it might be said that the Minister in reviewing the Annual Report is reviewing work for which he is himself to some extent responsible. He must, therefore, put the best construction on the year's results and gloss over as far as possible the year's failures.

It is curious that a period of Conservative Government, with its steady relaxation of controls and removal of restrictions, should have increased government control over the nationalised industries. It has been an inevitable development, and not the result of deliberate policy on either side. The nationalised industries have been caught in the tide of inflation and their ever-mounting costs have forced on them repeated increases in the prices of their products. These have been most unpopular and have cut across government efforts to hold prices steady. Willynilly, therefore, the industries have had to postpone increases and where that has not been possible they have sought to cover themselves by securing ministerial approval – not always easily obtained, to judge from complaints about delays. Also the costs of their capital programmes have steadily risen, making earlier estimates out of date and forcing them to seek additional finance. After 1956 this finance has been provided by direct loans from the Treasury; a fact which has given ministers more authority.

The products or services of the Public Corporations are in general use. Most people require them and therefore an increase in price is widely felt. As their products – fuel or transport – are basic they enter into industrial or commercial costs and therefore promote increases in the prices of many finished products. The Government is always on the alert to restrain or postpone such proposed increases. This is particularly the case when the unpopularity of such increases might rebound on the Government which condones or authorises them. As is shown by the delay in authorising increases in coal prices in the spring of 1955, a Government before a General Election will hold up such unpleasant decisions until the electorate has voted.

Labour Governments, up to 1951, naturally favoured the nationalised industries which they had created. The industries were facing exceptional difficulties in getting under way. So was every industry in the private sector. But the Public Corporations were faced with the tremendous task of coping with an acute postwar shortage of material, equipment and trained labour, at a time when the demand for their products was unlimited. But, and this was their particular problem, they had, at the same time, to create a brand-new national organisation for the industries for which they had been made responsible. Anyone familiar with the problems of large-scale mergers will agree that many years are required before the new and enlarged unit can settle down. The nationalised industries were mergers on an unprecedented scale and they required at least a decade in which to reorganise themselves and create the new team spirit which was so necessary. But unfortunately the times did not allow of such a leisurely approach; they had to attack the most daunting problems with organisations newly formed and completely untried.

Naturally, therefore, the Labour Government did its best to help, but the help it could give was limited. The Government itself was struggling with enormous economic and financial difficulties and in September 1949 had to carry out a 30 per cent devaluation of sterling.

In October 1951 the Conservatives took over. They immediately made arrangements for denationalising the steel industry and for reducing the powers of the Transport Commission, particularly in road haulage and in the scope for expanding nationalisation in such fields as road passenger transport. Having done this, they announced on 3 November 1953 through the Prime Minister, Sir Winston Churchill, that they proposed to leave alone the remaining nationalised industries. His words deserve quotation: 'We abhor the fallacy, for such it is, of nationalisation for nationalisation's sake. But where we are preserving it, as in the coal mines, the railways, air traffic, gas and electricity, we have done and are doing our utmost to make a success of it, even though this may somewhat mar the symmetry of party recrimination.'

It was a strange experience for the Conservative Government to find itself saddled with responsibilities which it disliked. It had to defend and support these Public Corporations, whose creation it had strongly resisted as stepping-stones to a Socialist State. It had no alternative but to defend and support them; they were an important part of the national economy which could not be neglected. Perhaps transport was the one industry which did not get the attention which it required. But the Transport Commission, even after the slimming Transport Act of 1953, was still a vast and unwieldy body which inspired little hope and interest. It began to receive attention in the later fifties, when its financial position was beginning to look desperate.

But with the exception of transport, which had been neglected even by the Labour Governments, Conservative ministers soon found themselves defending and protecting the industries for which they were responsible. It is interesting that Lord Citrine, in complaining of cuts in the electricity capital programmes, only refers to cuts imposed by Labour ministers and makes no reference to cuts by Conservative ministers. Yet these ministers brought pressure to bear on him by demanding oil-fired power stations and, what was much worse, thrusting upon the electricity industry a programme of largely experimental nuclear stations which was far too large in the light of the knowledge available in 1955. Yet in 1957 the Government trebled the programme of this experimental type of electricity generation as a result of panic on oil supplies after the Suez débâcle. This enlarged programme of 6,000 MW. of nuclear stations has been a burden on the electricity supply industry, which they accepted with reluctance.

By the end of the fifties the Government was forced to consider seriously the financial position of the nationalised industries. In the Finance Act 1956 the Government had scrapped the arrangement whereby the industries financed themselves by issuing of stock, and had substituted direct loans from the Treasury. This had the inevitable effect of making the Government very conscious of its financial responsibilities; but it was not until April 1961 that it issued its White Paper on the Financial and Economic Obligations of the Nationalised Industries (Cmnd. 1337), which is discussed in detail in the next chapter.

The course of the 1960s has steadily made the Boards more and more dependent on government policy and has brought them into closer relations with ministers. This stems from their ever-increasing financial problems. Two of the industries, coal and railways, are in financial difficulties – the latter desperately so. Electricity has a vast investment programme which is a great strain on the Treasury. Gas, which sailed along in fairly quiet waters, attracted little notice till the North Sea revealed great supplies of natural gas. These naturally led to substantial programmes of development, which mean capital expenditure several times as large as normal investment in gas and which added to the burdens of the Treasury. The Airline Corporations, always subject by their very nature to government control, became even more so when they required foreign currency to buy aircraft. Even the newly born British Steel Corporation started life with the certainty that it would incur losses for a time.

The following chapter describes the working of the 1961 White Paper on Financial Obligations. It had a definite effect in controlling the finances and prices of the gas and electricity industries; a slight effect on coal and none at all on railways and transport. The importance of the White Paper lay in the fact that it provided a yardstick for the financial behaviour of the industries, which the Treasury produced on every possible occasion. No longer was it possible for the various industries to go their individual ways; there was, to change the metaphor, a blue-print to conform to which every attempt had to be made.

The advent of a Labour Government in October 1964 made still further difference. Within a year of its arrival the Government had produced the National Plan, which was based on the assumption of an annual growth in the economy of 3·8 per cent for the following five years. A Socialist-planning Government laid stress on the growth of public expenditure or 'collective consumption' during that period, and public expenditure included, of course, the provision of finance for the nationalised industries. As these industries were basic, it was clear that the predicated economic expansion could not take place unless the industries bestirred themselves. So the industries got down to revising their development plans to get into line with the National Plan. In fact little happened, because capital development in these industries takes years to mature; in any case the National Plan was quickly defunct.

But apart from the abortive National Plan, the Government

was faced with awkward situations which did necessitate some planning for the nationalised industries. The fuel-supply position was becoming difficult. Consumption of coal was declining and by 1966 two new competitive fuels were appearing. A new form of nuclear generation of electricity based on the air gas cooled reactor was planned which became a serious threat to conventional generation by coal. As electricity supply was the only market where coal had hoped for a substantial expansion – even up to 100 million tons – this new type of nuclear station boded ill for the future of the coal industry. Secondly, the North Sea supplies of natural gas would reinvigorate the gas industry and make it into a formidable competitor.

So the Labour Government set about planning a fuel policy. Its first White Paper in October 1965 (Cmnd. 2798) was a feeble document, sketching the historical background and consisting mostly of pious generalisations. The main proposals in the White Paper were put forward to help the troubled coal industry. The White Paper was followed by the Coal Industry Act, which wrote down the capital of the Coal Board and made grants towards expenditure on redundancy payments, etc.

To help coal, electricity supply increased in 1963–4 its consumption of coal, their policy being 'to use coal-fired in preference to oil-fired stations where the extra cost of doing so is not excessive in the expectation that the need for such preference will disappear as the coal industry succeeds in concentrating output in low-cost coal-fields and thus strengthens its competitive position' (Electricity Council, 1964–5 Report, para. 112).

The Fuel Policy White Paper of 1965 demanded that this policy should continue, subject to annual review. The gas industry was also requested to take more coal, though it was admitted it could only give 'modest assistance'.

This is an interesting example of government influence over nationalised industries. Both gas and electricity are asked to put up their costs by generating from coal instead of oil. The two industries complied in the hope that cheaper coal would ultimately relieve them of the burden. Instead, the price of coal was increased on 1 April 1966, burdening the Central Electricity Generating Board with an additional £28 million coal costs in 1966–7. This was obviously the last straw and the electricity industry insisted on new arrangements. From 31 July 1967 to 1 April 1971 the gas and electricity industries were to be subsidised by the taxpayer to a maximum of £45 million to compensate them for the additional costs incurred by burning extra unwanted coal.

The Coal Industry Act 1967 which contained this novel provision provided other financial help to the Coal Board. Another clause provided that the Government should pay from £5 to £8 million to the Coal Board to reimburse it for losses incurred in deferring closures of coal mines between 1 September 1967 and 27 March 1971. These deferments would take place in order to keep down the volume of unemployment, and the Coal Board would have to satisfy the Minister of Power that it had incurred a loss; a not very difficult task.

Despite these and other financial grants provided for in this Act, a public clash of views took place between the Government on the one hand and the Coal Board and the National Union of Mineworkers on the other, when the Government published their second White Paper on Fuel Policy in November 1967 (Cmnd. 3438). This was a far more thorough and comprehensive document than its predecessor of October 1965.

This second White Paper, employing modern economic and statistical methods, attempts to forecast the possible use of all kinds of fuel up to 1975. It takes account of the striking finds of North Sea gas and the development of the second generation of nuclear power stations, based on the A.G.R. reactor. The calculations are therefore based on four primary fuels. Even the employment of the most modern methods involves some assumptions which may falsify the forecasts; among them may be mentioned the anticipated growth of the Gross Domestic Product at an average rate of 3 per cent per annum. Previous forecasts of energy consumption have sometimes been falsified within a few years.

But for the purpose of our argument, the significance of the second White Paper lies in the fact that the Government, having made the best possible assessment of energy requirements up to 1975, is prepared to back its calculations by making the nationalised fuel industries fit into the picture. Subject to slight modifications, the policy laid down in the White Paper of November 1967 went through.

In December 1957 the author wrote the following (*Nationalisation in Britain*, 1st ed., p. 283):

What we are in fact suggesting is that the Government should come out into the open as the mentor of the nationalised industries on questions of national importance. At present we have the fiction that the

Boards are Public Corporations going their own way and occasionally informing the responsible ministers of what they are doing. But more and more it has become clear that the operations of the nationalised industries are a vital part of the economic industrial and financial policy of the country. The public expects the Government to guide these industries.

That paragraph was written when the nationalised industries had been operating for about a decade. In their second decade the Boards came more and more under the control of the Government, as we have described in this chapter. The Conservative Governments were slow to move towards greater control, but they took long steps with the White Paper of April 1961 on Financial and Economic Obligations and with the Transport Act 1962 which ended the Transport Commission; they had already abolished the Central Electricity Authority in 1957. Thus two of the 'monoliths' set up by the Attlee Government were replaced by looser and more flexible organisations, which were more susceptible to government influence and more capable of adaptation to changing circumstances. The only monolith left was the National Coal Board, and it is not surprising that the Government found the Board, with its powerful political and trade union backing, the most difficult of the Public Corporations to bring into line with national policy.

Besides the White Papers on fuel policy the Labour Government has made other important changes in the nationalised industries. In 1967 they issued a White Paper entitled Nationalised Industries: a review of economic and financial objectives, which is discussed in Chapter 9. This was followed by the Transport Bill 1967, which was enacted in the 1967–8 parliamentary session. This Bill was claimed by the Minister of Transport as part of a Socialist policy. Earlier in 1967 the Iron and Steel Act had reached the Statute Book and set up the British Steel Corporation – a monolith of a new type as the industry which it controlled was neither a service nor extractive; its product, steel, was a basic material required by almost every industry in the country. This was, of course, another Socialist measure passed in fulfilment of an undertaking given fifteen years earlier and frequently repeated.

In September 1967 the Government, taken aback at the outcry provoked by a nationwide increase in electricity charges, announced that in future all proposed price increases by Public Corporations must first be reported on by the Prices and Incomes Board. This was a very important change which took away the last shred of independence in making price or tariff changes. Even the bulk supply tariff of the Central Electricity Generating Board was for the first time publicly examined and reported on. The Reports so far issued by the Prices and Incomes Board show that it is taking this task very seriously and it is possible that these Reports may lead to further changes.

During the life, therefore, of the Labour Government the nationalised industries have come under closer and closer government control. Transport, in particular, as planned in the Transport Bill 1967, will be operated by a series of interlocking Public Corporations over all of which the Minister of Transport presides. As in many cases these Corporations will depend on the Minister for financial help, even in their operations, the Bill naturally gives the Minister a more detailed power of policy control than is usual in the Nationalisation Acts.

The Boards will, of course, remain in control of management and day-to-day activities, but we must expect that the significance of these terms will diminish substantially. The Boards will more and more become executants of policy laid down centrally – even if it is a policy which they dislike. The tendency, which is common in many countries, for Public Corporations to become subject to central control is developing apace in Britain. Legally and theoretically the Boards are different from Departments of State; but as instruments of government policy they are becoming indistinguishable.

An important consequence of the growth of the public sector and of the increasing government control over that sector is that the power of the Executive has been greatly enlarged. How great that enlargement has become is not generally appreciated, especially in Parliament. Apart from the Select Committee on the Nationalised Industries, which has limited value, the House of Commons has not equipped itself or revised its procedure to enable it keep watch on the enhanced power of the Executive in the economic and financial field. It is doubtful whether the House of Commons could supervise the Executive to any degree without a drastic revision of its procedure, which would be bound to cut across the powers and responsibilities of ministers. Naturally no Government would welcome such a curtailment of its powers. We can expect, therefore, that the ever-growing problems of the Boards will more and more conduce to the increase of the powers of Governments and to the weakening of the supervisory influence of Parliament. The existence of the nationalised industries has greatly enhanced the scope of the public sector. They have thus greatly increased the powers and responsibilities of the Executive – sometimes to an extent which ministers find embarrassing.

ADDENDUM

While this book was with the printer, there appeared in September 1968 the longest and most important Report of the Select Committee on the Nationalised Industries; it was entitled 'Ministerial Control of the Nationalised Industries'.

The investigation by the Select Committee was carried out over two Parliamentary Sessions – 1966–7 and 1967–8. As it was too late to work the Report into the text of this book the publishers kindly arranged with the printers to provide space for this Addendum. It follows Chapter 8 because the subject of the Report is dealt with in that Chapter.

The Report is on a massive scale, 1232 pages in three volumes. The first volume of 230 pages is the Report itself; the second contains the Minutes of Evidence in a huge volume of 730 pages – all in small print; 2,439 questions and answers and 22 Memoranda. The third volume contains the remaining Memoranda submitted to the Committee.

Reports of the Select Committee on Nationalised Industries tend to become longer. There is some justification for the very great length of this Report and its ancillary volumes. It deals with a most important general question and probes into all aspects of the relations between Government and the nationalised industries. To the student of this subject there is a great mine of information in the Report, for which he must feel grateful. Only a Select Committee set up by the House of Commons could have the authority to extract all this information from ministers, their Departments and the Boards of the nationalised industries. Nevertheless one cannot help feeling that the great length of the proceedings and the great mass of evidence submitted were so overwhelming that the Select Committee found it difficult to stand back and decide which issues were more and which were less important. The result is that their main recommendation at the end of the Report comes as an anti-climax; it will be most interesting to see in the next few years what steps Government will take in carrying out this main recommendation. One may hazard the forecast that very little will be done – for reasons explained later in this Addendum.

The reader of Chapters 8 and 9 will understand that the relations between Government and the nationalised industries changed materially in the second decade of 1958 to 1968. This change was effected without any serious amendments to the founding Statutes; formally the powers of ministers in 1968 are little different from what they were in 1948. But informally the picture is very different and we are all aware that great changes in government control and guidance have taken place over these twenty years. But as the changes are informal, it is difficult for the onlooker to describe, analyse and comment on them in a worth-while manner. One can see the results of the increasing controls of ministers, but one cannot describe the manner in which these controls are exercised. What is more, one cannot assess whether some attempts to increase controls have not succeeded and most important of all what is the attitude taken by the nationalised industries to the increasing powers of the Departments. Then there is the interesting question of the relations between the Treasury – the Senior Department, which holds the purse strings – and the 'sponsoring' Departments, who supervise the various industries.

On this subject of increasing controls the Report lets in a flood of light and we can trace in detail what changes have taken place in the relations between each Department and the industries for which they are responsible. The attitude of the Departments vary- and naturally so. The Select Committee discovers that the Ministry of Transport is 'frankly interventionist'; Mrs Castle, giving evidence, made that attitude quite clear and embodied it in the Transport Bill which she introduced in November 1967. But that was nothing new; Mr Marples was just as interventionist in 1960 when he clamped down on the Transport Commission after an investigation by Sir Ivan Stedeford's Advisory Group and decided to wind up the Commission by the Transport Act 1962. Incidentally in doing so, he disregarded a voluminous Report of a Select Committee on the Transport Commission. 'Intervention' is inevitable when a publicly owned industry depends on a huge subsidy from the taxpayer, which on Treasury calculations, nearly equals the yield of one shilling of income tax. When the Transport Bill takes effect in January 1969, these subsidies will continue, though wrapped up in various ways.

The Select Committee is aware that the nationalised industries are a difficult problem, because they owe allegiance to two very different principles – the 'public interest' and 'commercial

G

obligations'. The Committee believes that these two guiding principles can be kept in separate compartments, provided that the techniques for carrying out the 'commercial obligations' are clearly and firmly laid down by the Government and adopted by the Boards of the industries. Any divergence from these techniques which may result from ministerial action requiring that the 'public interest' should be followed by the Boards would then be clearly seen, published and paid for by the Minister concerned.

This is a simplified statement of a long and involved argument which runs the length of the Report. The one substantial achievement of Select Committees over the years has been to publicise the unprofitable actions taken by Boards at Government behest and to insist that Government compensates for the losses incurred. That principle has now been adopted in the Coal Industry Act 1967 and the Transport Bill which will shortly become an Act.

The Select Committee, when considering the techniques for carrying out 'commercial obligations', is interested in the proposals in the Treasury White Paper of November 1967 (Cmnd. 3437), 'A review of economic and financial objectives' for the nationalised industries. There one can find the latest economic devices for correct methods of investment and for pricing policies which can be regarded as sound commercially.

The Select Committee takes the view that ministers who supervise the industries from both aspects, tend, on the whole, to fall down in implementing the doctrines in the Treasury White Paper; there are, for instance, many reasons why ministers may depart from strict marginal cost price policies – though the Committee does admit that marginal costs may not be so simple or specific 'that they can be quoted off the cuff'.

Nevertheless the Committee is so impressed by modern economic techniques that it decides that the machinery of government must be reorganised. It proposes therefore the creation of a Minister of Nationalised Industries, whose main function will be the 'laying down the adopted pricing and investment policies for each industry'. From this function would flow naturally the other functions of supervising their efficiency, approving their investment programmes, deciding on their financial objectives and so on.

The present 'sponsoring' Departments would be left with residual powers, as they would be generally responsible for the sectors in which the various industries operate.

This proposal was put to the Treasury, which strongly objected to it on various grounds. Here we need only refer to its main objection, which was that it 'did not think it was possible to separate the responsibility for securing public interests from the responsibility of seeing that the industries are efficiently run' (para. 922 of the Report). This is profoundly true. How can a Minister of Transport be responsible for transport policy generally and yet not be responsible for the supervision of the publicly owned transport industries, which are such an important part of the nation's transport system and which compete with other forms of transport?

One senses that the Select Committee, having laboured so long and so hard, felt it must come out with some strong recommendation, which it describes as 'tidying-up' (para. 937).

Unfortunately the nationalised industries do not lend themselves easily to 'tidying-up'. In their make up there are incompatible elements. It is just not true, as is suggested by the Economic Adviser to the Select Committee, that 'most people approach the nationalised industries as political phenomena' (*The Times*, 16 September 1968). Who regards his local railway line or gas board as a political phenomenon? Such attempts to simplify a most complicated issue are not helpful.

Let us recall the statement to an earlier Select Committee on 11 July 1957 by Sir James Bowman, Chairman of the National Coal Board, which is quoted on page 166 in Chapter 7.

In the eleven years since Sir James made this statement, very powerful forces have subtly and inexorably changed the relations between Government and nationalised industries. These forces will, if anything, become stronger. This is a deep-seated revolution which seriously affects the national economy. The Select Committee has concentrated on machinery and 'tidying-up', which are not so important as it seems to think.

9 Finances and Economics of the Nationalised Industries

BEFORE the war the industries working under public ownership, such as the Central Electricity Board and the London Passenger Transport Board, had to find their own capital without the help of a Treasury guarantee. In the case of the London Passenger Transport Board this applied even to the stock required for compensation to the owners of the assets taken over by the Board. At the time Mr Morrison stressed the fact that he was not calling on the Exchequer to underwrite the capital of the new Board: he displayed some pride in this form of independence, which he abandoned in the post-war nationalisation schemes.

There is a genuine difficulty in a nationalised industry resorting to the capital market – it cannot offer anything in the nature of an equity stock. By definition such an industry is in public ownership; equity shareholders, however, are the ultimate owners of the company's capital and can, for instance, decide by their vote to sell the company, or put it into liquidation. A nationalised industry is set up by Act of Parliament and its constitution can only be amended, or its life terminated, by another Act of Parliament. There cannot, therefore, be anything in the nature of ordinary shareholders with their usual rights. This posed an awkward problem for the London Passenger Transport Board, who compensated by its 'C' stock the holders of ordinary shares in the undertakings taken over. The London Passenger Transport Act 1933 provided that if the interest paid to the 'C' stockholders fell below 5 per cent for a period, they could appoint a receiver. This contingency fortunately did not arise, and it would have been interesting to see how a receiver handled a public transport monopoly which presumably was not paying its way.

In 1959 the possibility of the nationalised industries raising money on the market without a Treasury guarantee was reviewed by the Radcliffe Committee Report on the Working of the Monetary System (Cmnd. 827). It concluded (paras. 591–5) that such a method of raising funds was unrealistic. The Government in its White Paper of 1961 (Cmnd. 1337) on the Financial and Economic Obligations of the Nationalised Industries accepted this conclusion – somewhat reluctantly. It points out (para. 27) that 'the amounts of money needed are much too large to be raised in the open market without Government support and the industries are, of necessity, closely associated in the public mind with the Government, so that it would be difficult for the market to regard them as independent financial concerns. Whatever may be the possibilities for the future, an improvement in the financial record as contemplated under the present proposals would be a pre-requisite.' The improvement planned in 1961 has, as we shall see in this chapter, taken place to some extent but as against that there are the growing capital demands of the industries and the diffi-culties of the gilt-edged market.

The post-war Nationalisation Acts followed a common pattern and provided that the Treasury should guarantee all stocks issued as compensation payments, both principal and interest. This mandate on the Treasury only applied to compensation stocks; on any other stocks issued by the nationalised Boards the guarantee was left to the discretion of the Treasury, which could guarantee them 'in such manner and on such conditions as they think fit' (Electricity Act 1947, Section 42 (1)).

The Coal Industry Nationalisation Act differed from the other Acts. The stock issued in compensation to the colliery owners was to be government, and not National Coal Board, stock. This emphasised the fact that the mines belonged to the nation and the miner could not feel that he was working to find money to pay interest to a rentier stockholder. This stock was funded by annuities payable by the National Coal Board over fifty years. Furthermore, the National Coal Board was to be financed by advances made from the Minister of Fuel and Power, who, of course, received the wherewithal from the Treasury. As we shall see later, the Government were compelled, in 1956, to extend this Coal Board arrangement to the other nationalised industries.

The sums required for compensation payments were consider-able, as is shown by the following table:

Transport	£1,217 million
Electricity	£540 million
Gas	£265 million
Coal	£388 million
Iron and Steel	£244 million

The valuation of the assets of the colliery companies by District Valuation Boards was not completed till 1956, and compensation payments were therefore spread over a period of nearly ten years. But for the other industries compensation could be made immediately after vesting, as there were no valuations and as compensation was on the basis of market value of the shares. The raising of these vast sums in a short period posed difficult problems to the Treasury. They were issued to the shareholders in the companies of the industries taken over. If these holders had been content to leave these government-guaranteed stocks in a drawer and draw the interest, all would have been well. But many holders wished to sell, and in any case in a period of inflation the holder would be tempted to sell and invest the proceeds in equities. Consequently, from the day of issue these stocks stood at a discount which has steadily increased.

There were complaints that the terms and conditions of the stocks were cut very fine by the Treasury. As a result the dispossessed shareholders found themselves with a smaller income than they had hitherto enjoyed. Ministers replied that, by obtaining gilt-edged stock in lieu of equities, the owners were exchanging an uncertain for a fixed and secure income. It was only natural, therefore, that a reliable income should not be so large as the previous uncertain income. For security something must be surrendered. This is an ironical commentary on the course of gilt-edged stock prices in the twenty years since nationalisation. The income as fixed in 1947 or 1948 may have remained the same in nominal money values, but inflation has eroded the value both of capital and of income.

Despite the fact that, in stock issues for purposes other than compensation, the Treasury guarantee was optional, all such issues by the nationalised industries have carried the Treasury guarantee. They are, therefore, classed as gilt-edged stock and are treated as such by the market.

Most of the Boards, when established, set about preparing long-term plans of capital development, the financing of which depended on these issues of stock. In earlier chapters reference has been made to the difficulties of scrutinising and controlling these programmes of capital development. *The Economist*, in two articles on 16 March and 13 April 1957, dealt with these difficulties. Each nationalised industry produces a vast programme collected from its officials, scrutinises it and then presents the mass of figures to the competent Minister and the Treasury. But the departments can do little with these figures. As *The Economist* points out (16 March 1957, p. 929):

The civil servants and the politicians whom they serve are still, as they have always been, almost completely at the mercy of the technicians on whose say-so these programmes are based. The technicians, on grounds of 'the national interest' as well as sheer prudence, dovetail their plans into the demands and promises of the other big industries that go in for similar long-range investment planning; but this formal consistency is disarming because it makes any section of the whole harder, and not easier, to check. Even given complete technical competence and economic information, the task would be a formidable one.

The Economist, in the same article, made this further comment:

Nor is the economic information with which these programmes are presented really meaningful. The prices upon which any estimates of return are based are political prices, not prices based upon relative costs; and in such circumstances it is inevitable that nationalised investment priorities will veer according to politics and fashion, not according to economics.

This was shown in the 1950s by the differing treatment meted out to the transport industry on the one hand and the fuel and power industries on the other. The latter industries could hardly ask too much. Ministers repeatedly expressed regret that investment in coal was not moving fast enough. Had the Coal Board doubled its capital expenditure, a sigh of relief from the whole Cabinet would have been audible. Shortage of coal, which was sold below real costs, held high priority in government thinking. The vast electricity capital programme occasionally produced murmurs of doubt; but the memory of the 1947 fuel crisis – which was not due to a shortage of electricity generating plant, but to a shortage of coal – and the subsequent miseries of load-shedding, which were due to a shortage of plant, silenced the murmurs and the programme marched on in all its amplitude.

Lord Citrine, chairman of the Central Electricity Authority from 1948 to 1957, complains that 'Right through my Chairmanship the policy of restricting our capital development was continued' (*Two Careers*, p. 297). It is, of course, true that in most of the ten years of his chairmanship the Government made some cuts in electricity investments, but this was inevitable; on the whole the cuts were marginal. The proof was that in the mid-fifties electricity plant was adequate and the immediate post-war difficulties had faded away.

Lord Citrine's complaint is a good example of the difficulty of scrutinising the capital development programme of the nationalised industries. In the case of electricity, fortunately, we have an independent view in the Report of the Herbert Committee (Cmd. 9672) whose conclusion is: 'In our opinion, the control today, either for seeing that unnecessary projects are not undertaken or for ensuring that value is received for money spent on necessary projects, is somewhat weak' (para. 352).

Lord Citrine mentions (*Two Careers*, p. 296) that he 'had a few trenchant arguments about this [i.e. the cuts in capital investment] with Hugh Gaitskell when he was Minister of Fuel and Power and more when he was Chancellor of the Exchequer. I took the line that we must aim at supplying consumers with all the power they needed, whatever might be the state of the weather. But Gaitskell was adamant that this policy was economically unjustified.'

We have two 'Plans for Coal'; the first was estimated to cost £650 million over fifteen years and the second £1,000 million in ten years. The second Plan was revised in 1959 and the estimate for capital expenditure for the six years 1960–5 was £535 million.

Then there is the gigantic capital development in generating electricity. Early in 1957 it was decided to treble the nuclear power station programme in the period up to 1965. These nuclear stations, which were to have a capacity of 6 million kilowatts, would cost £900 million; they were added to a programme of conventional power stations, transmissions, etc., estimated to cost £2,000 million in the same period. Thus the total bill for electricity investment from 1957 to 1965 would be about £2,900 million.

No evidence has been produced that all possible methods of mitigating this vast programme have been considered. The Central Electricity Authority did much to reduce the costs of constructing power stations; technically, the developments were very good. But it gave little sign of a policy of determination by means of tariffs to maximise the use of its expensive capital equipment. The extent to which the plant is used has improved little since nationalisation; the adjusted system load factor rose from 43·5 per cent in 1948–9 to 46·8 per cent in 1957–8. One can only conclude that in the 1950s a policy to improve the load factor did not exist. Why should it when capital was so easily come by? It was not till some years after the C.E.A. had gone that off-peak tariffs were widely offered to the electricity consumer.

We must conclude that the nationalised industries strive for simple objectives which have in them a strong uneconomic element. Up to 1957 the Coal Board was out to maximise output of coal at all costs; it is doubtful whether there was any calculation what the marginal (say) 10 million tons per annum really cost to produce.

Similarly, electricity policy was to maximise generating and distribution capacity. As we have seen from Lord Citrine's remarks quoted above, the plan was simple – capacity so ample that not even on the worst day of the most severe winter would it be necessary to cut loads. As a public utility service Electricity Boards intensely dislike inability to supply and they are to be respected for their high standards in this respect. But as we have seen, responsible persons like Mr Gaitskell doubted the economic justification for providing plant necessary to obviate reduction in load a few times in an occasionally very severe winter.

The second defect in the 1950s was the inability of the national-ised industries to find from their own resources an adequate contribution to their capital requirements. During that period private enterprise found about two-thirds of its capital require-ments from its own resources; nationalised industries about one-third. Much of the capital development programme of the National Coal Board was not development, strictly speaking, but maintenance of capacity which the Board, in its evidence to the Select Committee, estimated was diminishing at the rate of four million tons a year. Sir Oliver Franks (now Lord Franks) in a speech in January 1957 pointed out that in 1955 the nationalised industries required more than £300 million to maintain their capital intact, but that their total surplus was barely half that amount.

When the Select Committee on the Nationalised Industries began in the late fifties to investigate in turn the various industries, its Reports revealed in detail the government technique – or lack of it – in scrutinising the vast plans of capital development put out by the industries.

In its Report on Coal (H.C. 187-1 (1958)) the Committee made the following comments on the system of control revealed by its enquiries:

Your Committee are in no doubt that the Ministry are right in their refusal to attempt any kind of technical reconsideration of the Board's proposals (para. 29).
On the other hand, Parliament has made the Minister responsible for providing the money for the Board's Investment plans. . . . If these

discussions with the Ministry are meant to replace the negotiations for raising money on the market, there is a strong case for making the two as nearly equivalent as possible; and your Committee question whether any private borrower without a firm record of profitable investment could expect to raise money at regular intervals without giving further details than the Board at present give the Ministry. Following this line of argument, the Ministry should not try to make a full technical appraisal of the proposals, but they should apply an economic test, and should demand the information necessary to do so (para. 30).

The Select Committee points out that

the Board must find themselves taking decisions on projects of border-line profitability. There would seem to be a strong case that the Ministry – who are the judges of 'where the public interest lies' should as a matter of course be judges in these cases; and there can be no doubt that they should be told of the projects of border-line profitability for which they are being asked to lend money, so that they can apply some financial test. . . . The Ministry should at least make a greater financial check on the anticipated return on money they lend than they do at present (para. 31).

If a change were made along these lines, it would admittedly run counter to the views of the Board, the Treasury and the Ministry – all of whom, in different ways, approve the present system (para. 32).

Your Committee therefore recommend that a change should be made, and that the Board should present the Ministry each year, not only with the average yield expected from the total investment, but also an account of the major schemes estimated to give the lowest yield, and the reasons why those schemes were put forward (para. 33).

This recommendation was accepted by the Government soon after (*Hansard*, vol. 591, col. 849).

Before we discuss the value of this new machinery of control, let us look at the searching Report of the Select Committee on British Railways (H.C. 254 (1960)). There the Select Committee found, to its surprise, that the Ministry of Transport had had the same relations to the British Transport Commission as the Ministry of Power had had to the National Coal Board. 'Your Committee are surprised that the Ministry of Transport and the Treasury have not until recently examined the returns to be secured from the schemes for which they were lending public money' (para. 387).

The Select Committee's investigation had shown that, as the financial position of the Commission had deteriorated, the Government was forced to exercise a closer control over the capital made available for investment.

When, as in recent years, the Commission's finances have been a subject of general concern, the department's control has come right into the open. It amounts today to a situation where the Minister can, if he so wishes, exercise a control over the Commission's Capital plans for the railways that is similar to the control which he exercises statutorily over the Country's road programme. But although the Ministry have been able to exercise power of this kind when they believed it to be needed, the lessons of the early years of modernisation is that more control might well have been exercised then (para. 73).

This Report of the Select Committee was debated in the House of Commons on 26 October 1960, and Sir Toby Low (now Lord Aldington), chairman of the Select Committee, explained this recommendation in some detail (*Hansard*, vol. 627, cols 2423/4):

We were not suggesting that the Government should usurp the functions of those operating the coal mines or the railways. We were merely suggesting that in lending money for these industrial purposes, the Government should act as a banker and ask the proper questions. It is important, too, that in getting the information, the Government should be able to work out what kind of return is anticipated on this large investment. Anybody who has read the Report about the London-Midland electrification will have seen the sort of difficulty that can arise even inside the Commission, between the Commission and the Select Committee, between the Commission and the Government and the various Government witnesses about how one tests what the yield of an investment will be. It was, however, rather disconcerting to us that we could not get any consistent advice from anyone as to the proper way of working it out. One hopes that that sort of thing would be put right.

Sir Toby Low admits, therefore, that the yardstick his Committee had devised for coal development, which the Government had adopted, was not so valuable after all; no one knew, in fact, how to construct the yardstick.

Coal development, as the Coal Board explains in its accounts, is a speculative operation; so it set up a Central Obsolescence Fund. Two examples may be quoted of the use of this Fund. On 30 June 1958 the Queen visited the Shaw Colliery at Rothes in Fife; in 1963–4 this colliery was closed and the amount written off and charged to the Central Obsolescence Fund was £6·5 million (N.C.B. 1963–4 Report, vol. II, p. 79). At end August 1968 Kirkby Colliery, Notts., was closed. The official notice explained 'about £3½ million has been spent on reconstruction work in the past five years, but unforeseen geological problems have arisen' (*Daily Telegraph*, 22 April 1968). Private enterprise, faced with such losses, would have gone bankrupt. A nationalised industry, however, can easily include such capital expenditure in its development plans; no one can query it.

Sir Toby must have been conscious of the fallibility of his Committee's yardstick because he went on to make an important suggestion:

I do not know whether the machinery of Government has yet developed enough to take these difficult industrial development decisions which they are now required to take in looking after the nationalised industries and providing the money in this way, but I would hope that, at least, consideration is being given to the possibility of strengthening the machinery by introducing, with a purely advisory function, a nationalised investment advisory council, consisting of men experienced in finance, in industry and perhaps in science; and as is done with the Export Credit Advisory Council, I would ask for the co-operation of the T.U.C. I do not put forward that as a recommendation about which I feel strongly, but it is certainly something which should be considered. After all the kind of decision that is needed in approving a scheme of £160 million is foreign to the ordinary training of members of Government Departments.

Sir Toby's suggestion is important because it is the first time that an admission has been made by a responsible person with some knowledge of the subject that there is lacking an essential piece of machinery in relation to the nationalised industries. Before 1960 there was a kind of conspiracy of silence and Governments acted on the assumption that the plans of capital development put out by the industries were both technically and economically sound. In any case they found themselves helpless before the vast mass of detail in which these plans were embodied, and, having no staff capable of understanding, much less examining, such plans, they took refuge in the philosophy of the nationalisation statutes and underwrote – though sometimes with hesitation – the vast financial obligations of those plans. It was the patent failure of the British Transport Commission to come anywhere near its forecasts on the outcome of the modernisation programme that led the Government in 1960 to challenge the whole basis of the long-standing relations between the Department and industry and to make the Department assert control in the manner described in paragraph 73 of the Select Committee's Report quoted above.

In April 1961 the Government took a decisive step by putting out a White Paper on the Financial and Economic Obligations of the Nationalised Industries (Cmnd. 1337); this document marks a decisive change.

It begins by pointing out that though more than a decade has elapsed since nationalisation, there has been no general review of the manner in which the financial and economic principles in the nationalising statutes have been applied in practice. In other words each industry has gone its own way.

The Government's general policy is summarised under two heads. First it must ensure that the industries can carry out their responsibilities so as to make the maximum contribution to the country's economic well-being. Secondly, it is made clear that though the industries carry some non-commercial obligations, they are not social services and are not absolved from economic and commercial justification.

The White Paper then refers to the financial obligations in the Acts of nationalisation. There is a general formula under which they are required to earn revenues, on an average of good and bad years, which would be sufficient to meet all items properly chargeable to revenue, including interest, depreciation, redemption of capital and provision of reserves. Only after all these are met could there be a surplus in the statutory sense. As all their capital is fixed-interest obligations, and there is no equity capital, this surplus differs from profits in the commercial sense; but the industries were intended to make a 'profit' as they were to build up reserves.

On this the White Paper makes three comments of interest. First, the redemption of capital was clearly an onerous burden and successive Governments had not sought to enforce provision. Secondly, depreciation had been on the basis of historic and not replacement costs. Thirdly, though they had built up some reserves, in most cases they were not adequate to provide for the replacement of the assets used up in production. The Government thus confirms the statement made by Lord Franks quoted earlier.

The Government then examines the financial record of the industries from 1954 to 1959. Most of them had earned less than 5 per cent per annum net after providing depreciation at historic cost; two had earned 8 per cent net. They appended a table showing that increasingly the public corporations depended on the savings of the private sector to provide capital for their development. This must result in higher taxation or higher borrowing by the Treasury. As the industries, largely under pressure from public and Governments, have kept their prices as low as possible, demand for their products and demand for capital to enable them to increase production have been artificially stimulated. Low prices have also contributed powerfully to low returns on capital compared with the private sector, which, on the average, was earning 15 per cent. A note of warning is sounded on too close a comparison between the private and public sector, as the latter is largely public utilities which traditionally earn lower returns and which are in some cases burdened with non-commercial obligations.

The Government then set out its proposals for the future under three headings: Revenue Account, Capital Account, and Prices and Costs.

As regards the revenue account, it was proposed to take a given year period and make an arrangement with each industry; they differed so widely that no general formula was applicable to all. The arrangement should be that, over five years, surpluses on revenue account should be adequate to cover deficits; surplus or deficit would be struck after charging to revenue items normally chargeable, including interest and depreciation on a historic basis. Revenue should also provide for extra depreciation to cover the difference between historic and replacement costs (including arrears) and also adequate allocations to reserves as a contribution towards capital development. This last was particularly desirable in electricity, which was expanding fast and had huge requirements of capital for development. The Corporations would thus have to earn a higher rate of return on their borrowings than the rate paid by the Exchequer.

From these arrangements the Transport Commission was excluded. In a White Paper of December 1960 (Cmnd. 1248) on Reorganisation of Nationalised Transport Undertakings, the Government had proposed to abolish the Commission and to split its undertaking between a number of Boards, each responsible to the Minister of Transport. Needless to say there were no arrangements for payments for depreciation or obsolescence. The railways were bankrupt and it was recognised that, even after this reorganisation, they would be operating at a deficit which would be met by an annual grant from the Minister of Transport. This reorganisation is dealt with in detail in Chapter 3, 'Transport'.

As regards the capital account the previous arrangements for discussion between the industries and the Departments on the development plans of the industries would be strengthened. Each year the Government would fix an upper limit to be spent two years ahead of investment. This would be after a general discussion of plans for five years ahead to enable the industries to enter into long-term commitments. If any proposal for investment were expected to yield a relatively low return, the Government would expect to be specially notified.

The change of procedure in the Finance Act 1956, whereby the industries could no longer issue stock with Treasury guarantee had, by 1960, had serious effects. The Exchequer now had to find the finance for their capital development from its own resources – either from taxation or by borrowing. As early as 1956 the Ministry of Power had begun to issue an Annual White Paper on Capital Investment in the Coal, Electricity and Gas Industries. In November 1960 the White Paper, Public Investment in Great Britain (Cmnd. 1203), brought together for the first time in a single document information about prospective public investment and notes on the various programmes. The scope of the White Paper included not only the programmes of the nationalised industries which, with the Post Office, accounted for half of all public investment; the remaining half dealt with public service capital expenditure, i.e. roads, housing, education, etc., and, of this half, about four-fifths were programmes carried out by local authorities. In April 1961, in the same month as the White Paper on the Financial and Economic Obligations of the Nationalised Industries which we are analysing, there was issued another White Paper (Cmnd.1338) on Government Expenditure Below the Line, i.e. expenditure financed by loans. This White Paper had been promised by the Chancellor of the Exchequer in the debate on 10 November 1960 on Public Investment in Great Britain referred to above. Finally in July 1961 the Plowden Committee on Control of Public Expenditure reported (Cmnd. 1432) and in its Report the Committee considered and rejected various methods of strengthening parliamentary control over the expenditure of the nationalised industries. There was clearly in the early sixties great concern not only in Parliament and the Government but also among the public at the finances of the Public Corporations and the rapidly rising level of their capital expenditure. The first ten years of nationalisation, when there was no co-ordination of the demands of the industries, were now gone. Lord Citrine informs us (*Two Careers*, p. 299) that 'we raised on the open market £825 million'– between 1949 and 1955. The market could hardly be described as 'open' as no electricity loans were possible without Treasury guarantee. It was the last electricity loan of £200 million in August 1955 that convinced the Treasury that it must keep full control of all borrowing by the Public Corporations in view of its responsibility for managing the National Debt; hence the change in method of borrowing in the 1956 Finance Act, which has become permanent.

The White Paper on Financial and Economic Obligations of the Nationalised Industries concluded with some paragraphs on pricing policy of the nationalised industries. It refers to 'the existing informal arrangements whereby Chairmen of Boards ascertain in advance the views of the appropriate Minister when they prepare to make substantial changes in the level of their prices'. The White Paper goes on: 'In the Government's view these arrangements should continue. If a Board decide to modify their own proposals by reason of views expressed by the Minister, it would be open to them to require a written statement of those views, which could be published by the Minister or the Board, and to propose an appropriate adjustment of their financial objectives where, in their opinion, this modification would significantly impair their ability to meet them.' So much for the repeated complaints against these 'informal arrangements' by the Select Committee on Nationalised Industries, which are dealt with in Chapter 7.

The White Paper concluded by saying that 'the Government believe that the closer definition now proposed for the financial and economic obligations of the industries should help improve their performance and morale'. Let us now see how far this hope was realised.

As a result of this White Paper the Government entered into discussions with the coal, gas and electricity industries in order to fix their financial objectives for the five years, April 1962 to March 1967.

Electricity was by far the most prosperous industry and expanding fast. The financial objective fixed for that industry was a gross return of 12·4 per cent on average net assets. This would have been made up as to 5¾ per cent for depreciation, 4½ per cent for interest and 2¼ per cent for surplus. As the 'surplus' was always ploughed back into the industry, and there was no possibility of distributing it to workers or consumers, the industry decided to drop the term 'surplus' and replace it with 'balance of revenue'. It was agreed that in the earlier years of the quinquennium the rate of return would be somewhat lower than the 12·4 per cent, but that it would increase in later years. The figure 12·4 was an aggregate average figure for the whole industry; it varied slightly between Board and Board. Depreciation was related to replacement and not historic costs.

The five years are now over and we can see what happened. In the first four years the financial objective was practically attained – 12·3 per cent. The average gross yield for the four years was £353 million on average net assets employed of £2,863 million. But in the fifth year the gross return fell to 10·9 per cent, making the average for the five years 12·0 per cent; another £66 million would have had to be earned to reach the agreed financial objective.

The electricity industry hoped during this quinquennium to achieve a 50 per cent financing of capital development from internal sources and 50 per cent from borrowing from the Government. It did not quite achieve this objective, as is shown by the following table:

	£ million Capital required	Electricity Provided internally	Borrowed
1962–3	380·6	181·8 (47·8%)	198·8 (52·2%)
1963–4	464·5	222·4 (47·9%)	242·1 (52·1%)
1964–5	520·8	234·5 (45%)	286·3 (55%)
1965–6	594·5	277 (46·6%)	317·5 (53·4%)
1966–7	616·4	237·1 (38·5%)	379·3 (61·5%)

In September 1967 there were substantial increases in electricity tariffs and a major consideration in making these increases was the necessity of getting back to the 12·4 per cent objective which was to be continued for the year 1967–8.

In the case of gas, a lower financial objective of 10·2 per cent was agreed. The gross returns achieved in the five years were 9·3 per cent, 10·0 per cent, 10·8 per cent and 9·1 per cent; the average for the five years was 9·8 per cent. The Gas Council attributes the decline in the last two years to the rapid changes in production technology and the delay in securing price increases. The following table, prepared on the same lines as the electricity table above, shows the steep rise in capital requirements and the increasing difficulty in maintaining a reasonably high proportion of self-financing:

£ million Capital required	Gas Provided internally	Borrowed
1962–3	59·3	36·8 (62·1%)	22·5 (37·9%)
1963–4	106·5	45·3 (42·5%)	61·2 (57·5%)
1964–5	100·2	54·1 (54%)	46·1 (46%)
1965–6	118·7	51·8 (43·6%)	66·9 (56·4%)
1966–7	208·4	44·8 (21·5%)	163·6 (78·5%)

The speed of expansion in the development of the gas industry will accelerate greatly up to the early seventies. Much of the expenditure required, e.g. on the building of high-pressure grids or conversion of consumers' appliances to take natural gas, will yield no quick returns. The income of the gas industry in 1966–7 was less than half that of the electricity industry – £557 against £1,141 million – and a great expansion of capital expenditure must therefore inevitably be financed mainly by borrowing.

In paragraph 91 of the White Paper on Fuel Policy (Cmnd. 2798) the gas industry was warned not to expect to continue to receive the favourable treatment of a lower financial objective than was agreed with electricity. That warning was given before the great discoveries of natural gas in the North Sea which have overnight transformed the future of the gas industry. It is agreed that it is in the national interest that a prompt use on a great scale should be made of this splendid new fuel. To do so, the gas industry must step up investment very rapidly and for several years it will require very large sums to provide the equipment and facilities for using the natural gas. The gas industry will not be able to expand its revenue as rapidly as it expands the capital programme and it must therefore, for some time, depend on heavy borrowing from the Government to finance this programme. It is very largely a once-for-all programme; an increase in financial objectives cannot make the gas industry find more capital from its own resources. In these conditions the 1965 warning is out of date.

What were the arrangements agreed with the coal industry as a result of the 1961 White Paper? When it was issued the industry was in difficulties; demand for coal had been declining since 1957 and coal consumption had fallen below 200 million tons in 1959. In these conditions it was out of the question to fix a financial objective, as in gas and electricity, in the form of a percentage return on average net assets.

It was accordingly agreed that from 1963 the N.C.B. target should be to break even, after paying interest and making 'proper' provision for depreciation. As the Board had provided for depreciation at 'historic' cost, 'proper' was defined as an additional £10 million a year, which would be presumed to cover the gap between historic and replacement cost. Even while this modest target was being agreed, the N.C.B. was pressing for a capital reconstruction but, for the time being, the Government refused.

The £10 million extra depreciation was paid for the first year. But in a statement in the House of Commons on 12 April 1965 the Minister of Power 'announced that in the present circumstances of the Coal Mining Industry the Board, for the time being, were relieved of the obligation to make a contribution of £10 million towards replacement costs' (1964–5 Report, vol. II, p. 25). No addition was therefore made to the Accounts of 1964–5, which, with the aid of this retrospective concession, showed a surplus of £0·1 million.

The N.C.B. by 1965 was in serious financial difficulties. It was not allowed to put up prices and 25 per cent of its costs were fixed, which meant an increasing burden with falling sales. So the Coal Industry Act 1965 provided for capital reconstruction, which relieved the industry of £415 million of its capital debt. The Board was thus relieved in 1965–6 of interest charges of £21·5 million and depreciation charges of £14·1 million. This sum of £415 million was treated as a fresh loan from the Minister of Power which was placed in a 'Capital Reconstruction and Reserve Fund' which could be used to write off certain losses of the Board, including the losses up to £25 million incurred in delaying price increases from 1965 to 1966. In 1965–6 a sum of £223·1 million was thus written off, including £90·8 million for the accumulated deficit of the Board and £99·2 million for colliery assets which were no longer of value. In 1966–7 a further sum of £52·3 million was written off.

A further provision of the Coal Industry Act 1965 was a grant to the Board of half the 'social costs' involved in pit closures, subject to a maximum of £30 million in the five years ended March 1971.

With this financial assistance the White Paper on Fuel Policy of October 1965 expressed the hope (para. 54) that the 'coal industry thus streamlined will continue for many years to be a main supplier of primary fuel on a basis which will enable it to make a major contribution to the strength of the national economy'.

But within two years of the White Paper another Coal Industry Bill was introduced. The coal industry was being run down so fast that the Government's help of 50 per cent of the social costs was not enough; so the limit was raised from £30 to £45 million, and the portion to be met by the Government increased from one-half to two-thirds. Also the Government would supplement the wages of elderly miners who became redundant by an estimated amount of £35 million by March 1971. The Government would also reimburse the N.C.B. for losses incurred by delaying the closure of economic pits at the request of the Government. Finally, the Government would bribe the electricity supply industry with £45 million during the period 31 July 1967 to 1 April 1971 to burn coal which was too expensive for them to burn.

These contributions to 'social costs' arising from pit closures are badly overdue. Coal-mining is a highly localised industry with whole communities dependent on the pit. It is hoped that industries can be persuaded to go to those areas where pits have been closed. But if, as seems likely, these efforts will not be very successful, the 'social costs' which the Government will have to meet will be much greater than the sums so far offered.

The financial objectives fixed in the light of the White Paper of April 1961 were for the five years April 1962–March 1967. The Government announced that the same financial objectives would apply for a sixth year ending March 1968. New financial objectives will therefore be announced for the period beginning April 1968.

In November 1967 the Treasury issued a White Paper entitled Nationalised Industries: a review of economic and financial objectives. The purpose of the White Paper is set out in the last paragraph, which reads as follows:

This White Paper is intended to show how investment, pricing and efficiency policies will be taken into account in settling financial objectives, rather than to make any change in the basic relationship between the Government and the nationalised industries. It reviews the features and principles which are common to all nationalised industries and which underlie their relationship to the Government. The circumstances of the industries are, however, very divergent and will be taken into account in formulating detailed policies for the sectors concerned.

The major changes envisaged in this White Paper are largely the work of the ample staffs of economists now to be found not only in the Treasury, but in the Departments responsible for the nationalised industries. This is shown by the emphasis on discounted cash flow at a test discount rate of 8 per cent which the industries are required to employ in all their projects for capital investment. The White Paper explains, however, that even if a project satisfies this criterion it does not automatically follow that it should be launched. 'The test rate of discount is essentially a device to ensure that the calls of the public and private sectors upon resources do not get out of line with each other in the long term. The Government are concerned with the phasing of investment which needs to be considered in the light of real resources available' (para. 16). Return to the pre-1956 arrangements of resort to the stock market is ruled out because 'these would involve serious problems of market management and would not create any additional savings' (same para.).

This reference to savings shows the Government's concern at the financing of the massive developments of the nationalised industries and in the case of several of them at the financing of their deficits as well. Table 2 of the White Paper shows that in 1966-7 the industries spent on fixed investment in the U.K. £1,492 million, of which £812·6 million was borrowed from the Treasury; in addition railways and other transport boards were paid £142 million to cover their deficits for the year. These figures will increase in 1967-8 and subsequent years. Gas will require much more than hitherto in order to make use of natural gas from the North Sea. Steel is now nationalised and is at the start expected to incur a deficit which can only be met by the Treasury.

The White Paper (para. 5) stresses that the nationalised industries have a vital role to play in promoting the Government's objectives which include the raising of 'the rate of new capital formation' and 'increasing the profitability of new investment'. With steel nationalised, 'their new assets are now valued at nearly £12,000 million. Their annual investment is equivalent to the whole of that for private manufacturing industry; they contribute about 11 per cent of the gross domestic product and they employ about 8 per cent of the total labour force'.

The nationalised industries are only part of the public sector; there is also the public service sector – local authorities, etc. – who invested more than £1,000 million in 1966-7.

The net income as a percentage of average net assets earned by the industries as a whole (including the Post Office) is very low – 3·9 per cent in 1966-7. In the last twelve years it has been as high as 4·1 per cent and as low as 2·2 per cent. This conceals wide variations, with the Post Office and electricity earning between 6 and 8 per cent and the railways unable to meet their operating costs, let alone their interest charges. But from the point of view of the Treasury at the centre, they are one massive problem which yearly becomes more difficult. From this net income the Corporations have to meet their interest charges and earn some surplus to reinforce their depreciation allowances and provide a reasonable amount for self-financing.

This inability of the nationalised industries to finance themselves is a major problem in government finance. Whether the money is raised by taxation or by borrowing, it has to be found from the private sector, which has to provide a sufficient surplus from which the taxes can be raised or a surplus of savings from which the loans can be made. If the borrowing is not raised from genuine savings, it becomes a potent factor in inflation and in depreciating the value of the pound. Furthermore, excessive borrowing tends to push up the rate of interest at which the money is borrowed. This increases the cost of servicing the National Debt and also imposes a crippling burden on the nationalised industries, which in recent years have been borrowing at rates well over 7 per cent. This rapid increase in the burden of interest charges naturally tends to keep up or push up the price of their products.

In view of this rising rate of interest, will not the Treasury have to step up the test rate of 8 per cent which it has prescribed for the Public Corporations to use in their calculations of discounted cash flow?

Unlike private industry with its cushion of equity capital, the capital of the Public Corporations is all in fixed-interest capital which is a prime charge on income, unlike equity capital which is a residual beneficiary when income falls. As a consequence, those nationalised industries which fall on bad times, such as coal and railways, cannot support the heavy burden of interest charges and the State has no alternative but to write down their capital and thus relieve them of their obligations to service it. This, of course, is a euphemism for transferring the written-down portion to the National Debt and the servicing is transferred from the consumer of the product, who has ceased to consume, to the taxpayer, who cannot escape in the same way as the consumer. No one can be compelled to buy coal or travel by rail; we all pay taxes.

The serious strain on the gilt-edged markets arising from the requirements of the nationalised industries is shown by the surprising decision of the Treasury on the terms of steel compensation stock. It has been usual to pay such compensation by long-dated stocks – at least twenty years. But in July 1967 to issue such a long-dated stock for the large sum of £500 million would have meant setting a high interest rate, of the order of 7 per cent. To everyone's surprise, therefore, the Treasury issued a short-term stock of $3\frac{1}{2}$ years currency at $6\frac{1}{2}$ per cent, thus postponing the awkward decision till January 1971.

After this review of the financial history of the Public Corporations over twenty years, can we now examine their economic performance?

Ever since the Corporations have been established there has been an outpouring of economic dissertations, many of them in economic and financial journals, scrutinising the behaviour of the Boards and suggesting devices whereby they might strengthen their economic competitiveness and follow more closely the pattern of commercial behaviour of private industry. As British public enterprise has come to be regarded as a model to be studied, particularly in the under-developed countries which are promoting the Public Corporation as an instrument of economic expansion, these criticisms have received worldwide attention. The United Nations has, for instance, held seminars at which the best methods of organising and operating publicly-owned industries have been studied.

In part, this flood of economic criticism has been due to the fact that during the years 1947 to 1961 Governments were slow to make up their minds and formulate a policy which would lay down commercial and financial guide-lines. That is not to say that during those fourteen years the Government did not play an important part in relation to the nationalised industries. It provided the capital for development; it had an influence on prices; it attempted to step up or slow down its capital programmes, led along by that old will-o'-the-wisp – counter-cyclical investment; they thrust highly expensive projects, such as nuclear power, on to unwilling industries. But in all this, there was no clear-cut policy. Partly it was due to the fact that the Conservative Party – who were in power ten of the fourteen years – could not bring itself to accept the (to it) unpleasant fact that this important public sector was now permanent, that in fact it was responsible for guiding and controlling it and that, therefore, it was incumbent on it to hammer out a clear-cut policy which everyone would understand and accept. This was not achieved till April 1961 when the White Paper on the Financial and Economic Obligations of the Nationalised Industries was issued.

That White Paper could only work in relation to a selection of the Corporations. In coal it broke down almost immediately and in railways it never applied. Throughout the sixties the Government has been attempting to evolve a suitable policy for guiding and regulating those two industries and this task is as yet far from complete.

What were the main issues in the economic discussions, carried on largely in academic journals or bankers' reviews?

The criticisms of the economists may be briefly summed up as follows. Nationalised industries make small profits because their prices are kept down as near as possible to costs – often by government pressure. Their products, thus too cheaply priced, are consumed on too great a scale. Demands for these products therefore rise faster than demands for products more commercially priced. This in turn leads to the need for increased investments in order to produce more of these cheap goods. This is encouraged by two factors – inadequate screening of investment projects and borrowing from the Government at gilt-edged and not commercial rates of interest.

There is considerable truth in this. The nationalised industries are basic, whose products are used by everybody. Government and the industries, in an era of rising prices, were most anxious not to attract too much public criticism. For example, railway passenger fares were kept down; the domestic consumer of electricity got it cheaply – each electricity Annual Report boasted of the fact. The responsibility for this state of affairs lay squarely on government shoulders. Each industry was out to maximise production. It was not enough for Government to prune here and there and seek out projects bringing in a low return; it was its responsibility to go behind the facts of increasing output and increasing investment programmes and find the fundamental causes of the increases. Only now are government departments beginning to question the ancient shibboleths of electricity expansion, but the electricity industry does not mean to tackle the domestic consumers tariff till the seventies. Meanwhile, for lack of a modern pricing policy the vast electricity investment programme marches on.

The economists were going too far in attempting to draw too

close an analogy with the behaviour of the private sector. For instance, Mr Polanyi, in his valuable study *Comparative Returns from Investment in Nationalised Industries,* bases the study on the assumption that 'the criterion of profit earned is appropriate for nationalised as well as private industry and consequently, that the comparisons of financial yields summarised in this Memorandum provide at least approximate indicators of efficiency in the use of capital'. He has no difficulty in proving that had the yields in the public sector been as high as those in the private sector, the growth of the economy would have been greater and many of our economic ills averted. This might be true, but Mr Polanyi's simple criterion begs many questions. Granted that the nationalised industries get their capital too easily and too cheaply and are not therefore subject to the discipline of the private sector in the use of scarce resources; yet economists who point this out complain that energy is sold too cheaply. But is there not some economic gain in cheap energy and has anyone measured that gain to the economy as against the loss resulting from the misuse of capital?

The measurement of the economic performance of the national- ised industries is a most complex and difficult task. As those industries, by their very nature, cannot be purely profit-making undertakings, they cannot behave like the private sector. They could be made more efficient than they are, but to what extent and by what means requires close and patient investigations of facts which are not easily available. But such treatment is very different from refusing to accept them as statutory and monopolistic Public Corporations with all the connotations implied in such a de- scription.

A nationalised industry can never follow a strictly market policy. If it does, it incurs an odium altogether out of proportion. We must bear in mind that they started, at least, with distinctive traits of monopoly and there is nothing more obnoxious than a statutory monopoly charging what the traffic will bear. In 1954 the Coal Board put selective price increases on coking coals required by the steel and gas industries. This was reasonable on commercial grounds – better quality of coal, more expensive to produce and so on. But it led to great bitterness because the steel and gas industries maintained they were being exploited by a monopolist, and that bitterness has persisted to this day and has cost the coal industry heavily. Both steel and gas were determined to weaken the hold of the monopolist and have been largely successful.

Reading the analyses of some of the economists, one is forced to the conclusion that they have little knowledge of the practical problems facing the Public Boards. What is the use of suggesting that a low-cost pit should go out and compete, expand its market in order to maximise its output? The pit manager, or even the area general manager above him, has no responsibility and cannot have any for selling the coal; often he cannot know who is the final consumer of the coal he produces. The marketing of coal is rightly centralised and most of it has been sold by the Coal Board under bulk contracts to large consumers such as the Generating Board, Area Gas Boards, railways, steel companies, cement companies and so on.

An American economist who has gone to great trouble to examine the analyses and judgements of the economic theorists, has come to the following conclusion on their efforts to work out for the Public Corporations an ideal equilibrium pattern – ideal, that is, in the economic sense. His conclusion is: 'All the foregoing suggests that a preoccupation with internal efficiency for public corporations, especially from the viewpoint of commercial criteria, lends itself to superficiality, sterile controversy and misemphasis among policies' (W. G. Shepherd, *Economic Performance under Public Ownership*, p. 145).

The fundamental economic problem of the nationalised industries is a simple one. All the industries, by their very being and nature, are compounds of commercial undertakings and social agencies. For some of the industries the social aspect is slight – in gas for example. In electricity an obligation to promote rural electrification was written into the Electricity Act 1948, the intention being that the great majority of consumers who are urban should help out the small minority of rural consumers. British European Airways maintains services to the Scottish Highlands and Islands, on which it incurs a loss. But it is in coal and transport that social obligations loom so large that they can bedevil commercial considerations. Lord Beeching in his various Reports proved conclusively the heavy losses incurred in running branch lines; but in numerous cases the Minister of Transport refused consent to the closure. The Government justified this policy in its White Paper, which is referred to earlier in this chapter. A review of economic and financial objectives for nationalised industries (Cmnd. 3437). 'There are cases like the railway branch lines where the Government may take social and regional considerations into account in requiring an industry to undertake continuing operations which are themselves unprofitable' (para. 14).

Government has long been aware that some of the activities of the public corporations, actual or proposed, are financially unprofitable but have a substantial social value. In the 1961 White Paper on Financial Obligations etc., it skated over the thin ice. 'Cost may be significantly affected by the amount of commercially unprofitable activities carried on by individual undertakings. These activities will, so far as practicable, have been taken into account in fixing the financial standard for each undertaking' (para. 32). This soon meant, as we have seen earlier, that for railways the financial standard did not exist and for coal it vanished under the impact of capital reorganisation.

But in the six and a half years between April 1961 and November 1967 a new economic technique of social cost/benefit evaluation was appearing, though the 1967 White Paper pointed out (para. 15) that 'there are often difficulties and uncertainties involved in making the calculations'. For years London Transport had been pressing the Government to authorise the construction of the Victoria Line. They admitted it could never be profitable but would help greatly to reduce congestion in London. In the end the Government gave way. Presumably they were satisfied that the social benefits arising from the relief of traffic congestion, which the Victoria Line would provide, justified the authorisation and the inevitable subsidy on its working.

But with respect to the new technique of social cost/benefit analysis, this decision can only be regarded as a further step down into the morass of subsidies into which public transport has sunk. Mr Polanyi well describes this new technique as 'a largely arbitrary total of assigned money values corresponding to the supposed physical benefits selected from a very wide range of possible positive and negative valuations' (*Comparative Returns from Investment in Nationalised Industries*, p. 12). Furthermore, when the analysis has been carried out one can never know whether the benefits have, in fact, been obtained. One suspects that ministers have been blinded, willingly or unwillingly, by the science of the economists standing at their elbow.

The 1967 White Paper goes further in laying down a policy involving social benefits. In paragraph 14 it lays down the new doctrine that 'Indeed it must take a wider view than that of the industry itself, since the Government's objective is to secure the maximum social return on the capital invested, while the industry's concern is properly with the financial return.' This confident reference to 'maximum social return' is somewhat weakened by the passage in the next paragraph quoted earlier about the 'difficulties and uncertainties involved in making social cost/benefit calculations'. Anyhow the Transport Bill 1967 takes this policy very much further.

If the Government is to find the difference between 'social return' and 'financial return', it will be far more closely involved in financing the Public Corporations than ever before. When an industry is finding an activity unprofitable, and can adduce social or regional considerations (e.g. fear of increasing unemployment in a certain region), it will naturally demand a subsidy to offset the loss on the activity. Part of the revenue of the Boards will come therefore from the consumer and part from government grants. That is now happening with almost every Board. It does not pay the Electricity Generating Board to burn more coal; in fact it incurs a loss in doing so. So the Coal Industry Act 1967 provides the substantial sum of £45 million for the period 31 July 1967 to 1 April 1971 to cover the excess costs which would have been avoided if another fuel had been used.

This is a fairly simple and clear-cut operation for a definite period. But in the case of transport – by rail or by road – many of the usual operations are unprofitable. Accountancy arrangements on the railways have been condemned in the past because they do not enable clear calculations to be made on the profit or loss of any particular activity. This, of course, arises from the intricacies of joint costing, which, in a highly integrated industry such as railways, can be baffling. In 1960 the Select Committee found that the Transport Commission could not say whether any of its regions ran at a profit or a loss. But it is easier to find losses than profits and the Government will have to exercise very stringent control to keep down mounting subsidies. With a substantial number of activities showing losses and with the constant incentive to itemise them for the purpose of attracting government subsidies, it is difficult to see how either management or staff are going to be commercially-minded and to go all out for making profits. Even though applications for subsidies to cover losses will be most critically examined at the Ministry of Transport, and even though there will be attempts to fix limits for the subsidies, morale on the railways will not be improved. It is not likely that there will develop the purposeful thrust and vigour which is likely to turn the railways – or even a substantial part of them – into a commercially viable undertaking. To use Mr Harold Wilson's phrase, there will be too many 'begging bowls' around.

The Transport Bill 1967 (which is going through Parliament when this book went to the publisher) provides for further subsidies to various forms of public transport. Every subsidy, apart from its effects on management and workers referred to above, creates its own group of beneficiaries. As soon as the subsidy is reduced or withdrawn, these beneficiaries become a pressure group – very vocal in defence of their 'rights'. Subsidies are an easy way out of a temporary difficulty but the consequences can be lasting. If the Transport Bill is to be the pattern of future financial relations between Government and nationalised industries, then we must expect their industrial and commercial efficiency to fall still further. Up to 1960 government policy adhered to the original doctrine – written into the statutes – that the Public Corporations took the rough with the smooth and no subsidies were envisaged. In the 1960s that doctrine has been weakened, to the detriment of the industries themselves and of the national economy.

10 Men of the Boards and their Staff

THE Socialists, when planning nationalisation, paid little attention to the all-important human factor. There was a vague optimism among the theorists of Socialism that once an industry was transferred from private to public ownership a complete change would come over the outlook of all those engaged in the industry. Their attitude would become one of devotion to the public good. Sordid motives would disappear with the disappearance of the capitalist. A selfless race of managers would appear, whose object would be to manage the industry for the benefit of the community. The nationalised industries would, in their morale and outlook on life, provide a startling contrast to private enterprise, dominated by greed and the profit motive.

Sidney Webb, with his conspicuous intellectual honesty, did give consideration to the question of who were to manage the industries under public ownership. He envisaged a superior breed of civil servant who, with their great adaptability, would learn to guide the industries with the same unselfishness and devotion which they gave to their political masters. That is a doctrine which is now fashionable in India and other Eastern countries, where industrial managers are woefully inadequate. But in this country this belief in the value of the civil servant became subdued as more and more stress was laid on the Public Corporation which was to be run as a commercial concern.

The great protagonist of the Public Corporation was Mr Morrison. In his book *Socialisation and Transport* he considers the problem of who were to be members of the Boards of the socialised industries – he has always preferred the word 'socialised' to 'nationalised'. In chapters X and XI of his book he examines three possible sources of Board membership. They might consist of technical experts, they might be representatives of various interests, or they might be appointed by the responsible Minister on grounds of ability.

The first type, he rejected, because he decided that technical experts were more suitable to be officers of Boards than members. Create a Board of technical experts and you have a Board of departmental heads. 'The Board meetings would tend to be meetings of departmental officers, each concerned to argue the case of his own department and the others not desiring to appear critical of a colleague. Certainly we need capable minds on Public Boards, but I suggest that such minds need to be more public in character and to have more contact with the outside world than is likely in the case of the full-time technician' (*Socialisation and Transport*, p. 170).

The second alternative of representation of interests involved Mr Morrison in some dispute with the trade unions – particularly the Transport and General Workers' Union. To a Socialist Minister the most important 'interest' was the workers in the industry, and the Transport and General Workers' Union pressed that the workers should be represented at Board level. But the trade unions realised the force of Mr Morrison's argument that if representation were accorded to the workers in the industry, other interests such as consumers or local authorities would have a right to be represented; in the end the workers might be in a minority.

There was a tinge of Syndicalism in the attitude of the Transport and General Workers' Union, and the trade union movement came to realise that it was unwise to insist on representation. They would do better for their members by securing safeguards for consultation, etc., in the Nationalisation Acts, and this became the official policy of the trade unions.

So the Labour Party adopted the third alternative of Mr Morrison – appointment by a Minister on grounds of ability. As this was the method written into all the Nationalisation Acts, it requires examination.

The various Acts attempt to define ability; e.g. Section 2 (3) of the Coal Industry Nationalisation Act provided that: 'The chairman and other members of the Board shall be appointed by the Minister of Fuel and Power from amongst persons appearing to him to be qualified as having had experience of, and having shown capacity in, industrial commercial or financial matters, applied science, administration or the organisation of workers.' This section (and similar sections in the other Acts) brings out two points. The first and more important is that the Minister has unfettered discretion. If any criticism is made of one of his appointments, he need not produce the grounds on which he made his choice. The appointee has 'to appear to him' to be qualified and, after all, the Minister knows his own mind.

The second point is that there is no definition of 'experience' or 'capacity'. It is true that if a Minister appointed a person who was generally regarded as a failure in his previous post, he would expose himself to serious criticism. But ministers on the whole have behaved with care and responsibility in making their appointments and it would not be in their own interest to appoint a person who had been widely known to be a failure. So any amount of 'experience' or 'capacity' would be sufficient justification.

From time to time Labour Members of Parliament have criticised the appointment of men who, they claimed, were out of sympathy with nationalisation policy or had even opposed it. The most recent case was the appointment of Mr N. G. Macdiarmid to the British Steel Corporation. But Mr Marsh, the Minister of Power, easily rebutted the criticism. Mr Macdiarmid 'appeared to him' the best man for the post and that was that.

So the only method adopted of appointing Board members was to give the Minister unfettered discretion. This places a considerable power of patronage in the hands of certain ministers; this is dealt with in Chapter 8. Meanwhile let us consider how ministers set about their difficult task of making appointments.

It was obviously desirable when great radical changes were being made in the industries that the new controllers who would man the Boards should be the best whom the Minister could find. The task of handling, controlling and reorganising the nationalised industries was immense. The very size of the industries demanded qualities of the highest order.

It might be objected that there were industrial units in private enterprise as great as the nationalised industries. The important fact which is always overlooked is that a giant in private enterprise is the slow steady creation over a considerable period of time by men of outstanding ability and often of dominating character.

The overnight transformation of 800 colliery undertakings into one National Coal Board posed far greater problems than the gradual creation of I.C.I. or Unilever. By the time those units in private enterprise had reached their present size they had developed traditions and an *esprit de corps*. Their organisations had gradually been moulded to meet the requirements of their increasing size. Their reputation stood high and they could attract into their service the cream of the young talent, which became available from year to year. They provided a life career under leaders of great abilty and were in the the forefront of development – industrial, commercial and scientific.

Let us now turn, by contrast, to the nationalised industries. Some of them, such as airways and electricity, and (more recently) gas, have obviously a considerable future. But coal and railways had their great days in the nineteenth century, and though these industries still have an important part to play, they are diminishing in size and therefore there are considerable doubts about their future. What father would press a bright son to embark on a career as a coal-mining engineer or a railwayman? Even in the inter-war years they had not attracted an adequate share of the country's talent. In those years both coal and railways were depressed industries where prospects were doubtful.

Gas has only recently shed its Victorian image. In the last few years it has loosened its connections with coal and become a petrochemical industry. With the advent of natural gas from the North Sea a bright future is opening up before the industry, which is anxiously recruiting first-class talent to enable it to match up to its increased problems and opportunities.

Electricity is in a class by itself. It was a young industry – definitely twentieth-century. But the electricity supply industry was part of the greater industry of electrical engineering. In the past the electrical manufacturing companies offered greater scope and attracted more talent than the electricity supply industry, especially the municipal part of that industry, where salaries were not so good and many of the undertakings too small to provide suitable opportunity for ability.

Consequently when these industries were nationalised the top structure available in them was not of the best, and certainly not as good as that to be found in other industries. But even this top structure was not entirely available for manning the nationalised Boards. In some of the industries, such as coal and electricity, there was bitter opposition to nationalisation, and some of the abler managers, particularly those who were still young enough to contemplate a change, preferred to leave the industries and go elsewhere. Some of the Boards of the nationalised industries, therefore, started with only part of the top structure, and that often not of the highest quality.

The provisions of the Nationalisation Acts did not encourage able men to stay on and take posts on the Boards. The Acts

H

contained provisions which seriously militated against the attraction of men of the highest ability. Among these provisions may be listed the following:

1. The term of appointment to the Boards is usually only for five years. The appointments were made by a Minister who had unfettered power of dismissal. There was no formal guarantee that the appointment would be renewed after the five years had expired. There was bound to be some uneasiness on that score. At a time when everyone was becoming concerned about pensions, and private industry was developing 'top hat' pension schemes, the appointments to the nationalised industries carried no pension rights. This was only at the beginning and soon had to be corrected.

2. The salaries were fixed by ministers in consultation with the Treasury. A standard was adopted and at first salaries of the members of major Boards were fixed at £5,000, or at the same level as Cabinet ministers. Such a salary might seem high to the man in the street, but private industry had found it necessary to pay much more to attract talent. An element of rigidity must enter into a scheme of public appointments, and the Treasury must keep its eye on the lower salaries paid to the Civil Service. The salaries of members of Public Corporations must be published and be open to criticism by Parliament. Inevitably they tend to remain fixed and changes are difficult to make. It is not surprising, therefore, that from 1947 there was no change in the salaries of the members of the Boards, until 1957. A further increase was made in 1964.

3. Even if the Treasury had felt in a generous mood, which is difficult to imagine, the fact that the appointments were made by a Labour Government meant that the salaries would be fixed on the low side. The Labour movement and the trade unions have always paid their servants absurdly low salaries. A Labour Government fixing salaries for public Boards would have to have regard to the views of its backbenchers. When the supporters of the Labour Government, particularly trade union officials, were offered appointments on the Boards, they felt suddenly rich; the salaries were beyond their wildest dreams.

So the combination of Labour views on remuneration and Treasury policy made it inevitable that Board members' salaries would not be high enough to attract the best, and that there would be no flexibility which would allow for variations to suit individual cases.

In any case the Minister's task was incredibly difficult, however carefully he made his choice. He was appointing to a new Board men who had never carried such vast responsibilities, even if they had worked in the same industry. But if they came in from other industries, the most careful appointments were little more than a gamble, as the Minister could not possibly foresee whether they would be of value in their new posts.

There was the further difficulty that the nationalised industries were run by Boards, and that for a Board to be successful, all its members had to be imbued with the team spirit. A group of eight or nine men, some of whom were strangers to each other, could only with difficulty become a closely-knit team; it would, in any case, take time. This difficulty was intensified if the Board were run by Boards, and that for a Board to be successful, all defined field of activity and was in fact the head of a department, sitting on the Board. All inter-departmental quarrels forced their way up to Board level with disastrous results for team-working. The abler the men appointed, the more likely that quarrels would develop. The chairman of the Boards would, in these circumstances, have an intolerable burden thrust upon them. As we saw early in this chapter, Mr Morrison had foreseen this possibility.

The Report of the Advisory Committee on Organisation, appointed by the Coal Board (the Fleck Committee), stresses the importance of teamwork on a Board (para. 66):

All the members appointed to the Board should have for each other that degree of trust and respect, without which a Board cannot work in harmony. However competent individuals may be in their own fields, it is no use appointing them to the Board if their personalities are such that they cannot work together as a team. In this respect the experience of the Board in the past eight years has not been happy. Therefore the necessity of ensuring that the members of the Board are able to work together is an aspect of the reorganisation which will necessarily engage the Minister's attention.

No doubt ministers did what they could to select men whom they regarded as most able, but the conditions described above militated badly against them. As they were barred from tempting men into the industries by individual offers, the had to be content to draw their appointees from fields of recruitment which regarded the conditions in the nationalised industries as attractive.

Apart, therefore, from the less enterprising and capable men who were in senior positions before nationalisation, the main fields of recruitment were appointments of a political character and civil servants.

Trade union officials and civil servants did not mind working in the semi-political atmosphere of nationalised industries. The latter were familiar with the problems of living with ministers and did not find the salaries and emoluments which were offered unattractive. To a civil servant a Board member's salary with a modest expense account was an improvement on his own terms and conditions of work. To a trade union official with an extremely modest salary, usually a few hundred pounds a year, a full-time appointment on the Board of a nationalised industry meant riches; in any case a Minister was a better master than a trade union committee. Each Board had, of course, to include one or more trade union officials. When the trade unions gave up their claim to be represented on the Boards it was always understood that some appointments to the Board would be made from their ranks.

Ministers have repeatedly complained that it is not easy to get the right men for the Boards, and one may reasonably assume, therefore, that some of the appointments have been made with reluctance. There have been repeated protests, e.g. in the Report of the Herbert Committee, that the salaries paid to members of the Board are too low to attract able men from industry or commerce, and in 1957 a substantial increase in salaries was granted. Curiously enough, Mr Morrison then protested that not all the Board members are worth the increased salaries (*Forward*, 23 August 1957, p. 1). Mr Morrison must know that nationalised industries are a form of public service and it is out of the question for men of the same grade to receive different remuneration. If you decide that some men cannot 'make the grade', get rid of them, but do not pay them less. That way lies bitterness and discord. After all, everyone would know that you were paid less than your colleagues and you would have to carry openly the badge of inferiority. In any case, for the reasons given in Chapter 8, ministers dislike individual salaries.

In making appointments to the first Boards, ministers had a clean slate to write upon, and they could select men from all walks of life. There were very few industrialists appointed from outside the nationalised industries because the conditions of appointment were not then and are not now attractive. We shall see that when it came to the British Steel Corporation very special measures were necessary.

So the Labour ministers in the early days appointed distinguished trade unionists, Co-operators, civil servants, and officers from the armed services, to supplement the appointments from the industries themselves. And this is where Mr Morrison's original classification breaks down; under 'ability' must be included 'technical experts'. His picture of a group of 'able men' – ability quite undefined – under whom the technical experts serve is quite unreal.

An industry must have at the top some men who have spent their life in the industry. Newcomers are not really part of the industries; they know it themselves and everyone in the industries knows it. Thereby they do not command the unquestioning support accorded to the leaders in the great units of private industry. It would take them years to become leaders, and as many were appointed at an advanced age – sometimes over sixty – they can never acquire that identification with the industry which comes from growing up in it and with it.

It was no small loss that in some of the industries able men preferred to go out rather than to serve their new masters. At the time the Labour Government regarded this departure as an advantage, as many of these men were known to be opposed to nationalisation. But as the years went on the significance of the loss became apparent.

In later appointments there has been a steady tendency to fill vacancies by appointments from within the industry. Ministers no longer have a clean slate to write upon. Indeed, the Report of the Fleck Committee definitely lays down the principle that full-time appointments should come from within the industry. The recommendation (para. 68) is worth quoting:

We think it ought to be accepted that in future most of the full-time members of the Board must be drawn from within the industry. We are satisfied that the direction of the industry must be largely in the hands of men with experience in the industry. In any case, full-time membership of the Board is unlikely to attract leaders of the required calibre who are already engaged in industry and commerce, because these people will already be filling responsible jobs and receiving high salaries. Moreover, the top posts in private industry and commerce are free of the political and public criticism which membership of a public body is bound to attract. Normally, therefore, the industry will have to breed its own full-time Board members.

In effect this creates a Board of 'technical experts' which Mr Morrison distrusted.

The dangers of this inbreeding, as we shall see, are great. Nationalised industry is a form of public service and its contacts with the nation which is presumed to own it, and which constitutes its consumer, should be wide, strong and sensitive. But what the Fleck Committee is proposing is in fact a self-perpetuating corporation of producers; the Committee is well aware of this, for paragraph 57 says:

The coal industry, both management and trade unions, has always tended to regard itself as different and separate from its fellows, and now that the industry has a monopoly of coal production, the increased tendency towards self-centredness should be countered by the presence on the Board of men of wide experience of affairs. If, as we hope, the full-time members were drawn from the younger ranks of the industry, the experience and balanced judgement of the part-time members would be of course of strength to them.

This brings us to the obscure and often forgotten part-time members of the Boards. Their role is to bring into the board-room a breath of air from the outside. They should be persons of experience of the world outside the industry, and should be able to contribute from that experience something valuable to the Board's deliberations.

The Fleck Committee indeed projected a very important role for the part-time members. It urged them to take a definite part in the Boards' work; it suggested they should have access to the Minister, jointly or severally; their presence on the Board would inspire the community with confidence. It even made the remarkable proposal that they should act as advisers to the Minister in making the full-time appointments (para. 63).

The part-time members, by reason of their independent position, and the knowledge they acquire of the Board's affairs, can be of special assistance to the minister in advising him on the appointment of full-time Board members, who must normally be drawn from the industry itself. We suggest, therefore, that before appointing a chairman or a deputy chairman of the Board, or making new appointments of full-time Board members, the minister should consult the part-time members.

If ministers adopted this policy – and we cannot know if they have done so – some serious consequences might follow. The part-time members would in fact be the watchdogs of the Ministers. The relations between them and their full-time colleagues might become strained and awkward – especially as the time for re-appointments approached. Ministers can seek advice in many quarters and if they wished to consult part-time members there is no reason why they should not; but it would be well, if there were changes on reappointment, that they made it clear that they sought advice in many quarters.

But the Fleck Committee was postulating a role for the part-time members which they were not able to fill. The type of person whom it was anxious to obtain may be willing to serve, but is usually very busy with many calls on his time. Part-time membership taken seriously, as the Committee suggests, would be a great strain.

It would be difficult, therefore, for them to play a valuable part in the work of a Board unless they gave up some of their other responsibilities. With the best will in the world their grip of the numerous and complex problems facing their industry must be slight compared with that of the full-time members. The latter have the advantage of having lived in the industry and are no doubt supported by the senior officers of the Board, who think like them and with whom they are in constant collaboration. The professionals, if we may so call them, will naturally act in close co-operation and the amateurs – as we may call the part-time members – will find themselves on the periphery of policy. They cannot come to close grips with intricate problems because of lack of background and detailed knowledge; they therefore prefer to contribute now and then from their special experience. On the whole, therefore, it would be surprising if part-time members can be of great value to a Board of a nationalised industry. Their influence can be no more than marginal. The public are misled if they assume that the presence of three or four part-time members on a Board makes any difference to the policy of a nationalised industry.

Part-time members only accept the appointment from a sense of public duty. The remuneration is negligible, but when added to their existing income it becomes derisory under the impact of income tax and surtax. If, therefore, part-time members conclude that conditions make it difficult for them to fulfil a public service they lose interest and resign. No explanation was ever given of the resignations of Lord Heyworth and Mr J. H. Hambro from the National Coal Board in February 1955, but one can assume they had decided they had no longer a satisfying part to play as members of the Board. The type of part-time member who will not resign is the ex-trade union official or retired public servant, who finds the work and status of interest, and to whom the remuneration is of some value. But these are not the part-time members sought by the Fleck Committee.

Let us revert to the tendency to appoint Board members from the ranks of the industry as recommended by the Fleck Committee. Such a policy has its attractions to ministers. The burden of making the appointments is heavy. If consultations before the appointments are limited to a few men in the industry concerned the burden is sensibly lightened. Further, a familiar figure obtaining promotion is more welcome to the industry than an outsider. The public will also be pleased. They know nothing of the men in the industry, but they will know that an 'expert' has been appointed; and 'experts' are always welcome. What the public do not like and become suspicious about is when a stranger is brought to an important appointment in a nationalised industry. Even if it is not a case of 'jobs for the boys', which was a frequent allegation against the Labour Government, there are suggestions of personal reasons and newspapers are full of dark hints, which are ventilated by members in parliamentary questions.

So this tendency is bound to become stronger as the nationalised industries become older. A glance at the appointments of the last few years, particularly to the Area Boards, such as gas and electricity, shows that new appointments are usually promotions from within the industry, if not from the staff of the particular Board. It is not unusual for a chief engineer or a secretary of a Board to become chairman of another. As the newcomers originally appointed retire, their place is not taken by other newcomers but by men who have spent their life in the industry.

This tendency has not pleased the Trades Union Congress. According to their half-yearly report in 1959, *What the T.U.C. is Doing*, they discovered that the numbers appointed to the Boards for their trade union experience had fallen from one-seventh to one-eleventh, and they sought a meeting with the Prime Minister to discuss this issue. Mr Macmillan explained that it was government policy 'to confine full-time membership of these Boards to people who have come up through the industry'. This policy thus received the Prime Minister's blessing, but the T.U.C. 'did not consider this a satisfactory reply'.

Further confirmation of this policy is to be found in the White Paper of 1960 on the Reorganisation of the Nationalised Transport Undertakings (Cmnd. 1248). Paragraph 33 of that White Paper reads as follows:

The Government consider it important that, so far as possible, the nationalised transport undertakings should produce their own leaders.

Promotion from within the undertakings to the highest levels should be within the grasp of those who prove themselves capable. In particular there should be much greater opportunities in future for those in all parts of the railway service to make their way to the top. At the outset, however, some major posts may have to be filled from outside.

It is as well that the last sentence has been added because it is doubtful whether the railways during the previous thirty years had attracted their fair share of ability. The reorganisation of the railways requires a very high level of talent, which it is very unlikely can be found at present among the railway staffs.

This tendency may be said to be for the good of the industry. But is it good for the nation? The industry is nationalised: it is presumed to operate in the national interest. Its leading figures should be conversant with national issues and should be able to explain the policy of the industry to the public, and convey the wishes of the public to the industry. This problem of public relations is vital, and the failure to solve it one of the weakest aspects of nationalisation. Even the Fleck Committee regarded public relations as a part of the activities of the secretary of the Coal Board, and as the secretary was not responsible to any member of the Board no member of the Board had anything to do with public relations. As is suggested in Chapter 12, public relations are sufficiently important to occupy the whole time of a member, with the chairman lending a hand.

To fill top posts from the ranks of the industry will, therefore, please the industry, make the Minister's task comfortable and obviate criticism from the public and Parliament. It might be said that it is all-important to have a contented industry and that to achieve that object is to serve the nation's interest best. But some serious questions arise which require ventilation. How far will this tendency produce a highly organised and self-perpetuating technocracy, out of touch with national issues? How far would such a technocracy, working closely with the trade unions, promote the interest of the industry at the expense of the consumer? How far can the Minister, faced with a well-organised industry, dare to insist on the national interest, which is his responsibility? As the stream of precedents broadens and appointments from inside become more numerous, is the Minister not abdicating his functions under the Acts to find the most able men in a variety of fields? Are we not back on Mr Morrison's first alternative of technical experts, whom he rightly distrusted and whom he felt would be more appropriate as senior officers under the Boards, rather than as members of Boards?

All these are serious questions which have hardly been venti-lated. These industries are statutory monopolies with the consumer at their mercy. The nation, which is at once their shareholder and consumer, is a kind of *tertium quid*, ignored by management and trade union who, as the producers, have a close and common interest. Let us remember that public ownership was always demanded as something good for the worker in the industry, rid of the capitalist. All the driving force towards nationalisation comes from the workers' organisations. If they and management can see eye to eye, both parties are happy, and we have a contented industry. But the cost may be great and the nation, as consumer, pays. Even if the nation, as consumer, does not put as high a value on the service rendered as the men in the industry insist on receiving, then the nation still has to pay – as taxpayer. The deficit of the railways does not prevent the Railways Board seeking a contented body of workers by improved conditions or increased wages, and the price of contentment – as both Board and railway-men know – has always been forthcoming from the Treasury.

In the sixties the tendency to appoint members of Boards from inside the ranks of the industries has hardened into a regular practice. A new aspect of this tendency has been to appoint a senior officer of a Board to membership of the Board, leaving him to draw his salary as an officer and not fitting him into the usual scales. As the salaries of officers of Boards are confidential and not shown in official publications, we do not know whether they receive more or less than other members of the Board. It is a way of conferring status on a valued official.

The greatest problem in manning the Boards is finding a suitable chairman, particularly of the important national corpora-tions. In this respect there have been several experiments in the last ten years and, no doubt, more experiments will be made.

The chairmen are the key posts. They represent the industry to Government and Parliament, to its millions of consumers and to the personnel of the industry. Some of the nationalised industries have found their monopolistic strength crumbling away and have developed a crisis outlook. The industry's attitude to that crisis is personified to everybody in the policy of the chairman. Sometimes ministers realise that there is no person in those industries capable of handling the crisis; importation of a chairman from outside becomes imperative.

In the fifties the occasional chairman from outside would be a distinguished member of the Services. Thus the Transport Commission was headed by a general, British European Airways by an air-marshal and B.O.A.C. by an admiral. By 1960 both the Coal Board and the railways were in serious difficulties and ministers decided that a new type of chairman was required. In the case of coal, the Conservative Government appointed a Labour Member of Parliament Mr (later Lord) Robens. But this was not as striking a break with tradition as the appointment of Dr (later Lord) Beeching. He was a director of I.C.I. and a member of Sir Ivan Stedeford's Special Advisory Group, which had made a confidential Report on the railways to Mr Marples, the Minister of Transport. An arrangement was made whereby Dr Beeching was seconded from I.C.I. for five years to be chairman of the Transport Commission and later of the Railway Board, and Dr Beeching was to continue to draw the remuneration he had been receiving in I.C.I. – £24,000 a year.

The announcement of this figure led to a storm. The highest-paid chairmen of nationalised Corporations – coal, electricity and atomic energy – received at that time £10,000 a year. Dr Beeching's salary was therefore well out of line. Mr Marples defended the appointment and the salary on the ground that the plight of the railways was so serious that an exceptional chairman was required to take exceptional measures and that he had to be paid the market rate.

Dr Beeching's appointment was followed by another exceptional appointment at the Transport Commission, which however attracted little attention. Mr P. H. Shirley, a financial expert from Unilever, was appointed a member of the Transport Commission at a salary of £12,000 a year, which, at the time, was higher than any salary paid to any chairman of a nationalised corporation. Presumably this was again a case of a person transferring from private to public enterprise at a salary received in private enterprise.

Dr Beeching left the Railways Board at the end of his five-year term in 1966 and Mr Shirley left in 1967.

In the sixties there have been other cases of higher salaries paid to chairmen where it was felt necessary to attract the right man from private enterprise. For example, Sir Giles Guthrie, a merchant banker, became chairman of British Overseas Airways Corporation in January 1964 at a salary of £15,000.

Salaries for Boards of Public Corporations became a very

awkward issue when steel was nationalised in 1967. It was imperative to have as members of the British Steel Corporation some of
the top men in the steel industry, who had been drawing salaries
considerably in excess of those paid to Board members in other
nationalised industries. So the Minister of Power secured Cabinet
agreement to a complete new scale of salaries, which puts the
nationalised steel industry in a class by itself.

The Chairman of the B.S.C., Lord Melchett, only wished to be
appointed for two years till April 1969, and draws a personal
salary of £16,000. His deputy chairmen are on a scale of £20,000 to
£24,000; members of the Board are on a scale of £15,000 to
£19,000; in both cases these salaries are abated by one-eighth up
to 26 April 1969. These salaries are paid to members who had no
previous connections with steel, such as Mr Ron Smith, who was
previously General Secretary of the Union of Post Office Workers.
Such salaries must cause heartburning among the members of
other Public Corporations.

The Cabinet, having given way on steel, refused to do likewise
elsewhere. When an attempt was made to secure a new chairman
of the Railways Board at a salary higher than his predecessors,
consent was refused and the vice-chairman of the Board was
promoted to chairman at the normal salary of £12,500.

In the next few years this salary problem for Board members
will become more difficult than ever.

There is great difficulty in attracting first-class men from
private enterprise to the Boards. On the contrary, in recent years,
able men have resigned from the Boards to join private enterprise.
As time goes on posts on the Boards become, if anything, less and
less attractive. In the fifties the Corporations were on the whole
left alone. Government control was light and fairly remote and the
Corporations insisted on the charter of autonomy which is to be
found in the nationalisation statutes. But gradually government
control and interference, as we have seen in Chapter 8, became
more detailed and persistent. The Labour Government regards the
'public sector' as an instrument under its close control and therefore the chairmen of the Corporations are repeatedly instructed to
fit their activities into the framework of government policy, with
its numerous changes. This, at times, causes serious embarrassment
to the chairmen, which has been publicly expressed by Lord
Robens. If anything, therefore, it will become more and more
difficult to attract suitable persons from private to public enter-

prise, which will have to learn to live more and more on the stock of personnel to be found in its 'staff'.

There is, however, one type of experimental appointment to chairman or deputy chairman which has developed in the sixties and may possibly go further. In some cases a capable person can be secured as chairman or deputy chairman on a part-time basis; he is thus left free to continue with his previous activities for part of the time. There are a few part-time chairmen or deputy chairmen but, on the whole, these appointments are with the lesser Boards where the burden of work can be assumed to be less onerous than with the important national Boards controlling a major industry. If it became the practice to appoint an officer or a member of the Board to be chief executive – like a managing director – there would be more scope for part-time chairmen or deputy chairmen.

If in the future most Board members are to be recruited from the 'staff', the quality of that staff is very important. We can therefore now consider how the staff have fared in the last twenty years.

The staffs of the Boards may be defined as all the personnel employed by the Boards, other than the industrial workers. There is no clear-cut line of demarcation between staff and industrial workers because there often is, and should be, movements from the ranks of the workers into those of staff. This is particularly so in the case of coal. The only test that can be applied is the organisation of which a person is a member and to which he looks for protection. Thus in the case of coal, a member of the staff would not be a member of the National Union of Mineworkers but of the British Association of Colliery Management or the N.C.B. Labour Staff Association, or the Clerical and Administrative Workers' Union. This definition is rough-and-ready because there may be some clerical workers in the National Union of Mineworkers. Further, in the case of coal, staff would be dealt with by the Staff Department set up as a result of the recommendations of the Fleck Report. Paragraph 124 of that Report defines staff as 'everyone engaged in managerial, technical, administrative, supervisory and clerical work. This definition would include under officials and others in supervisory posts at the colliery and clerks.'

Staff, therefore, are not a homogeneous body. They would range from clerks, whose pay and status would not differ much from that of an unskilled manual worker, to men with outstanding qualifications and experience whose pay would not be much less than that of Board members.

It goes without saying that the staff of a nationalised industry are of supreme importance and that the success or failure of the industry will depend very largely on the quality of the staff who, in fact, manage the industry.

The nine members of the National Coal Board do not manage their great industry. This is done in 1966–7 by an army of 44,000 technical, administrative and clerical staff. In addition there are the under-officials – overmen, deputies, etc. in the pits – who might be described as the non-commissioned officers of the force of about 410,000 workers employed in March 1967 in coal-mining.

Despite the obvious importance of staff, little was heard of them during the debates and discussions which led up to nationalisation. Frequent references were made in Parliament to the views of the trade unions – mineworkers, railwaymen, etc. In the debates on the Iron and Steel Act 1949 much was made by Labour speakers of resolutions and demands of the Iron and Steel Confederation. Similarly frequent references were made to the owners of the industries which were nationalised. Colliery companies, power companies, iron and steel companies – all were attacked by Labour Government speakers. But neither Government nor Opposition ever referred to the views of the staff; there was an uncharted desert between the handful of owners on the one hand and the army of industrial workers on the other hand, who were pressing on to the promised land of public ownership. After reading the debates in Parliament one might legitimately conclude that there was nobody in these industries apart from owners and industrial workers.

The reason for this is obvious. Staff, as we said above, are not a homogeneous body, as are the industrial workers. The more important of them – engineers, scientists, etc. – would belong to their professional institutions, which by their constitutions were barred from handling such matters as remuneration and conditions of employment; they were only concerned with the professional standards and qualifications of their members. The lower ranks of staff such as clerical workers, were often in no organisation at all; consequently when nationalisation suddenly descended on them they found themselves without a spokesman. In some industries, such as gas and electricity, they were split between municipal and company undertakings, and so might belong to different trade unions.

Labour Party programmes have always referred to 'workers by hand or brain', and one must assume therefore, that they were as much concerned with staff as with the industrial worker. But they knew little about the staff, who were not organised to express their views.

So all the staffs of the industries concerned were silently swept into public ownership; their views almost entirely unknown, even to themselves. Mostly they were worried, puzzled and frightened men. Their careers were in the industries and in mid-career they found the whole organisation changed overnight. With the exception of the railways, a few colliery groups and a few large gas and electricity undertakings, they had worked in small and local units. They now found themselves members of vast national organisations reaching away to London, with numerous and novel authorities in between. Naturally they were at a loss. The industrial worker on the other hand suffered no such 'sea change'; he still worked in the colliery, power station or goods yard and his complaint was, if anything, the opposite; nationalisation had not changed his bosses who were now even slower in adjusting grievances.

There was, of course, no fear that anybody in the industry taken over would lose his post. All the Acts provided that any whole-time worker in these industries should receive compensation if, in any way, his position was worsened after nationalisation. So financial loss was obviated. In fact this obligation to take everybody over and give equivalent employment or compensation in lieu led to redundancy in the earlier years.

The new Acts forced the staff to organise themselves in a way they had not previously contemplated. Hitherto they had worked for numerous employers, whose terms and conditions of employment varied. For instance, in the gas and electricity industries the company undertakings tended to pay better salaries than the municipal. Collieries varied in size and profitability; colliery managers would move on to a larger and wealthier companies. But now there was only one employer in each industry. It is true that in electricity and gas there were the Area Boards, but even there the Central Electricity Authority and the Gas Council were given overriding power to conclude national agreements with organisations of workers.

Each Act laid upon the new Boards the duty 'to seek consultation with any organisation appearing to them to be appropriate with a view to the conclusion of such agreements as appear to the parties to be desirable with respect to the establishment and maintenance of machinery' for settling terms and conditions of employment and promoting safety, health, and welfare of employees (Electricity Act 1947, Section 53 (1)). It was imperative, therefore, for the staffs to bestir themselves and form their own associations for negotiating with their new employers. In some cases such associations existed and they soon became sufficiently comprehensive and representative to obtain recognition from their appropriate Board. In other cases associations had to be formed.

As a result each industry is now equipped with a group of negotiating bodies which cover the whole industry, except for a small number of senior staff who are on individual contracts which are deemed to be non-negotiable. In electricity, for example, there is the following set-up. Besides the National Joint Industrial Council for manual workers, there are the National Joint Board for engineering staff, the National Joint Council for administrative and clerical staff, the National Joint Committee for building and civil engineering workers and finally the National Joint Managerial and Higher Executive Grades Committee. In some of these cases there are District Councils and Works Committees. The representation is complete for all grades of employees.

The staff cannot complain, therefore, that they have no opportunity of making their voice heard. Gradually the great variety in conditions of employment on vesting day has been systematised and standardised. There is now a complete hierarchy of staff in all the nationalised industries and every employee knows exactly his position, his relations with his fellow workers and his prospects of promotion.

Thus the Nationalisation Acts rendered a service to the staff by requiring the Boards to find the appropriate organisation with which to negotiate on conditions of employment, etc. The staff have therefore been enabled to strengthen and consolidate their positions, not only in relation to the Board which employed them, but also in relation to the trade unions of the industrial workers, which were, of course, highly organised on vesting day and were deemed, both by themselves and the Labour Party, to be the main beneficiaries from the transfer to public ownership. The staff were able, by their own negotiating machinery, to fight for their standards in a period of inflation, when the improved remuneration and conditions of the industrial workers narrowed the differentials between staff and workers.

So as a whole, staff are now organised and can reasonably protect themselves in general matters such as conditions of employment.

But what was the effect on them as individuals of the transfer to public ownership?

Here we are much more in the dark because staff are, on the whole, fairly silent and their representative associations not addicted to publicity in the same manner as the powerful trade unions which represent the industrial worker. Detailed information on individuals is hard to come by and there is scope for considerable research on the subject. The Acton Society Trust has made some excellent case studies on the subject, particularly in *Management under Nationalisation*. These have let in valuable light on the outlook of a few individuals who may or may not be representative of the tens of thousands of staff who are now working in the nationalised industries. As they are only a few individuals, the following analysis must perforce be based on general considerations applying to the nationalised industries as a whole

We can, on the whole, ignore the clerical grade. Their outlook and prospects were bound up with the undertaking in which they were serving on vesting day. In this respect they were not unlike the manual worker, who did not anticipate moving from his place of employment. The difference between them was that before nationalisation the clerical, unlike the manual, worker was poorly organised. The Nationalisation Acts conferred a boon on him in forcing him to organise himself; had he not done so he might have suffered in the inflation which followed.

The staff of the railways probably suffered least. A national body, the Railway Executive, was clapped on to the four main-line railways, which were thereby amalgamated into one unit; and the Railway Executive was only an agent working with powers delegated by the British Transport Commission. The Railway Executive was organised on a functional basis, but as the main-line railways, were very large organisations, it was impossible to amalgamate them in the same manner as colliery companies or gas and electricity undertakings. There was no alternative, therefore, but to allow them to continue to function at a level, so to speak, lower than high policy. Accordingly, right from the start six Railway Regions were created and the Transport Commission decided 'that the detailed supervision, maintenance and operation of the railway system should be vested in departmental offices in six Regions' (1948 Annual Report, para. 141). The Regions were given fair autonomy:

In each region there is a Chief Regional Officer, who reports direct to the Railway Executive, is responsible for the general administration of the region within the policy and general instructions of the Executive and co-ordinates the activities of the Regional Departmental Officers. . . . The internal organisations of the regions varied considerably at the outset, but apart from the Scottish Region, which is being built from the beginning, they were in essence the headquarters organisations of the former companies (para. 142).

So apart from the most senior officers, the technical and administrative staff on the railways were not too bewildered at the change-over. Nevertheless, criticism at the centralising tendencies of the Railway Executive continued to mount, and the Conservative Government, by the Transport Act 1953, abolished the Railway Executive. As a result six Area Boards were appointed from 1 January 1955, with powers delegated by the Transport Commission. These Boards have the authority to delegate further and have experimented accordingly. These arrangements have, on the whole, continued with the British Railways Board, which started functioning on 1 January 1963.

One may reasonably conclude, therefore, that in the case of the railways, the managerial, technical and administrative staff found themselves with landmarks not very seriously changed. They may now be depressed at the failure of the railways to pay their way, with all the attendant consequences of working in an industry making repeated losses.

It was in the three fuel industries – coal, gas and electricity – that the change-over was most drastic. In the main, the units in those industries had been small; overnight the units disappeared and were replaced by large publicly-owned corporations. Coal was the complete change-over; one National Coal Board took over 1500 pits. In gas, the twelve autonomous Gas Boards did at any rate maintain their own local organisation, but the national body, the Gas Council, having the power to conclude national agreements with trade unions, etc., was of importance. Nevertheless, the employer was the autonomous Area Gas Board. In the case of electricity, the Central Electricity Authority created, for its own functions of generation and main transmission, a national organisation and hierarchy of staff. It also had the power of concluding national agreements which affected the staffs of the Area Electricity Boards.

In these three industries, therefore, the change in the conditions of the staff was overwhelming. From being a member of a small staff with strong local and even personal affiliations, he became a member of a large staff spread over a wide territory or even over the whole country. Hitherto his relations with his fellow members of the staff and his superiors had been simple and direct. Now they were involved and complicated. Sometimes it was difficult to know who were his superiors. Suppose he were an engineer working with an Area General Manager in the coal industry. His superior was the Area General Manager. But if an engineer came down from division, still more if the divisional engineer were accompanied by an engineer from headquarters, what was he to do with their proposals? Act on them as instructions? Refer the matter to the Area General Manager, who might be too busy to be troubled? Or what?

Difficult as was the position of the technical official, the position of the manager was much more so. In a colliery, gas or electricity undertaking, the manager was the 'boss'. There might be a board of directors or a municipal committee to whom he was responsible. In difficulty he would go and talk it over with this managing director or committee chairman and, as long as he had him on his side, he knew he could proceed. In fact in many of the smaller undertakings the manager had a seat on the Board and was even managing director; authority was centralised in one person.

This independence was now gone. He might now be called District, Divisional, Sub-Area Manager or some other such term. There were usually above him at least two superiors if not three. Many decisions which he had hitherto made on the spot were now beyond his competence. Even if he could make a decision he would have to put it through some consultative machinery.

He was now working in a publicly-owned industry and one of the main results of public ownership was consultation. Nationalisation envisaged not only technical reconstruction but also 'industrial democracy'. This might mean 'workers' control' but the very least it could mean was joint consultation, which was written into all the Acts. At all levels the new industries proliferated consultative committees.

In electricity for example there were 'in 1967 two National Joint Advisory Councils (one for England and Wales and one for Scotland) twelve District Joint Advisory Councils in England and Wales, and some 500 Local Advisory Committees (including those in Scotland) to promote, improve and encourage measures affecting the safety, health, welfare and the education and training of employees in the industry and to allow discussion of other matters of mutual interest including efficiency' (Electricity Council 1966–7 Report, p. 48). All these bodies were, of course, established in consultation with the trade unions and the last ten words of the above quotation give a very wide latitude in selecting subjects for discussion. For instance, in 1965–6, much time was given in Advisory Committees at all levels to discussing the ill-fated National Plan and its effect on the electricity supply industry and its employees.

The manager of a unit – a coal mine, a power station or a gas works – would in the early days find difficulties in his relations with his workers. The Acts enjoined, as we have seen above, consultation with the workers. Even if a manager had the formal authority to take a decision without reference to the appropriate Advisory committee, it might be wiser if he did not. On the other hand, if he referred to the Committee, he might be starting a series of arguments which might wend its way upward to a N.J.A.C. If he were doubtful about the outcome, he might decide to let matters rest.

One of the consequences of nationalising an industry is the tendency to promote the employment of specialist staff. It pays to do so if the unit is large enough. For a unit of 500 workers an industrial relations officer would be absurd; for 10,000 men it is desirable, if not necessary. One or two collieries could not bear the cost of a specialist in coal preparation; twenty pits on the other hand would provide him with full-time work on the important task of improving the quality of the saleable coal. Clearly, therefore, if the Boards were to discharge their statutory responsibilities to reorganise their industry, great numbers of specialists were required, who were unknown in the small units formerly prevalent.

In the years after vesting day, the new Corporations were living on the technical and managerial ability inherited from their predecessors. But in the course of the 1950s it was clear that it was important to attract, train and hold young men who could rise to responsible staff positions.

The National Coal Board had probably inherited less managerial ability than the other nationalised industries. It was faced with serious problems of maintaining and expanding coal supplies at a time of increasing demand. It set to work, therefore, to comb its own industry for all the ability which could be found in it and to give that ability all the opportunities for promotion and higher responsibility. By the Ladder Plan and Technical Scholarship Scheme it catered for all grades of specialist and manager. In 1957 it set up a Staff College whose purpose 'is to contribute to improving management in the industry by helping those in line of command or departmental management to develop attitudes of mind likely to enable them to deal more successfully with their various problems' (N.C.B. Report for 1957, para. 297).

Since 1948 the N.C.B. has offered 100 scholarships a year in engineering at the universities, open to applicants both in the industry and outside; the total awarded by March 1967 was 1,195. In no year did 100 suitable applicants come forward. In 1966–7, 39 were awarded – 29 to school-leavers and 10 to men already in the industry.

Also since 1950 the Board has had an Administrative Assistant Scheme, which trains men, both from the universities and from within the industry, for non-technical management posts. The training is intensive and includes underground work and experience in the coalfields as well as at the Board's Headquarters. More than 150 men have been recruited into the scheme and many of them have risen to senior posts in the industry. The Board plans to maintain selective recruitment in the concentrated and reorganised coal industry of the future. There were seven new entrants to the Scheme in 1965–6 (1965–6 Report, para. 159) but there is no mention of further entrants in the 1966–7 Report.

The Coal Board, in launching all these schemes, was aware that newcomers from the outer world have much prejudice to overcome and are not very welcome to the 'self-centred coal mining industry' as the Fleck Report describes it. It must know that the miners and their union view these outsiders with the greatest suspicion and have repeatedly protested at the increasing number of staff appointments made by the Board. The National Union of Mineworkers has even formally conducted an enquiry into the swelling number of staff appointments which the 'miners carry on their backs'.

The Acton Society Trust conducted a field investigation into the outlook of the miners in a coalfield which it called 'Pollockfield', and reported their findings in a pamphlet called *The Worker's Point of View*. This investigation was carried out in the spring of 1951 and will be referred to more fully in Chapter 12. But it is interesting to see what the miners thought of the staff. 'It is said that administration is largely an organisation for providing well-paid sinecures for persons who have influence with the previous owners' (p. 11). 'The intensity of hatred and scorn which is felt for the administration is perhaps conveyed by some of the names which are given to them; glamour boys, fantailed peacocks, little Caesars. These feelings find more formal expression: thus the Midland Area of the National Union of Mineworkers discussed at an Annual Conference the need to clear out many of the "people doing superficial jobs and earning £1500 a year" ' (p. 12).

These words were written soon after nationalisation and it is to be hoped that the educative efforts of the Coal Board have subdued these violent prejudices. But the conservatism of the miner is very deep-seated, and his dislike of outsiders was shown by Mr Blyton (now Lord Blyton), a miners' M.P., who said on 28 February 1957, 'we hope there will not be built up a civil service of college boys and jobs taken from men who have worked in the pits and understand the industry'.

As a contrast during the 1950s we can take the attitude of the Central Electricity Authority, which was wound up in December 1957. The Herbert Committee investigated its policy of staff recruitment and found it sadly wanting (chapter 14 of Report). The Authority ran a training scheme for engineering graduates recruited from the universities. In 1949/50 it recruited 104 graduates, of whom 21 resigned during training. The numbers fell steadily in succeeding years: 69, 39, 37, 25, and 8 in 1954/5. The Herbert Committee was disturbed at this trend because 'the industry undoubtedly looks to the entrants under the graduate training scheme for the men who in later life will provide the nucleus from which senior appointments will be made'. The scheme covered student apprentices who were not necessarily graduates, but their numbers also continued to decline. In 1949/50 there were 401 in all (including the 104 graduates), but in 1954/5 there were only 93 (including the 8 graduates). Despite the attractions of electrical engineering, the Herbert Committee found that the prospects, after some early promotion, were rather uncertain. It points out (para. 325) that a young entrant from out-side has to compete for the senior posts with older men with longer experience in the industry. 'In these circumstances there is no certain prospect of the graduate being given the planned training and experience in various posts on the generation and distribution sides, which we consider to be essential for eventual leadership of the industry.'

The Committee advocated 'a deliberate scheme under which men are carefully selected, trained and advanced in particular posts, so that they emerge in their middle life as potential leaders of the industry'. 'But the Authority have told us that they do not believe in the earmarking of individuals for particular jobs as "this would be invidious in a great national undertaking, and contrary to the best industrial practice".' The Committee disposes of the last part of the statement and contends 'that the Authority's confidence that under the present arrangements future leaders will be automatically forthcoming is ill-founded'. It concludes that unless a change of policy is adopted 'we do not consider the industry will be able to provide a future top management of the requisite calibre from its own ranks, and the minister and the industry will be impelled continually to make appointments from outside' (para. 328).

This policy of the C.E.A. could even be described as reactionary, because it ignored the increasing opportunities in the 1950s for young men to go to the universities; in future there would be many fewer bright youngsters entering industry direct from school. As we have seen in Chapter 4, the reorganised electricity supply industry reversed this policy of the Central Electricity Authority. It has embarked on a policy on an extensive system of training and recruitment. University graduates are recruited, financed by industry scholarships awarded to persons both inside and outside the industry. The advent of nuclear generation has made high technical competence more than ever necessary for the staff of the Generating Board.

During the 1950s competition to recruit the able young men and women from the universities became intense. During this period the prospects of the gas industry were not bright enough to enable it to join in the competition. But in the last few years the 'image' of the industry has changed and its prospects are promising. Now it is able to recruit university graduates, the number rising to 119 in 1966–7. It is interesting to see that gas, like the coal industry, recruits a percentage of arts graduates.

The National Coal Board is continuing its well-known policy of training and recruitment, but, as the industry's future becomes more questionable, it will probably find it difficult to recruit young people of the same quality as hitherto. That will be a sad experience for a Board which, earlier than most of the Corporations, set out to attract young men of ability and promise.

There is one imponderable factor which may be of importance in hindering the recruitment of able young persons. In his contacts the writer has more than once been told by staff members that they find unpleasantness in the derogatory attitude of their neighbours towards the industries in which they work. The public tend uncritically to lump the nationalised industries together. When, therefore, the 'image' of one of them is poor, e.g. the railways, the discredit tends to rebound on the other industries. It is impossible to assess the weight of this factor. But at a time when industries and professions are strenuously competing to recruit the able youngster who can now make his choice, this factor must have some adverse effect on the standards of future management of the nationalised industries.

11 The Workers in the Nationalised Industries

NATIONALISATION springs from the urge to improve the lot of the workers in the industry to be taken over. We have seen in Chapter 1 how Sidney Webb was pressed by Arthur Henderson to produce a programme for nationalising all industries, so that the whole working class could be uplifted. Why confine the undoubted benefits of nationalisation to miners and railwaymen?

Largely as a result of the Report of the Sankey Commission in 1919 the Miners' Federation of Great Britain adopted nationalisation as their definite programme and patiently pursued that objective till it was realised in 1947. They were far and away the most determined among the unions. Their sufferings in the inter-war years seemed to them to have no end, except in the national ownership of their industry. Compared with them the railwaymen's unions were lukewarm. The workers in the gas and electricity industries, which were public utilities affording regular employment, showed no enthusiasm for expelling the capitalist. In any case two-thirds of the electricity industry and about two-fifths of the gas industry were already in the public ownership of the local authorities, and the companies in those two industries were closely controlled by statute and regulation.

There were cross-currents. Syndicalism never obtained any hold on the trade unions in Britain as it did on the Continent. In the 1920s Britain had an intellectual version of Syndicalism in Guild Socialism, which produced ambitious schemes for the workers 'by hand and brain' taking over and running the industries in which they worked. But these paper schemes made no impression on the stolidity of the trade unions, and after the General Strike of 1926 Guild Socialism died of its own emptiness.

In the 1930s when Mr Morrison pressed the claim of the Public Corporation as the chosen vessel for managing nationalised – or, as he preferred to call it, socialised – industries, there was a demand from some unions, led by the Transport and General Workers' Unions, that the unions should nominate members of the Boards.

But in 1944 the Trades Union Congress, in the *Interim Report on Post-War Reconstruction*, abandoned this claim. It realised the serious difficulties of this proposal which would have led to claims from other interests to be represented. So it left the future Labour Government a free hand in appointing the Boards. But among the qualifications listed in the Acts, to which ministers should have regard, appeared 'experience of and capacity in the organisation of workers'.

Accordingly, among the members of the new Boards there appeared at least one leading trade unionist. His responsibility was usually industrial relations on behalf of the new Board. When the Coal Board appointed Divisional Boards, a trade unionist was always included, with similar responsibilities. Some of these distinguished trade unionists became chairmen of their Boards. Lord Citrine was chairman of the Central Electricity Authority throughout its whole existence. A Conservative Government in 1955 appointed Mr (now Sir) James Bowman deputy chairman of the National Coal Board and in 1956 he became chairman.

Sir John Benstead was an original member of the Transport Commission and went on to become deputy chairman. In electricity not only did Lord Citrine hold the most important post but Mr Gibson was appointed chairman of the North-Western Electricity Board. In gas Sir John Stephenson became chairman of the Eastern Gas Board and several leading trade unionists became deputy chairmen or members of other Gas Boards.

Throughout it has been assumed that the responsibility for the conduct of industrial relations must rest with a former trade union official. The assumption rests on the belief that such a member, having negotiated all his life with the employers on behalf of his fellow workers, will be the best man to represent the new employers in the negotiations with his old trade union. But it is doubtful whether such a belief is justified. His successors are bound to prove to their trade union that they are as capable negotiators as the veteran who has joined the employers. In any case there is the deep and intense solidarity among the workers. The trade unionist member of the Board is no longer one of 'us'; he has become one of 'them'. On that ground alone he is suspect. His conduct is most carefully watched. As he is no longer a member of the union, will he, naturally, try to make a career in his new post? Is he therefore using a lifetime of experience of fighting on their behalf to resist their claims? Is he letting his fellow Board members into secrets which should be kept in working-class circles? Might it not be preferable to deal with the type of men with whom they had always been familiar – a straightforward representative of the employers? His outlook was, on the whole, easier to understand and negotiations could be planned and carried out on traditional lines.

This whole subject of industrial relations in nationalised industry is complex and deserves far more careful and thorough study than it has received. But it is a difficult subject. The outsider has so little knowledge of what goes on; he can only see the results. Until we obtain some inside knowledge from someone with experience in the subject, we can only speculate about what happens. Unfortunately persons with experience of industrial relations seem relectant or unable to put their views on paper.

The newly appointed Boards were to adopt a 'New Model' policy towards their employees – not only manual, but also clerical, technical, scientific and administrative. They were to 'promote the welfare, health and safety of persons' in their employment. It is their duty, 'in consultation with any organisation appearing to be appropriate, to make provision for advancing the skill of persons employed by them and for improving the efficiency of their equipment and the manner in which that equipment is to be used'. So they had to work out, in consultation with the trade unions, schemes for training and education, and for general improvement of the standard of efficiency.

When it comes to settling terms and conditions of employment, the duty is laid upon the Boards 'to consult with organisations which appear to them to be representative' and to conclude with them 'agreements providing for the establishment and maintenance of joint machinery for the settlement by negotiation of terms and conditions of employment, with provision for reference to arbitration in default of such settlement in such cases as may be determined by or under the agreements' (Coal Industry Nationalisation Act, Section 46 (1) (a)).

The Acts also contain more general provisions on consultation with the workers. For instance, Section 46 (1) (b) (ii) of the Coal Industry Nationalisation Act lays upon the Coal Board the duty of consulting organisations of their employees so that they could discuss 'the organisation and conduct of the operations in which such persons are employed and other matters of mutual interest to the Board and such persons arising out of the exercise and performance by the Board of their functions'.

Both the Transport and the Electricity Acts contain provision for the setting up of machinery for 'the discussion of other matters of mutual interest to the Commission (Electricity Boards) and such persons, including efficiency in the operation of the Commission's services'.

So all the Acts provided for consultation between Boards and employees on all questions of mutual interest, and as a result each industry has equipped itself with an elaborate collection of joint bodies.

Most of the industries which were nationalised had some national machinery for negotiation with the trade unions on wages and conditions. But, as we have seen in Chapter 10, non-manual workers had to organise themselves into associations which would negotiate on their behalf with the national body which now became their employer.

But whereas negotiations with the trade unions on wages and conditions were nothing new, joint bodies for consultation were radically different. As we have seen from the above quotations from the Acts, the field for consultation was very wide. It is not surprising, therefore, that in the preliminary negotiations the trade unions should take the view that the new consultative bodies should have executive functions. What happened in electricity may be quoted. The Herbert Committee's enquiries led it to the following conclusions:

Unlike the national negotiations of terms and conditions of service, joint consultation on a national basis has no tradition behind it and was in fact virtually a new idea in 1947. The discussions between the Authority and the trade unions preliminary to the establishment of machinery for joint consultation revealed a difference in views of its purpose, the unions urging that the new consultative bodies should have executive functions. The Authority did not consider that they or the Area Boards could divest themselves of executive responsibilities which under the Act lay with them, but gave an assurance that, although the machinery must have a purely advisory character, the Electricity Boards would maintain their representation at a level which would ensure that its recommendations were likely to gain acceptance (para. 178).

As a result of these provisions on consultation, the nationalised industries have equipped themselves with a three-tier structure of consultative committees. At the top there is a National Committee; then there are District or Regional Committees and finally local committees at the pit, power station or gasworks. The workers' representatives on the National and Regional Committees are trade union officials, who are appointed in the same proportions as members of their unions bear to the total number of workers in the industry. The local committee contains workers' representatives elected by ballot, though local union officials may be members *ex officio*.

In electricity the Electricity Council and the two Scottish Electricity Boards have established in consultation with the trade unions two National Joint Advisory Councils (one for England and Wales and one for Scotland), twelve District J.A.C.s for England and Wales and some 500 Local Advisory Committees (including those in Scotland) to promote, improve and encourage measures affecting the safety, health, welfare and the education and training of employees in the industry and to allow discussion of other matters of mutual interest including efficiency (Electricity Council Report, 1966–7, p. 48, fn.). There are about 10,000 members of District J.A.C.s and Local A.C.s and the N.J.A.C. keep in touch by means of a quarterly booklet.

In gas there are also 'some 400 Joint Consultative Committees' (Gas Council Report, 1965–6, para. 184). These function under the auspices of the National and Area Joint Councils, but unlike the case in electricity, they deal not only with consultation but also wages and conditions of employment.

In the case of the Transport Commission the usual machinery for consultation was set up, but in 1955, impressed by the need of improving productivity, the Commission set up a British Railways Productivity Council. This consisted of senior members of management and senior representatives of trade unions who met monthly under the chairmanship of a member of the Commission. In subsequent Annual Reports from 1955 to 1959 there are references to the efforts of this Council to improve productivity.

The Report on British Railways from the Select Committee on Nationalised Industries, published in 1960, lists in paragraphs 281–7 the achievements of this Council. Some success had been achieved in the maintenance of the permanent way and in office work. But as the threat of redundancy has always hung over railway staffs, their co-operation is naturally very difficult to obtain.

The Productivity Council continued to function with the British Railways Board, which took over in 1963 from the Transport Commission, but information as to its activities is scanty. The general question of productivity in recent years has become interlocked with agreements on pay and conditions of employment, and will therefore be dealt with later in this chapter.

Can we make an attempt to assess the results of this elaborate machinery for joint consultation which was set up in all the nationalised industries in obedience to Acts of Parliament? What was the purpose of this machinery? How has it been regarded and worked both by management and workers? Are both sides satisfied with the results achieved, and if not, why not?

Joint consultation is not confined to the nationalised industries; it is known in private enterprise but there it varies considerably. But in the nationalised industries it was a sudden creation imposed by Parliament; in private enterprise it would be a slow and gradual growth, varying in form from unit to unit and having local roots and characteristics. This suddenness of creation presented a serious problem both to the management and to the workers and the trade unions which represented them.

As we have seen in Chapter 10 the management in the national-ised industries found the change-over produced a drastic upheaval in status and authority. Whereas previously they had worked in a clearly defined unit, often not very large, with their responsibilities known to all concerned, they now found themselves a small part of a gigantic unit whose operations might be on a national scale. Adjustment to such a severe change was difficult enough, but joint consultation added to the difficulties. A manager would now sit on a local committee and discuss with his workers' representatives many problems which hitherto he had settled for himself – often without having to report to anyone. He would find himself faced with men who felt that they had won a victory in securing the nationalisation of their industry, and now expected to reap the fruits of victory. He was responsible to his superiors for the efficient and economic operation of the unit of which he was manager; any falling off in that respect could hardly be attributed to the local committee.

Naturally, therefore, many managers would find it difficult to meet the demands of their workers' representatives. They were not sure what would be the consequences of compliance. The workers were organised in national unions; a concession in one committee would be quoted as a precedent in another committee. The manager might feel, therefore, that unwittingly he had committed his Board to a change or a form of expenditure which would spread far and would be unwelcome to his superiors. The easy way out would be for the matter to go to the District Council. From there the management representatives, if at all doubtful, would send the case to the National Council. So there would be a tendency for all but the most trivial matters to wend their way up to the top, with delay and frustration to the men who had raised the subject locally. In electricity, where the machinery for joint consultation is most elaborate, all the minutes of each council are automatically sent to its superior council; that would mean disagreements are automatically reported.

It is interesting to note that on British Railways the joint consultation rules forbade the reporting upwards of such disagreements. But in 1956 these rules were cancelled and 'an amended procedure agreed with the trade union representatives provides, in an important new clause, that should any difficulties arise at the normal level of consultation, these can be referred to headquarters level to smooth out' (1956 Report of Transport Commission, para. 61).

Joint consultation was provided in the Acts because the trade unions and the Labour Party took the view that industrial democracy should be the rule in publicly-owned industries. But what is 'industrial democracy'? The Acts provided for consultation on such matters as welfare, health and safety: that was straightforward. But what about the 'organisation and conduct of operations' and 'efficiency in the operation of the Commission's services'? Such phrases opened up a vast and unknown territory. Joint consultation was advisory to management and management might reject the advice. But that was not how many trade unions and their members saw it. They had won a long battle by bringing the industry under public ownership; they were given rights to be consulted on all kinds of matters hitherto outside their purview – vaguely described in the Acts. What were these new rights for except to enable them to make management conform to their views? Is it surprising that in electricity supply the unions should urge 'that the new consultative bodies should have executive functions'? (Herbert Committee Report, para. 178). Many influential workers had dreamed of 'workers' control' in the industries taken over. Trade unions in 1944 had decided to accept something much less, but they were not prepared to be put off with agreement on trivial matters, and for the rest, to be listened to politely by management with no result at all.

Management, in its bewilderment at all the changes which had suddenly befallen it, did not appreciate the significance of joint consultation, especially on the national level. But the trade union attitude was so confused as to be dangerous. Their concept that the Joint Consultative Councils were a medium through which their views were to be conveyed to and accepted by management was tantamount to a claim for power without responsibility – and such a claim was intolerable.

Fundamentally the trouble was that trade unions are not organised for this purpose of joint consultation. Enthusiasts may contest that 'from the beginning, the trade union movement had had in its collective consciousness – perhaps more accurately in its "collective unconsciousness" [*sic*] – a blurred outline of some future state of industrial democracy' (A. M. F. Palmer in *Problems of Nationalised Industry*, ed. W. A. Robson, p. 132). But even if the movement as a whole had dreamed of industrial democracy, it was a difficult matter when individual trade unions were suddenly put into a position of influence, for which they had not prepared themselves.

To begin with there was the problem of deciding which union should be represented on the Joint Consultative Councils. Only in coal-mining could one union claim to represent the workers as a whole, and even the National Union of Mineworkers had 'splinter' unions, such as the Colliery Winders, to handle. But that was the only case of 'one industry – one union'. The ambitions of the National Union of Railwaymen to become the industrial union for the railways have repeatedly been frustrated by the Locomotive Engineers and Firemen on the one hand and the Transport Salaried Staffs on the other. Even in gas, where most of the manual workers belong to the National Union of General and Municipal Workers (the original Gas Workers' Union), they form only a small fraction of that large general union.

Each union, therefore, took care to claim the maximum representation on the Joint Consultative Councils which could possibly be justified by the number of its members in the industry. Having secured the fullest representation possible, they would then support most strongly those cases where their members benefited most. In other words, inter-union rivalry was brought into the councils from the outside world.

Another difficulty was the character of trade union representation on the National and District Councils. Naturally the trade unions appointed their officials, national or district. But these men already had full-time posts. Now they found themselves faced with attendance at councils or committees dealing with a vast range of multifarious subjects, most of which had been referred up from below. They had to master these subjects because they had to come to a decision. Often their training and experience unfitted them to cope with a particular issue.

In the debates in Parliament there was a strong demand that the iron and steel workers should be represented on the British Steel Corporation. This was steadfastly refused by the Minister of Power, and the Iron and Steel Act 1967 is silent on this point. But it contains, of course, all the usual provisions regarding consultation, etc. which have been discussed in this chapter.

Nevertheless, one concession on workers' representation has been made by the Corporation. It is organising the steel industry into four groups, which will be managed by Boards; these are non-statutory and are appointed by the Corporation. An undertaking was given that there would be some part-time workers' representatives on these group Boards, and three workers have been appointed to each Board.

In the twenty years since the nationalised industries came into being there has been a great improvement in the standard of living of workers in all industries. Despite rapid inflation they have been able to take advantage of full employment to move ahead of the depreciating value of their pay packets. How have the workers in the nationalised industries fared compared with the workers in private enterprise?

Unlike coal and railways, the gas and electricity industries have been able to afford steady employment without fears of redundancy. In the 1950s the gas industry was static and could not therefore offer bright prospects of expansion and favourable treatment; but that has passed away with the developments of the sixties. In the next few years the gas industry will undergo a revolution and many of its workers will require retraining. But there should be no difficulties over that, as industrial relations in the gas industry have always been excellent. The National Union of General and Municipal Workers, which caters for industrial workers in gas, has always shown an intelligent approach to the problems of the gas industry.

Electricity supply has been the most prosperous of all the nationalised industries. They have had difficulties with their trade unions and there have been unfortunate incidents such as go-slows at some power stations. For a period the Electrical Trades Union was Communist-controlled.

I

During 1963 in the course of negotiations with the trade unions for a revision of scales of pay, hours of works, etc., a scheme was produced for giving the industrial employees 'staff' status. In the course of 1964 and 1965 this scheme was negotiated and agreed between the Electricity Council and the trade unions and brought into force by stages. The scheme was described by a Court of Enquiry as 'admirable and imaginative in conception' and its main features can be briefly summarised as follows:

1. All industrial employees were to receive annual salaries instead of hourly rates of pay.
2. They had the same sick pay benefits as technical and administrative staff.
3. There was an employee co-operation agreement. 'The new salaries incorporated payments for employee co-operation with management to improve job efficiency and service to the consumer by eliminating overtime working, wherever possible, by the best possible utilisation of the number of men and man hours to complete any particular job and by the acceptance of practices which improve individual and collective efficiency.' This is described as 'essentially a long-term project' (Electricity Council Report 1964–5, para. 193).
4. There was a variety of new work patterns. A staggered working week allowing the five days work to be spread over the seven days of the week as required, Saturday and Sunday being treated as normal working days. The winter/summer stagger allowed an agreed number of working hours to be transferred from winter to summer, when conditions were better for outdoor work. Allowances were paid for inconvenience caused.
5. There were also improved holidays for longer-service employees and a reduction in the standard working week from 42 to 40 hours from 5 July 1965.

This change-over was applied gradually. In 1966–7 42 per cent of the industrial employees were working on staggered work patterns. One clear result of the agreement was a reduction in overtime working. In October 1964 the average weekly hours of adult male employees were 49·4 per week – that is, overtime amounted to 7·4 hours per standard working week of forty-two hours. By January 1967 the average had fallen to 41·4 hours – that is, overtime amounted to 1·4 hours on a forty-hour week. This substantial reduction in overtime showed how much productivity per hour was increased under the new scheme.

The National Board for Prices and Incomes scrutinised this

scheme in its Report on Productivity Agreements (Cmnd. 3311). As regards its effect on pay the Board's conclusion is (para. 180): 'Weekly and hourly rates of pay in Electricity Supply have risen by considerably more than those of almost any other industry in the country, but increases in weekly earnings have been relatively modest and below the national average.' In other words the chronic trouble about 'wage drift' – the more rapid advance of earnings than of wage rates– has been checked in electricity supply.

There were transitional costs of £4–£5 million in implementing the agreements, but without the agreements there would have been the 'recurring effect of increases in labour costs, which would have been considerable'.

The Prices and Incomes Board summarises the three main gains of the agreements as follows:

1. A closer assimilation of manual staff to other groups.
2. The elimination of waste associated with high overtime and the opportunities for better planning which this opened up.
3. The achievement of a contract of employment which now properly reflects the pattern of need (Appendix D of Report).

The last gain is particularly true of the C.E.G.B., far more than in the case of the Area Boards. The Generating Board introduced stagger patterns of work promptly and sweepingly and by June 1967 they affected 90 per cent of its manual staff. The effect on the workers in power stations is that they have rotated a five-day week spread over seven days. Weekend working has been brought much more under control by the elimination of overtime.

There is a great contrast between industrial relations in coal and those in the railways. In the latter industry the public are hardly ever free from a threat of a strike – either official or unofficial, local or national. Though there have been unofficial strikes in coal, the National Union of Mineworkers has never forced the Coal Board to negotiate under threat of a strike. What are the reasons for the different behaviour of the trade unions in the two industries?

The public are vastly more sensitive to trouble on the railways than to trouble in the mines. An unofficial strike in a pit or group of pits hardly earns a mention in the press. Its effect, if any, is local and few members of the public are inconvenienced. With the railways an unofficial strike of some workers at any point of the railway system immediately has noticeable effects. These are news and the treatment of this news by press, radio and television serves to magnify the impact and strengthen the resolve of the strikers to stay out. As a result, threats of unofficial strikes on the railways in some years are almost continuous.

From 1947 to 1957 the miners were in a strong bargaining position. The output of coal was never enough. On the whole, the nation had a guilty conscience about the sufferings of the miners in the inter-war years. Demand for coal was inelastic and frequent price increases did not seem to check the demand. Thus between 1947 and 1957 wages about doubled and in line with this went the cost of raising a ton of deep-mined coal and the price obtained for it. The figures were:

	1947	*1957*	*1966–67*
Earnings per manshift	28/10	60/-	92/4
Costs per ton of saleable coal	41/3	81/6	98/5
Proceeds ,, ,, ,,	40/3	82/-	100/7

But between 1957 and 1966–7 increases in price became infrequent. There was no general increase between September 1960 and April 1966. It was only the 50 per cent increase in productivity between 1957 and 1966–7 which enabled miners to secure increased earnings. But otherwise their bargaining position was weak. With huge stocks of coal lying unsold on the ground a strike would have been futile and the miners and their leaders were aware of the change in their strength and practised restraint. Between 1957 and April 1968 manpower in the industry declined from 710,000 to 361,000. This tremendous decline in manpower meant that the Coal Board had to meet reasonable demands for increased pay and improved conditions; otherwise the rundown of the industry would have accelerated disastrously.

The history of industrial relations on British Railways is sad if not tragic. There are several factors about those relations which should be mentioned.

    1. It is difficult to understand why it was not till the end of 1966 that there was 'a Board Member with special responsibility for industrial relations'. To suggest that this appointment in 1966 'is evidence of the importance which the Board attach to improving their relations with the staff' (1966 Report, para. 25) takes one's breath away. The N.C.B. had such a Board Member in January 1947 when they started. It is true that Sir John Benstead, who had been General Secretary of the National Union of Railwaymen, was a member of the Transport Commission from 1947 to 1961. But

the Commission was not organised on functional lines and Sir John did not appear to be charged with industrial relations.

2. Railway management was faced with three trade unions, between which there was often 'tribal warfare' as *The Economist* once described it. Rivalry was especially strong – even bitter – between the Associated Society of Locomotive Engineers and Firemen and the National Union of Railwaymen. Time and again during the last twenty years management would secure an agreement with one union, only to be baulked by another. The footplate men organised in A.S.L.E.F. (there was a minority of them in the N.U.R.) had seen their locomotives and fireboxes disappear and the changes to electric and diesel tractions had left them worried and resentful. In April 1966 the railways still employed 15,334 firemen with average earnings of £21.4.0 per week, though steam locomotives were rapidly disappearing and will soon have disappeared entirely.

3. Rates of pay on the railways are national rates of pay. A porter in a village in Herefordshire is on the same scale of pay as a porter in Birmingham or Euston. The result is that in areas of full employment where high earnings are prevalent the Railways Board cannot keep staff, whereas in country districts they are over-manned. But improvements in pay are geared to the requirements of the areas which are short of staff, so too much is being paid in the other areas.

4. In the inter-war years when the railways were a depressed industry, railwaymen (like miners) were badly paid. There was therefore much leeway to be made up. Railwaymen are now reasonably well paid – of course by working overtime, as is the case with many other industries. A comprehensive census undertaken in April 1966 showed that railway industrial workers earned on the average £20.14.0 a week compared with a national average of £20.5.0 a week. Railwaymen worked on the average 47·8 hours a week compared with a national average of 46·4 and their average earnings per hour was eight shillings and eightpence compared with a national average of eight shillings and ninepence. Railwaymen are no longer underpaid.

The most important development in industrial relations on the railways since the war was the Report of an independent enquiry into the relativity of the pay of British Railways staff with that of the staff of the other nationalised industries, public services and appropriate private undertakings. The enquiry was presided over by the Cambridge economist Mr Guillebaud and its Report, known as the Guillebaud Report, was published on 2 March 1960. This Report provided a system of wage determination based wholly on specific comparisons with the pay of workers in other industries. This principle was accepted by all concerned – Government, Transport Commission and railway unions.

It led to an immediate substantial increase in pay in 1960 and was followed by regular increases at frequent intervals. The effect of these increases was that reductions in operating costs were regularly absorbed by higher wages and improved working conditions. Between 1962 and 1966 'determined and continuous efforts to secure economies and to introduce improved operating methods have produced gross annual savings of £115 million' (Annual Report for 1966, para. 5). Because of higher wages and improved working conditions, these efforts of Dr Beeching's regime 'had a relatively small impact on the financial results'. In January 1963 railway staff numbered 503,000 and cost £334·4 million a year or 63 per cent of working expenses of the railways. In January 1966 the corresponding figures were 388,000, but the cost had risen to £351·4 million or 65 per cent of working costs. Naturally the deficit on railway working had only declined from £87 million in 1963 to £78 million in 1966.

As time wore on the Guillebaud principles came in for increasing criticism, especially in view of the intractable deficit on railway operations. In the end the Government referred the whole question to the National Board for Prices and Incomes, which issued its Report on 12 January 1966 (Cmnd. 2873). The Government had issued a White Paper on Prices and Incomes Policy which accepted that comparability must play some part in wage determination, but required that it should be given 'less weight than hitherto'. The Prices and Incomes Board concluded that the Railways Board should cease to determine claims for increased pay by reference to the Guillebaud principles. It pointed out that the comparisons had been between rates of pay and not between earnings; that there had been assumed an unchanged relationship between the different categories of railway workers despite changes in railway working; and finally that the Guillebaud principles had crowded out other criteria in determining wage claims.

The Prices and Incomes Board proposed instead that railway management and unions should get together to set up Pay and Productivity Councils. Meanwhile the offer by the Railways Board of a 3½ per cent rise made in the autumn of 1965 should stand, until the Pay and Productivity Councils had produced a programme by October 1966.

This Report of the Prices and Incomes Board was followed by a threat of a national railway strike, which was only averted at the last moment by the intervention of the Prime Minister, who undertook to start discussions on the basis of future negotiations on pay and conditions, which would include the problems of devising a new pay structure relating pay to productivity. As a sop to the unions the $3\frac{1}{2}$ per cent increase which had been arranged for October 1966 was brought forward to September 1966; but in view of the standstill on prices and incomes this increase was not paid till March 1967. Meanwhile the discussions on devising a pay structure related to productivity have continued under the aegis of the Ministry of Labour (now the Department of Economics and Productivity). At the time this book goes to press no definite result has emerged from these discussions. Productivity on the railways has therefore been under discussion since 1955, when the British Railways Productivity Council was set up. The results have been negligible.

A fact which should be noted is that increases in railwaymen's pay are not earned but are found by the taxpayer out of the annual grant paid to the Railways Board on the vote of the Ministry of Transport. The gross receipts of the railways in 1966 were £464 million; with an average number of 374,000 workers, the average gross output of each railwayman was £1,240 for 1966. The average earnings for 1966 was £1,086; the difference of £154 is clearly grossly inadequate to pay for all the substantial costs, other than labour, required to run a railway system. But there is hardly a suggestion that steps must be taken by increased productivity to reduce the burden on the taxpayer. The silly and miserable dispute about guards travelling in the rear cab of diesel locomotives shows the extent to which inter-union jealousy and bitterness can go; it seems impossible for the railway unions to understand how much they antagonise public opinion by their behaviour. Clearly there has been a serious decline in morale and responsibility, which is largely attributable to the persistent and huge open-ended subsidy, which so far had defied all efforts to control. It is doubtful whether the Transport Bill, now going through Parliament, will make much difference. Indeed, as we saw in Chapter 3, it is likely to bring other unions, such as the Transport Workers, into the endless inter-union disputes which bedevil industrial relations on the railways.

The general conclusion might be that workers in the nationalised industries have fared neither better nor worse than workers in the private sector. The full employment, prevalent since 1945, has put all workers in a strong bargaining position and many employers have paid in excess of their obligations, through fear of losing valuable labour. The only industry in which workers have derived benefit from public ownership is the railways. If the railways had not been nationalised the enormous subsidies from the taxpayer would not have been forthcoming and the railways would have shrunk to a fraction of their present size. Hundreds of thousands of railwaymen would have found other employment – to the benefit of the national economy.

12 The Consumer and the Nationalised Industries

NATIONALISATION brought up the question of the rights of the consumer. Before nationalisation the problem did not exist, though on occasion consumers, when roused, did band themselves together to resist a powerful public utility. There was, for instance, the famous case of the South Metropolitan Gas Company in 1936, when strong protests led to a public enquiry and a climb-down by the Company. But if you did not like coal *A* you bought coal *B*. Many of the gas and electricity undertakings were municipal and local opinion, through elections, could hardly have a decisive influence on their policy. Even when they were company undertakings, they were local in character and susceptible to local views. Railways were always a cause for grumble and it was often felt that railway companies were too vast to be human.

Nationalisation changed all that. The consumer had been helpless all through the war, being thankful to take what was given. In 1947 when the transfer to public ownership started, he was still under a war-time regime with slight modifications. He was still rationed in many basic necessities – food, coal, clothes, petrol, etc. Quality was often poor and quantity inadequate. And now for some of these necessities he found himself dependent on vast statutory Public Corporation, as remote and inaccessible as can be imagined.

All the nationalised industries were in difficulties when taken over and some were in very poor shape. Inadequate supplies of dirty and sometimes incombustible coal were matched by frequent instances of load-shedding, or voltage reductions which reduced your electric light to a glimmer. The volume of street lighting was reduced. Reductions in gas pressures made the boiling of a kettle a prolonged trial and to be sure of cooking your breakfast quickly you were wise to get up very early in the morning. And then there were the slow, dirty and crowded trains, often inadequately lighted and heated, which made the daily journey to and from work a misery.

From 1947 these services were provided by vast corporations working remotely aloof from their suffering consumers in vast office blocks or country mansions. Newspapers were full of stories of these palatial buildings with their growing bureaucracies. When the chairman of the Yorkshire Electricity Board was sent to prison for spending on his country mansion headquarters more than was authorised by his building licences, many felt that their worst suspicions had been justified.

So the nationalised industries started life on the worst possible terms with their consumers, who were simply the nation as a whole, and this all-important fact for some years dominated the public attitude. It was a most unfortunate start and only long and patient effort in bettering services could bring about improvement.

Nationalisation was not intended primarily to benefit the consumers. It is true that Labour ministers, in advocating nationalisation, made vague promises to consumers, but the Socialists who worked hard to promote transfers to public owner- ship were motivated by the desire to rescue the workers from exploitation by the capitalist. It was assumed that if the capitalist were expropriated and his excessive profits disappeared, not only would the workers benefit, but from the profits thus saved there would be benefits to the consumer. In any case the capitalist had made his excessive profits not only by exploiting his workers but by fleecing his consumers, to whom he sold shoddy and indifferent goods. The industries under public ownership would no longer be motivated by greed, but would be operated for the common good or, as we would now describe it, 'in the national interest'. The consumer, no longer fleeced by the capitalist, would receive better goods and better service from the publicly-owned industries, and his suffering at the hands of the capitalist would become a thing of the past.

Public ownership was a horn of plenty, and though definite benefits would accrue to the workers in the industries, there was such ample sufficiency that the consumers would benefit sub- stantially.

As we saw in Chapter 1 the Webbs, with their clear and logical minds, were anxious that 'the citizen consumer' should have a voice in running the publicly-owned industries. They were not prepared to let the producers dominate and on their proposed Boards the representatives of the producers were balanced by representatives of the consumers. It is interesting that in France, the birthplace of

Syndicalism, consumers are represented on the governing Boards of their nationalised industries.

By 1945 the Webbs were outmoded. Labour proposals did not envisage any domination of the industries by the workers; representation of the consumers was therefore out of the question. The proposed Public Corporations were to give the trade unions full scope for consultation, etc., but the unions did not ask for and were not given representation on the new Boards. Usually each Board numbered among its members a leading trade unionist, whose province was 'labour relations'; but he was a Board member and not a trade union representative.

Therefore consumers could not be represented. They were not organised and could not be organised. The basic industries which were taken over after 1945 had the whole nation as their consumers. But something had to be done for the consumer; it was impossible to leave him defenceless against these giant statutory monopolies on which he was dependent for necessities such as coal, transport, gas and electricity. So the various Acts provided for some form of consumers' council.

The earliest, the Coal Industry Nationalisation Act, provided for two Consumers' Councils – an Industrial and a Domestic Coal Consumers' Council. They were to be appointed by the Minister of Fuel and Power. Surprisingly the Act provided that the council should consist not only of representatives of the consumers, but of the traders in and producers of coal, i.e. the coal merchants, the National Coal Board and the Gas Council (for coke). These Councils were to be national bodies, though the Act gave the Minister power to appoint regional councils – a power he has never used. The staff of the councils were to be provided by the Minister. The Councils could make representations to the Minister about the policy of the Board and if he were satisfied of the soundness of their representations, he could give a direction to the Board to mend its ways; no such direction has ever been given. The Councils were to make annual reports to the Minister, which he was to lay before Parliament.

It is interesting to note that when the Iron and Steel Bill was laid before Parliament in 1966, it provided (Section 8) for an Iron and Steel Consumers' Council, which included representation of the British Steel Corporation; this was a parallel to coal. In the Lords an amendment was moved deleting this representation. The Government accepted the amendment and the government spokesman, Lord Shackleton, admitted that 'the need to increase the independence of the Consumers Council is decisive and that it is necessary to make plain that the Council is really an independent body' (House of Lords Report, vol. 280, 9 March 1967). But no steps have been taken to amend the 1946 Coal Industry Nationalisation Act. *Mutatis mutandis*, the other Nationalisation Acts set up similar bodies. The Transport Act 1947 (Section 6) provided for a Central Transport Consultative Committee for Great Britain. Transport Users' Consultative Committees were to be set up for Scotland and Wales and other regions the Minister might select. Nine Area Committees were accordingly set up for England.

In the Electricity Act 1947 a new title was found for the consumers' organisation – Consultative Councils. As the Central Electricity Authority was a manufacturer and wholesaler to the Area Electricity Boards, who distributed retail, it was only the latter who were equipped with these Consultative Councils. In view of the strong local authority influence in electricity, between 50 per cent and 60 per cent of their members were to be drawn from a panel of persons prepared by local authority associations for the Area. The remainder were to be representatives of agriculture, commerce, industry, labour and general interests of consumers of electricity. A significant change was that the chairman of the Consultative Council was to be a member of the Area Board; he could thus act as a link between Board and Council. This is the only representation of the Board on the Council and of the Council on the Board.

Each Consultative Council was to prepare schemes for local committees so as to enable the Council to keep in closer touch with the consumers. Such schemes have generally been made and local committees appointed.

While the Electricity Bill was going through Parliament there emerged a general desire to widen the functions of the Consultative Councils. They were accordingly given powers to enquire into any matter of interest to consumers, and not merely to act on representations. If they made a report to an Area Board and were not satisfied with the result they could approach the Central Electricity Authority, who could give a direction to an Area Board. If, in turn, they were not satisfied with the decision of the Authority, they could approach the Minister. If he, after due consultation with all concerned, was satisfied that some defect had been revealed, he could notify the defect to the Central Authority, which would then issue a direction to the Area Board to remedy the defect.

The Gas Act, as was to be expected, followed closely the model of the Electricity Act of the previous year, and the Consultative Councils for gas are, except in a few matters, similar to the Consultative Councils for electricity.

The main difference between the Gas and Electricity Councils is that the Gas Act 1948 provided for complete autonomy of the Area Gas Boards. Consequently there is no possible contact between the Gas Consultative Councils and the Gas Council; the former, if they wish to press a case, go direct to the Minister.

As we have seen in Chapter 5 the Gas Council's original powers were greatly extended by the Gas Act 1965. The advent of North Sea gas will undoubtedly mean that in the 1970s the gas industry will be much more highly integrated than hitherto and that the Gas Council will be in much greater control of the bulk supplies which they will distribute to the Area Boards. Lack of contact between the Gas Council and the Consultative Councils will become an increasingly serious defect, which should be remedied at an early date.

The Gas Consultative Councils have set up local committees in the same manner as in electricity.

These Consumers' Committees, or Consultative Councils, have not impressed the people they were intended to serve. The powers given to these bodies broadened out in the later Acts, and the Consultative Councils were intended to be consulted by the Area Boards before they made any changes in policy. They have been consulted fairly often. One had only to read the Reports of the Councils to see how Area Boards take care to lay before them the facts of the situation, and how in nearly every case the Council finds no alternative but to give their agreement. The Reports of the meetings between Boards and Councils usually find their way into the Press, and the public are therefore warned of what is going to happen – usually an increase in charges. But the drill seems ineffectual. The Boards do not regard the Councils as real partners; rather they are sounding-boards for decisions already reached by themselves. The Council cannot hope to challenge the facts presented to it by the Board. They are complicated and technical and with the best will in the world it finds that, save for an odd question or two, it must bow to the inevitable. Perhaps both the Board and the Council are victims of forces which have both of them in their grip. But it is the Board which has the initiative and makes the decisions; the Consultative Council plays the part of a chorus in a Greek play, making obvious comments, often platitudinous.

The Acton Society Trust, in its study *Relations with the Public*, has pointed out that these Councils have no direct contact with the public and cannot therefore reflect consumer opinion. If they were to do so, they would have to be much more highly organised. It is difficult to expect a body of unpaid public-spirited persons to embark on consumer research, especially when the Councils are only equipped with a secretary.

The failure of ministers to provide funds for these Councils led the Acton Society Trust to this conclusion:

> The reluctance, even of Labour ministers, to sanction expenditures on advertising opens them to the charge either that they had little faith in the utility of the councils, or else that they had too much and did not wish to provide an effective outlet for complaints; and indeed about the whole structure there is a depressing air of an empty and insincere gesture to the idea of popular control. But now that management and labour are organised in powerful blocks for the representation, and indeed the negotiation, of their views, can the consumer preserve his position unless he is also organised, not merely to represent his views equally effectively, but actually to negotiate on a basis of strength? (*Relations with the Public*, p. 25).

The Acton Society Trust also pointed out that there was no real two-way traffic between the Boards and the public. 'The flow of information to the Boards is haphazard and inadequate; the flow of information outwards is copious but since much of it is based on a superficial study of public interests and tastes, it too often seems irrelevant and is ignored. . . . The nationalised industries carry on largely with the momentum generated by private enterprise, and seem little aware of the dangers of gradually drifting more and more out of touch with public thought' (p. 10).

The Acton Society Trust drew attention to the fact that the National Coal Board, in its Report of 1950, only allotted 'three-quarters of a page to the consumer and there is no reference to any complaints such as those concerning dirty coal'. That was written in 1953.

But the section of the Annual Report of the Coal Board, 'Relations with Consumers', which the Acton Society Trust complains is only three-quarters of a page, disappears altogether from the Annual Reports for 1954, 1955 and 1956 which do not even mention the Consumer Councils. And it is not only in the Report for 1950 that there is no reference to complaints about dirty coal; there is no reference to any such complaints in any of the Board's Reports up to 1956.

In 1957, however, demand for coal was five million tons less than in 1956 – the first drop in demand since the war. This jolted the N.C.B., and in the Report for 1957 the section on 'Relations with Consumers' reappeared. *Inter alia*, this referred to the quality of coal supplied and advised on the machinery for dealing with complaints on quality. There was also a longish section on 'The Shortage of Large Coal' which had been a constant source of trouble.

But in 1958 consumption of coal fell by a further 10 million tons. This caused alarm and there appeared in the 1958 Report a section entitled 'Service to Consumers'. In 1959 coal consumption fell by a further 12½ million tons and in a new section in the 1959 Report entitled 'Coal in Competition' the N.C.B. showed that it had become fully aware of the necessity of wooing the consumer. The Board 'undertook a big expansion in their sales service'; this was supplemented by an increase in general publicity and advertising. The indifference to the consumer shown by the Board in the early fifties had now disappeared. Coal was now 'in competition' and the consumer was exercising his sovereign right of choice.

It is not surprising that when the nationalised industries have been under discussion the Consumers' Councils have been severely criticised. There was an interesting general debate on the nationalised industries in the House of Commons on 25 October 1950 (*Hansard*, vol. 478). It was the early days of nationalisation, but the general verdict on Consumers' Councils was adverse. Mrs White, for instance, criticised them on the grounds that they were nominated bodies remote from the consumer. They were divorced from local government and the public knew very little about them. Mr Summers (now Sir Spencer Summers) quoted from the Fabian pamphlet *Nationalisation and the Consumer* that the reports of the Councils were 'limp and platitudinous documents'. It is difficult to avoid the word 'platitudinous documents' when reading the Reports of the Councils. Another criticism has been that as the offices and staffs of the Councils are provided by the Boards, they must fall under the influence of the Boards and cannot strike out an independent line.

The fact that on the Coal Consumer Councils the National Coal Board is represented as well as the consumer, has given rise to criticism. The Board naturally sends able and expert representatives; the laymen representing the consumer must feel helpless when confronted with experts. Full and frank ventilation of grievances is difficult in the presence of representatives of the producer. The consumers should, it is suggested, be free from such tutelage.

This also applied to the Transport Consultative Committees, of which representatives of the Transport Commission are members. Perhaps the role of these committees has, on the whole, been the most frustrating of all. Nevertheless the Central Transport Consultative Committee has produced frank and forthright Reports. In the Report for 1958 there are three paragraphs (49–51) on 'Cleanliness of Trains' which are outspoken.

The system of ensuring that coaches are properly cleaned, both inside and out, is not as effective as it should be. . . . The war has been over for fourteen years and standards have not been fully restored. The time has come for a real drive to put this matter right, and to revive that pride in his job and his service which was a characteristic of the old-time railwayman, and without which no satisfactory standard can be maintained.

To judge from frequent complaints this spirited protest of ten years ago has had a limited effect.

A simple service to the consumer is the carrying of his luggage by a porter. One railway regional management announced in the Press that it was 'no part of a porter's duties to carry passengers' hand luggage; that porters only did so as an act of grace, and that by doing so they became agents of the passengers, so that the management was not liable for loss of, or damage to, the luggage' (1958 Report, para. 52). A more inept statement it would be difficult to conceive, but it had a solid foundation. The Central Transport Consultative Committee had gone into the matter and found:

that, after nationalisation, a condition had been inserted into the contract which the passenger makes with the Commission each time he purchases a ticket, providing that the relationship of principal and agent does exist between a passenger and a porter who carries his bag 'at the termination of a journey', and that the journey does not 'terminate' as one would suppose, when the passenger and his bag leave the terminal station, but at the moment that the bag is deposited upon the platform beside the train in which it has been conveyed (1958 Report, para. 54).

The protest did some good, because the 1959 Report records that the Transport Commission has now withdrawn the obnoxious condition.

But the Transport Commission, alone of all the nationalised industries, had to face the consumer in open struggle. Every time there was an application for an increase in charges, or fares, the Transport Tribunal held a public enquiry. The representatives of the Transport Commission had to make their case and submit to cross-examination by Counsel for all kinds of consumers – local authorities, traders' organisation, unofficial organisations of passengers and so on. The hearings often lasted many days, were carried out in public and were reported in the Press. Uniquely in 1952, when there was a great agitation about increases in fares, the Government intervened and issued a direction to the Commission.

In its Annual Reports the Commission repeatedly complained of the delays involved in these enquiries and hearings, and the losses experienced as a result. Indeed, until 1956 it was claiming that it would not have been in deficit but for these prolonged enquiries. Small wonder, therefore, if the Transport Commission felt it had been treated with particular severity in its relations with the consumer.

In 1955 the Herbert Committee examined the work of the Electricity Consultative Councils and in chapter 20 of its Report it gives the results of its scrutiny.

'In a quiet and modest way the Consultative Councils have done and are doing creditable work in safeguarding the consumers' interest, but there is little doubt, in our opinion, that the vast majority of electricity consumers throughout the country are completely ignorant of the existence or purpose of the Consultative Councils.'

The Committee makes suggestions for improving and strengthening the membership of the councils. It suggests a smaller proportion of local authority nominations and wider representations of other interests. It also considered the arrangement whereby the chairman of the council is *ex officio* a member of the Area Board and came to the conclusion that, on the whole, it was a sound arrangement. It suggested – and this is important – that councils should be allowed to spend some money on making themselves known to the public. The Minister would approve the expenditure and recover it from the Area Board. It also suggested that the various local committees should be strengthened and encouraged and thus 'progress can be made in making the councils more effective and also more acceptable to the public'.

These various suggestions, so far as they required legislation, were incorporated in the Electricity Act 1957, the First Schedule of which is devoted to the reorganisation of the Consultative Councils.

The Act lowered the minimum of local authority representation from 50 to 40 per cent, thus allowing for more members from industry, etc. As the Act abolished the Central Authority and made the Area Boards autonomous, the new arrangements provided for ultimate reference to the Electricity Council, which could advise the Minister; he in turn, if satisfied that a defect had been disclosed, could give a direction to the Area Board. It should be noted that the Electricity Council cannot give a direction to an autonomous Area Board. In fact, the procedure culminating in a direction either by the Central Authority before 1958 or by the Minister since 1958 has never been used; indeed the direction is an instrument for use in the very last resort and is unlikely ever to be used.

The Herbert Committee's recommendation that the Electricity Consultative Councils should spend money on publicity seems to have had very little effect. Their expenses are met by the Electricity Council, which ten years later in 1966–7 spent £61,530 on twelve Consultative Councils. This average of about £5,000 per Council can only cover the salaries of their small staffs and out-of-pocket expenses of their members, leaving a modest residue for publicity. The Councils have only gone in for some leaflets, posters or local advertisements; there is no indication that they have ever pressed to be allowed to go in for large-scale and expensive publicity.

The fundamental issue was well put, in the debate of 25 October 1950 referred to above, by Mr Lyttelton (now Viscount Chandos) when he said: 'Where a public monopoly is operated with all the force of authority of this House and Ministers who are responsible to this House, there can be no satisfactory protection for the consumer.'

That is the problem. The ordinary citizen, when he has a dispute with these gigantic statutory monopolies, feels helpless. He may deal with a local official of no high status, who may be courtesy itself. He may even deal with a senior official who is also helpful and courteous. But if he gets no satisfaction, he will probably succumb to the feeling that it is useless to pursue the matter. The officials have such limited power that with the best will in the world they cannot give him satisfaction. They have not sufficient discretionary power to vary the rules. Who has then? The Board itself, a remote body fifty or a hundred miles away.

A Board's relations with its consumers is a part – the most important part – of its relations with the public; in the case of a national Board, the public of course is the whole nation. Relations with consumers is an aspect therefore of public relations, and the weakness of the Boards in public relations has contributed to a general feeling of dissatisfaction among consumers. Ministers should consider, when making Board appointments, whether there is one person on each Board with the capacity for explaining the Board's activities to its public. He should be a senior full-time member of the Board with full knowledge of its policy and with the gift of public appeal. He will find it hard going and will have difficult times.

In the 1950s the National Coal Board had probably the poorest reputation for treatment of its consumers. In the 1960s, after Lord Robens became Chairman, the situation was transformed. If anything, the pendulum swung too far and Lord Robens's flair for publicity overstated the case against the government policy of allowing the coal industry to run down. At any rate one could see a public corporation deeply concerned about the future of the industry, for which it was responsible, and appealing to public opinion to support its case.

In the later fifties there broke out what might be described as a revolt of the consumer. It was more than a decade after the end of the Second World War and goods and services were becoming more plentiful. But the quality often left much to be desired. For many articles and services it was still a sellers' market. The millions of unorganised consumers became embittered at their treatment and complaints were loud and frequent. The nationalised industries were not the only suppliers who provoked complaints, but their size and omnipresence made them conspicuous.

This was the period when the unofficial Consumer Association was formed. In 1959 the Board of Trade was prodded into appointing a Committee on Consumer Protection under the chairmanship of Mr J. T. Molony, which reported in 1962. As a result of that Report the Board of Trade set up the Consumer Council.

In paragraph 12 of its Final Report the Molony Committee explained that its remit did not cover services and that as regards the Gas and Electricity Boards 'their functions, duties and monopolistic relationship to the public have been determined as a matter of governmental policy and there is no room to apply the ordinary consumer/retailer/producer principles'. The Committee went on to say: 'In all these nationalised industries Consumers and Consultative Councils have been set up – if, as appears to be the fact, few consumers know of their existence or purpose, such ignorance is also to be found in respect of other established means of consumer protection.'

The only aspect of the nationalised industries which the Committee considered was the sale of solid fuel, which was mainly carried out by merchants, though in some areas such as Lancashire the Coal Board sold retail. Up to 1958 the supply of coal to the domestic consumer was controlled by the Ministry of Power. In conjunction with the Coal Board, the Ministry agreed on grades of domestic coal and the price for each grade. So the consumer was protected to the extent that he knew the grade he was buying and the price he should pay. But there were frequent complaints that the coal contained incombustible material. If one looks back over the period 1945 to 1960, there is little doubt that the repeated complaints and publicity about coal quality did more than anything to drive consumers away from the use of coal.

The Coal Board was well aware that the coal reaching the domestic consumer was frequently unsatisfactory and, as we have seen earlier in this chapter, falling sales from 1958 made it much more consumer-conscious. In fairness to the Coal Board, it had worked hard during the fifties to improve the quality of its 'saleable output'. As the Molony Committee pointed out, the Board had spent by 1960 £60 million on coal preparation plant. By 1960 a procedure had been developed by the National Coal Board 'for giving fair consideration to complaints from merchants who have found it necessary to compensate consumers for sub-standard deliveries' (Molony Report, para. 214).

From May 1962 there came into force an 'Approved Coal Merchant' scheme, whereby Board and coal merchants collaborated in trying to secure for the domestic consumer a fair deal in the coal he bought.

This was, of course, reinforced by the pressure of steadily falling sales in the domestic market. In 1966–7 house-coal sales were 19·3 million tons; in 1956 they had been 30·6 million. The 1966–7 Report of the Coal Board tells us (para. 68) that 'one hundred and twenty Sales Districts were set up during the year. In each of these Sales Districts, a combined effort by the Board, the coal trade and appliance manufacturers and distributors is being organised to achieve a greater concentration of sales effort.' In these conditions complaints from the consumer became scarce.

In the last ten years the Coal Board has therefore become very consumer-conscious in its efforts to stem the decline in sales. The railways also, during that period, have been losing custom both in passenger and freight services, despite the five years' intensive work under the chairmanship of Dr Beeching to cut costs and make the railways viable. In one of his main objectives, the closing of un-economic branch lines, he was largely defeated by the resistance of the consumers. The determination – and even fury – which local interests displayed in fighting those closures was so great that successive Ministers of Transport did not dare to approve proposals, even if they meant substantial financial help to the railways. One senses that in this opposition the users of the railways were hitting back.

In this dogged resistance to the closure of railway passenger services the eleven Area Consultative Committees played a substantial part. Section 56 of the Transport Act 1962 had been of great help to the Committees, as they were authorised to make reports direct to the Minister of Transport, sending copies to the railway Boards concerned and to the Central Transport Consultative Committee. The 1962 Act only permitted the Committees to base their case on 'hardship' and excluded financial or economic considerations; but, nevertheless, they were successful in many cases, where the Minister refused consent to closure. These refusals increased with the advent of the Labour Government in 1964.

Sections 51 and 52 of the Transport Bill of December 1967, introduced by Mrs Castle, continues the work of the Transport Consultative Committees. In particular Section 51 stiffens the conditions for the Minister's consent to the closure of railway passenger services or stations. The Minister will now be em-powered to 'have regard to any matters which for the time being appear to him to be relevant, including any social or economic considerations'. Also the Minister can receive representations from railway employees affected by the proposed closure (Section 51 (1)). In view of these overriding powers of the Minister it is to be expected that proposals for passenger railway closures will seldom come forward.

The gas and electricity industries were in a stronger position than coal and railways. Electricity, in particular, enjoyed a genuine monopoly in the sense that it was indispensable to everyone. Technically both industries give first-class service; there were statutory regulations enforced by the Ministry of Power, which used its authority to make sure the regulations were observed. Both industries were strongly imbued with the Public Utility outlook; and deterioration or interruption of supply was deeply regretted.

But in the sixties there developed stronger resistance from consumers to increases in charges. From vesting day both industries had enjoyed freedom in the matter of charges, far more than coal or railways. Both industries derived great advantage from the fact that usually charges were increased by one Area Board at a time and thus only part of the country was affected. But with the advent of the Labour Government in 1964, and a policy of restraint of prices, gas and electricity found their freedom gone. Further, the pattern of the increases changed. Owing to delays in securing consent to making increases and, in electricity, owing to the changes in the bulk supply tariff of the Central Generating Board, it was decided to make the increases in charges countrywide. All Boards would put up their charges at the same time, but each Board would fix on the amount in the light of its own local circumstances.

So when in September 1967 all the electricity boards increased their charges simultaneously, there was a national outcry which forced the Government to act. They announced that in future all increases in charges by nationalised industries would be submitted for scrutiny to the National Board for Prices and Incomes, whose report they would require before deciding whether to authorise the proposed increases.

The Prices and Incomes Board started with the proposals of the Central Electricity Generating Board to revise its bulk supply tariff on 1 April 1968 and with the proposals of all the Gas Boards for an increase in charges. As the Report of the Prices and Incomes Board came out too late to help the revenues of the Gas Boards in 1967–8, the gas industry inevitably incurred a deficit in that year.

This intervention by the Government, which is dealt with in more detail in Chapter 8, is partly the reflection of the increasing power of the consumer. Where monopoly does not compel him to use the products or services of the industry in question he cuts down his purchases and the benefits of the increase in charges are whittled away. This has resulted in reluctance to approve increases as in the case of certain railway charges and London bus fares; instead the Government give a subsidy which, as usual, is alleged to be temporary.

In February 1968 the Consumer Council published a full and valuable Report on the work of the Consumer and Consultative Councils set up by the Nationalisation Acts. We now have a detailed enquiry into these Councils, after they have been working for twenty years.

The Report shows that these Councils, where they do get the chance, do everything possible to help the consumer; but the criticisms made on them earlier in this chapter are not seriously affected. It is not their fault that they are rather ineffective and to a large extent ignored by the consumer; they have not the staff, finance or expertise to be otherwise.

The extent to which they are ignored by the consumer is brought out in the statistics in the Report. In electricity 5,000 persons were contacted by a sampling survey, of whom 957 had some complaint. But of these 957 persons, only 35 per cent took the trouble to lodge a complaint, of whom 30 per cent went to Board offices and only 1 per cent to the Consultative Council. This is only natural; the consumer will go direct to the people who have the power to put right the defect of which he is complaining. The Consultative Council must inevitably appear somewhat remote and only to be contacted in the last resort.

It is interesting to note that of the 65 per cent of the 957 who took no action, nearly half did so because it was 'too much bother'. In the case of public transport, no less than 77 per cent of the 1,368 persons who had some complaint felt that it was 'too much bother' to take any action. Yet the newspapers carry numerous complaints about unsatisfactory bus or railway services.

The Consumer Council Report makes various proposals for strengthening the machinery of the Consultative Councils, but it is very doubtful whether the proposed changes would make much difference. As the Preface to the Report points out, the government decision of September 1967 to refer all price increases in the nationalised industries to the Prices and Incomes Board, ignoring the Consultative Councils, makes 'it abundantly clear that in neither gas nor electricity is the Consultative machinery adequately geared to deal with issues such as these, which are nationwide in their impact and have a consumer interest that is undeniable'. The fact is that the resistance of the consumer is now so strong that the feeble machinery devised in the statutes to protect him is ignored and the Government has to take direct and positive action. The changes in the relations between the nationalised industries and their consumers can be briefly summarised as follows.

In the first ten years, when goods were in short supply and of poor quality, the consumer took the products of the nationalised industries with grumbles and protests. Prices increased regularly and though the industries in some cases practised economies, the tendency was to pass on to the consumer the burden of rising costs; he had to accept it.

In the second ten years he has become more resistant. Where he can, he avoids having to resort to the products of the nationalised industries, as coal and transport are well aware. Where he cannot avoid being a consumer – particularly in electricity – he has become so vocal in his protests that the Government takes action or at least makes a show of taking action.

PART FOUR

13 Labour Policy on Nationalisation after 1945

As the Second World War was entering its later phases and victory could be glimpsed, the people of Britain began to lift their eyes to the future and to hopes of a better world than they had endured in the inter-war years. In a famous Sunday night broadcast in March 1943 the Prime Minister gave voice to these aspirations. Mr Churchill promised a four years' plan of social reform, including social insurance 'from the cradle to the grave' and a National Health Service. From the point of view of this book there was an interesting reference to state enterprise. 'If we can make state enterprise and free enterprise both serve national interests and pull the national wagon side by side, then there is no need to run into that horrible devastating slump or into that squalid epoch of bickering and confusion which mocked and squandered the hard-won victory which was gained a quarter of a century ago.'

The Prime Minister did not anticipate that the electorate, buoyed up by these hopes, would send him into the wilderness for six years and entrust themselves to the Labour Party.

For Labour the position after the Second World War was immensely more favourable than after the First World War; 1945 was a great improvement on 1918.

As we have seen in Chapter 1 the war-time developments of government controls, etc., had greatly encouraged Sidney Webb and his colleagues to start planning a Socialist Society in which the central feature would be the transfer of important sections of the economy from private to public ownership. Under Sidney's guidance the Labour Party adopted a new Constitution in 1918, in which one section was and is of great importance. This is Clause IV (4); it reads as follows:

To secure for the workers by hand or by brain the full fruits of their industry and the most equitable distribution thereof that may be possible, upon the basis of the common ownership of the means of production, distribution and exchange and the best obtainable system of popular administration and control of each industry or service.

The words 'distribution and exchange' were added in 1929.

Clauses similar to Clause IV (4) were subsequently written into the constitutions of many trade unions.

The 'Khaki Election' of 1918 put into power a Coalition Government headed by Lloyd George in which the dominant element was 334 Conservatives; the Labour Party numbered only 74, of whom 63 would not support the Coalition.

The political situation in 1945 was vastly different. There were 396 Labour Members elected, with a clear majority of 182 over all the other political parties. What was more – and this was very important – many of the leaders of the Labour Party had already been ministers since 1940 and had thus had five years' experience of working in a Government. They were seasoned men with great experience as Cabinet ministers. The levers of power were entirely in the hands of Labour.

What was also in their favour was the system of administration adopted in the Second World War. That system started where the First World War left off. It was a total war and government control of the economy had reached a pitch never before conceived possible. Systems of allocation and rationing were in force for every commodity and some of them were to remain for years to come. There was no intention when the war ended to dismantle this apparatus of controls; indeed it was not possible to do so, for most commodities were in very short supply. Indeed, for a time the Labour Government added controls; for instance the rationing of bread was introduced for a period, and national service was extended in 1949 from 12 to 18 months. Some of the controls, such as rationing of coal, went on until 1958.

It is not surprising, therefore, that the Labour Party were now convinced that a Socialist State could be created. As we have seen in Chapter 1, the General Election Programme *Let us Face the Future* included T.U.C. proposals on nationalisation in their 1944 *Interim Report on Post-War Reconstruction*. The Attlee Government, therefore, started immediately with the nationalisation of the coal mines, and in November 1945 Mr Herbert Morrison announced a programme of nationalisation which would keep Parliament occupied for several years. Each year there would be at least one major nationalisation Bill; in some years such as 1947 Parliament was hard put to it to enact two major Bills, nationalising transport and electricity. The series closed with the nationalisation of steel in 1949.

As time went on and the difficulties of the Labour Government increased, culminating in the 30 per cent devaluation of sterling in September 1949, the resistance to nationalisation increased, culminating in the long-drawn-out battle on steel. Equally the Government found it difficult to go ahead with various half-way measures for controlling industries, such as the Development Councils. The economy was beginning to recover and after ten years of regimentation since 1939, most people were anxious to loosen and reduce rather than to tighten and increase the controls which they encountered at every turn. Many of the controls met with widespread evasion; 'fiddling' became a common word and a common disease. For instance, petrol rationing was widely and systematically evaded and there was general relief when it was ended in May 1950. There was plenty of evidence that this evasion of petrol rationing was resulting in a serious lowering of moral standards. What has been cheerfully accepted as a necessity in a desperate war was despised and rejected five years after the end of the war. Mr Harold Wilson, as President of the Board of Trade, struck a popular note by announcing a 'bonfire of controls'.

When the prgramme of nationalisation, announced in November 1945, had been completed, the question arose what industries were next on the list.

In April 1949 a draft policy statement was issued with the title *Labour Believes in Britain*. This was introduced by Mr Morrison at the Labour Party Conference in June 1949 and endorsed by the Conference. It was substantially the Labour programme for the General Election of February 1950.

The programme contained a list of industries for further nationalisation. These were industrial insurance, cement, sugar, the wholesale meat trade, 'suitable minerals' and water supply. The chemical industry, which was 'vital' and 'basic' to the national interest, would be 'carefully examined' especially as to 'monopolistic concerns such as I.C.I.', which would be nationalised 'if it should prove necessary'. Mr Morrison maintained that these industries were carefully chosen and were not an 'abstract list'.

As we have seen in Chapter 1 industrial insurance was suggested by Sidney Webb in 1918 as suitable for public ownership. The staff who worked in industrial insurance fiercely resisted the new proposal, which was amended to 'mutualisation'. The proposal to nationalise sugar was also resisted by a successful 'Mr Cube' campaign run by Tate & Lyle.

But in February 1950 the General Election reduced the Labour majority to six, which was obviously inadequate for taking over more industries into public ownership. The second Labour Government, which lasted till October 1951, was clearly a tired Government, which did little more than mark time. Some of the leading figures in the first Government, such as Ernest Bevin and Sir Stafford Cripps, were dead; and the Government was further weakened by the resignations of Aneurin Bevan and Harold Wilson.

When the Conservatives took over in October 1951 they immediately took steps to denationalise the iron and steel industry, which had been vested in the Iron and Steel Corporation only in the previous February. The new Government also amended the Transport Act 1947 by limiting the powers of the Transport Commission in the fields of road haulage and road passenger transport.

The Labour Party responded by giving a pledge to renationalise the steel industry, and the events leading up to the implementation of this pledge in the Iron and Steel Act 1967 are described in Chapter 6.

After six years of strenuous governing Labour Party discussions and arguments on plans for further nationalisation died down. Naturally they defended the work of the Boards which they had set up; any criticism of their activities was strongly resented. After dealing with steel and the Transport Commission, the Conservatives announced that they would not interfere with the other nationalised industries; but they made no attempt to formulate a policy in relation to them, and Conservative Ministers who were responsible for the Boards defended them in the manner described in Chapter 8.

One Labour statesman who did give some thought to what was happening in the world of nationalisation was Hugh Gaitskell. He could see what many Labour members did not see – that the unpopularity of the nationalised industries was not merely due to Conservative prejudice. So in July 1956 he published Fabian Tract No. 300 entitled *Socialism and Nationalisation*. In the foreword he explains that most of it had been written in 1953 and that it had not been thoroughly revised.

This Fabian Tract was important because in November 1955 Mr Gaitskell had been elected Leader of the Labour Party. What was more, he could claim to be an expert on nationalisation. At the

Ministry of Fuel and Power he had been concerned with the Acts on coal, electricity and gas and had for a time been Minister responsible for the newly created Boards. As this almost forgotten Tract was the basis of the important discussion at the Labour Party Conference in 1957, which gave rise to many suggestions now prevalent, it is worth while to analyse it in some detail.

He starts with an outline of Socialist ideas and with the traditional case for nationalisation; the word 'traditional' is significant. Those traditional arguments, he admits, are no longer convincing because they relate to a society where all means of production are publicly owned; in other words you have to go to the Communist States to find the complete justification for nationalisation. Hurriedly abandoning this argument, which might mean that the Labour Government should not have gone in for piecemeal nationalisation, he proceeds to examine why the traditional case sounds so weak today.

The anticipation that nationalisation would have redistributed property was obviously not realised, because compensation had to be paid. Mr Gaitskell has never flinched from fair compensation. Nationalisation, however, does help the levelling-up process because 'first, the interest income, though guaranteed, is smaller than the profit income would have been. Secondly – and more important – nationalisation eliminates the possibility of capital gains' (p. 9). So in future a shareholder compelled to take gilt-edged stock in compensation, will know why. Incidentally, Mr Gaitskell tries to have it both ways. Later in his tract (pp. 18 and 19) he contends that the coal-mining industry and the railways were in such a desperate state that they had to be nationalised. 'Indeed it is quite possible that had the railways remained in private ownership, the Government would have been obliged to intervene on behalf of holders of trustee debenture stocks.' What chance then of capital gains for the poor holders of railway equities?

The second argument for nationalisation – full employment for the workers – sounded feebler in the fifties than in the inter-war years. Full employment everywhere; so why bother to nationalise? In any case if nationalised industries like coal and railways are declining, these must shed workers.

He devotes much more care to the third argument – that nationalisation means a transfer of power from irresponsible private owners to responsible public owners. In the past, Socialist literature has depicted the capitalist as exercising tyranny over the worker because of his strong economic position. But he readily admits that that picture, which might have been true of the past, is not true today. There is the great and increasing power of the trade unions. The power 'of employers over workers is nowadays very severely limited by the trade unions' (p. 11), whether the industry is privately or publicly owned.

So nationalisation has made little difference in this question of 'power', except in so far as the trade unions have been formally strengthened by the Nationalisation Acts.

In his analysis Mr Gaitskell refers to the fact that nationalised industries are by definition monopolies, and that in a monopoly both employer and employed are in a very strong position. That is all the more so when the monopoly is statutory, backed by the full authority of Government and Parliament. He goes on to say that 'it must be admitted that demands for nationalisation and workers' control are sometimes associated with the desire of a little group of workers to get more for themselves; if not at the expense of the shareholders, then at a cost to the rest of the community' (p. 12). But he points out that 'such attitudes have nothing in common with the ideals of socialism'.

He then suggests that the trade unions in the nationalised industries 'have done their best to assist in creating a new spirit in the industries which will give better results for the community as well as for those who work in the industries' (p. 12). It would have been helpful if Mr Gaitskell had produced evidence for this statement. Indeed Mr Gaitskell contradicts himself in the next sentence where he says, 'but generally speaking, they have preferred only to retain the traditional function of the unions'. Further he suggests, on page 33, that if, to promote public savings, the nationalised industries made larger profits, the result could probably be higher wage claims.

In considering the question of the 'power' of management, Mr Gaitskell suspects that there is little to choose between private or public ownership. He doubts, for instance, whether 'it would be possible to eliminate all power and influence of this kind [of the manager] in any society, however democratic or socialist'. As the nationalised industries have complete freedom on 'day-to-day' matters, the managers of those industries are allowed to exercise that power without being answerable for it.

Then there is the question of 'parliamentary accountability'. As a former Minister closely associated with nationalised industries

Mr Gaitskell is conscious of the dilemma which can be put simply as follows: the more independent the nationalised boards, the more they will exercise power without 'accountability'; the less they are independent, the greater the risks of government control and lack of enterprise.

This central dilemma is disposed of by the suggestion that 'on the whole present arrangements are best'.

The continued anxiety on the part of both Parliament and public over the fact that nationalised monopolies are difficult to control, is not examined in detail, and he suggests that the present informal arrangements between ministers and the nationalised Boards present probably the best answer. But, as we have found in Chapters 7 and 8, these informal arrangements are outside Parliament's control and represent an extension of ministerial power for which ministers cannot be called to account.

In his next chapter Mr Gaitskell deals with another age-long argument of Socialism, that in public enterprise 'competition for private profit' is eliminated and is replaced by 'co-operation for service'. This view was based on several grounds. There was the broad Christian conception that 'man was not vile by nature but only by reason of the system', and therefore if the ownership and control of industry were transferred to the community, the natural greatness of man would grow and flourish. Secondly, there was the strong objection to the profit motive which was identified with the greed and materialism of the capitalists, which set the wrong tone for society and poisoned the relationship between the capitalist and his employees. And finally there was the feeling that, in such a competitive system of life, it was the worker who was the victim and therefore competition was bad because it was oppressive to the workers.

Having, therefore, given the various grounds on which Socialists have thought competition undesirable, Mr Gaitskell enquires how much importance we must attach today to this group of ideas. What effect have they had on the workers in the nationalised industries? He admits that this group of ideas has produced very little change among the workers in any nationalised industry, but suggests that the workers have more of a sense of partnership, in that they do not regard the management with the same hostility as in private enterprise. No evidence is produced for this statement.

Mr Gaitskell suggests that there is lack of difference in management between publicly- and privately-owned industries. He points

K

out that a nationalised industry should make profits, that it pays taxes and that it is expected to reduce costs. Management is therefore closely concerned with the profit and loss account. Their work is essentially commercial. He suggests therefore that 'up to a point, management is governed by the same considerations as the direction of a private firm.'

This suggestion is really remarkably wide of the facts. A nationalised industry is a monopoly. If their charges do not provide adequate revenues they slide into a deficit. The responsibility on the directors of a private enterprise is far more direct and harsh than it is on a board of a nationalised industry. If a private company incurs losses, there is no Treasury in the background to help it carry on; it stands alone. The criticism of the Stock Exchange by marking down its shares and the fears and worries which descend upon its managers and workers are definite, tangible and compelling. Unsuccessful management nowadays invites take-over bids, with all its unpleasant consequences.

Mr Gaitskell comes to the conclusion that the earlier and traditional arguments for nationalisation are weakened but not destroyed. The text of his pamphlet (p. 18) unfortunately omits the word 'not', before 'destroyed'. He therefore proceeds to examine the need for nationalisation, based on the situation in 1945. Labour, in the period 1945–50, relied far less on the traditional arguments than on practical considerations, 'designed to show that nationalisation was the best and only way to achieve higher production, greater efficiency and protection against monopolies'. 'Protection against monopolies' as an argument for the nationalising of industries is certainly remarkable. Monopoly by Act of Parliament is apparently not monopoly.

Mr Gaitskell then asks (p. 20), 'what does experience show about the validity of the more recent practical arguments, supporting the 1945–50 programme?' He is not too happy about it and comes to the rather lame conclusion that 'there is a good deal of evidence accumulating which suggests that the improvements in efficiency in physical terms, and the structural economies which were predicted for the nationalised industries, are taking place' (p. 21).

The evidence of achievement which he produces is remarkable in its utter inadequacy. In the case of the railways, for example, he is proud of the fact that 324 stations and 1784 route miles have been closed to passenger traffic. The increase by 64 per cent in seven years in electricity generating capacity, he puts down to the drive and buying power of the C.E.A.; the latter is, of course, synonymous with the Treasury.

After reviewing these developments in nationalised industries without making much reference, except in the case of coal, to the substantial capital expenditure incurred to obtain these results, Mr Gaitskell comes to the weak conclusion that 'while competition is wasteful it is also stimulating and that it is very hard to be sure, on balance, whether in terms of efficiency the gain from eliminating it is greater than the loss'.

Mr Gaitskell then discusses some special aspects of nationalisation, such as the large scale of a Board's operations (which he does not like), and the great difficulty of finding the right type of men to man the Boards. As a former Minister he speaks feelingly on the latter issue. 'Not many people realise the importance of finding enough individuals of high calibre who are able and willing to take over the top-level jobs' (p. 27). Finally he stresses, as he did in the speech at Brighton on 3 October 1957, the necessity of convincing the electorate of the soundness of the case. 'Almost all the industries taken over between 1945 and 1950 had been the subject of elaborate public enquiries over a long period, and the need for a change in structure was something to which the Public were quite accustomed. The same cannot yet be said of many of the new candidates for nationalisation' (p. 30). The words 'almost all' are worth noting. There has never been an enquiry or report to suggest that the steel industry was 'ripe for nationalisation'.

Finally, Mr Gaitskell comes to the 'Future of Nationalisation'. 'The vital question is how far greater social and economic equality can be achieved without more nationalisation and public ownership' (p. 31). He comes to the conclusion that some additional forms of public ownership are necessary if we are to envisage a continued further advance towards a more even distribution of wealth. We cannot yet say whether further doses of nationalisation will do the trick of equalising wealth – at any rate nationalisation as we have it now. 'No definite answer can yet be given' (p. 34). Nor will penal taxation do the trick either – even in the form of a capital levy. That has two disadvantages. Simple redistribution 'would almost certainly increase consumption and reduce saving. . . . Secondly, if the economy continued to be conducted on the lines of private ownership and inheritance, a new class structure based on property ownership would before long emerge.'

So there must be 'a high proportion of publicly-owned property' to make our wealth equal.

Here Mr Gaitskell introduces some ideas which have been fiercely discussed:

The State may become the owner of industrial, commercial or agricultural property without necessarily exercising detailed control, even over an individual firm – much less a whole industry. This can be done either by taking in death duties – not cash or bonds but equity shares and real estate – or by using the proceeds of a budget surplus to purchase equity shares – or if political conditions allowed, by a capital levy which again could either be paid in shares or land and buildings, or if paid in cash, could be used to purchase these assets (p. 35).

Further suggestions are made, such as 'the establishment of 100 per cent State enterprises to carry out a project where private firms would not undertake a risk, or some form of mixed enterprise involving a partnership between the State and private firms' (p. 35).

The great attraction of all these schemes is that as the shareholder is functionless the State can quietly take over his place; that would involve no change of management. 'If, as I believe, the major weaknesses of nationalisation are the creation of units which are too large to get the best response from those employed in them, and in the weakening of competitive attitudes in management, that is another argument for being careful about structural changes which do just this' (p. 36). The pamphlet ends with the following sentence: 'Thus in the next phase, public ownership achieved by an alliance with fiscal policy, and not just nationalisation as conceived in these last twenty years, may well become a major instrument of Socialist policy.' To promote equality of wealth the Socialist State will copy one of the most criticised features of capitalism – the functionless rentier. We are back to Sidney Webb's discovery in 1890 described in Chapter 1.

Mr Gaitskell's pamphlet has been examined in some detail because it was a painstaking effort to face squarely the consequences of nationalisation. Mr Gaitskell's heart drew him towards public ownership but his analytical brain recoiled from the dubious results of the massive transfers of ownership made by the Labour Government. Mr Gaitskell was a Socialist and leader of a Socialist Party, and his Socialism was based on an intense desire for social justice. This he too readily identified with equality of wealth, and in order to promote this egalitarianism he was prepared to adopt all kinds of measures to enable the State to 'cash in' on everything that is profitable.

The Labour Party Conference in October 1957 was held in high hopes. The Conservatives had won two General Elections, in 1951 and 1955; to win three in a row had never happened and Labour, therefore, hoped that at the next one – probably in 1959 – they would return to power. The Conference had before it two documents on Public Ownership, many of the ideas of which can be traced back to Mr Gaitskell's Fabian Tract.

The first document called *Public Enterprise* is 'Labour Review of the Nationalised Industries'. The second, *Industry and Society*, is 'Labour Policy on Future Public Ownership'. The first document was passed after a perfunctory debate; there were ideas in it which were not welcome to some sections of the Labour Party.

Public Enterprise covers the same ground as the first thirty-four pages of Mr Gaitskell's Tract, but is a much more feeble document; it is superficial and very apologetic in tone, compared with Mr Gaitskell's careful analysis. There is an undercurrent of uneasiness in the document. For instance, 'the nationalised industries have scarcely been given time to settle down and get on with the job' (p. 8). Ten years is too short a period in which to attempt a conclusion. 'The re-equipment of these industries could not be carried through as speedily as was desirable' (p. 8). One could not guess from this document that these industries had received about £2,000 million for development.

Chapter II, 'Problems to be Solved', admits that all is not well, but there is no necessity 'for radical changes in either the basic industries or the general policies of the nationalised industries. . . . Even when we felt the present situation was not satisfactory we recognised that developments were already taking place which were likely to lead to improvement in the next few years.' So a number of suggestions are put forward, none of which are novel.

In the section on 'Boards and Management' the only concrete suggestion is to increase the salaries of Board members, which was carried out in the autumn of 1957. When the old type of manager disappears in the course of time and is replaced by the new type of manager trained by the Boards all will be well.

As regards 'consumer interests' the Boards are advised 'themselves to pay very great attention to their relations with consumers. In some cases they undoubtedly do so. But in others, largely, we believe, as a result of out-of-date traditions inherited from the days of private enterprise, this is not yet the case.'

The section on 'Labour Relations' makes no reference to the vital fact that the trade unions persist in treating nationalised industries in the same way as they treat private enterprise. No Labour document could, in decency, even hint at such an unpleasant fact. Instead the section deals almost entirely with joint consultation, and ends up with this exhortation: 'vigorous and extensive educational campaigns on the problems of joint consultation are needed. Many unions already provide courses for their officials just as the Boards do for their staffs. We hope that both will give this important work very high priority.'

'The problem of Parliamentary responsibility', it is admitted, 'is not an easy one to solve. But while we do not rule out changes in the long run, we believe that, generally speaking, the right balance in the matter has been struck.'

In the last section, on 'Economic and Financial Policy', there are signs of some harder thinking. Labour's National Executive Committee is obviously becoming worried at the financial implications of nationalisation. Subsidies, except in some very special cases, are ruled out; presumably the National Union of Railwaymen agreed. 'There is a strong argument that the electricity industry should supply more of its own capital.' It is interesting to note that the National Coal Board is pressed to budget for a substantial surplus each year, but the N.E.C. does not share Mr Gaitskell's apprehension that 'higher profits in the nationalised industries will very probably invite higher wage claims' (Fabian Tract 300, p. 33). In any case, what becomes of Labour's repeated claims that nationalisation means cheap coal, cheap electricity, etc.?

The general conclusions of this superficial document are that, on the whole, all is well and that there is a right balance of advantage and disadvantage. Where there is not, it is due to a hang-over from the bad old days of private enterprise.

The second Report, *Industry and Society*, is a much more important document. It is a blue-print for the future. It develops in detail the ideas thrown out by Mr Gaitskell in the last two pages of his Fabian Tract.

The first two-thirds of the Report consists almost entirely of a financial analysis of private industry and of the relative merits of different forms of investment.

The Report makes much of the emergence of 512 large companies, each with assets in excess of £2·5 million. In these large companies the shareholder is functionless. The management is therefore in control and

exercise enormous power without being responsible to anybody. The essential point is that the Boards of these companies should conduct their affairs in a manner which coincides with the interests of the community. This involves not only good relations with their employees and full consideration of the consumer interest, but also a sense of responsibility to the nation as a whole, through Parliament and the Government.

'The Labour Party recognises that, under increasingly professional managements, large firms are as a whole serving the nation well' (p. 48). No intervention will therefore take place 'where any firm is doing a good job'.

Where companies fall down on their job – be they large or small – they will be put under control. The most significant sentence in the whole Report is on page 42: 'in many cases indeed, it is possible to control industry without owning it'. This is a radical change in Socialist doctrine, which has been hag-ridden by the words 'public ownership'.

To decide whether a company is 'falling down on its job' it will be necessary to exercise continuous supervision. The number of companies whose shares are quoted on the Stock Exchange is over 3000, which includes the 512 large companies referred to above. In addition there are over 7,000 public companies, whose shares are not quoted. Presumably all these are to be supervised – even the small ones. What a gigantic task for the Board of Trade!

The suggestions in the last two pages of Mr Gaitskell's Fabian Tract had proliferated into a vast and confused mass of proposals which, if adopted, would become a threat to the national economy.

In the year preceding the General Election of October 1959 the Labour Party, under the leadership of Mr Gaitskell, took care to play down the issue of nationalisation. But their opponents took as much care to keep it alive and there was plenty of evidence from public-opinion polls and other sources that nationalisation was a most unpopular issue. The fact that, in the popular mind, Labour was identified with a large-scale extension of public ownership did much to bring about their third successive defeat at the General Election. This was a great shock, because it was unexpected.

Mr Gaitskell was convinced by the results of the General Election that this identification of his Party with large-scale public ownership was fatal to their prospects of an early electoral victory.

Readers of this chapter will not be surprised at his conclusion because the detailed analysis of his views shows how he had carefully turned the whole issue over in his mind for several years. At the special Labour Conference at Blackpool in November 1959 he came forward, therefore, with a demand for the revision of Clause IV, the text of which is given at the beginning of this chapter.

In his speech at Blackpool advocating the change, Mr Gaitskell made some most unpalatable admissions. 'Some of the existing nationalised industries are unpopular.' 'Nationalisation was a vote loser because of the confusion in the public mind about our future policy.' The public 'were led to suppose we were going to take over everything indiscriminately, right and left, when we got back into power, simply out of a doctrinaire belief in public ownership'. 'Perhaps we were not sufficiently precise about what we were going to do it.' 'I disagree with the extreme view that nationalisation or even public ownership is the be all and end all, the ultimate first principle and aim of Socialism.'

Having thus ruled out the dogma that Socialism means public ownership, Mr Gaitskell enunciated seven 'basic first principles of British democratic socialism'. These included such generally acceptable doctrines as 'concern for the less fortunate, social justice, classless society, freedom and democratic self government'. Nationalisation was only one of the 'means of realising these principles in practice'. But it was necessary 'not only to understand why public ownership and nationalisation are means to our ultimate ends, but also to explain this convincingly to the electorate'. So Mr Gaitskell lays down two principles which he wished 'to make clear to the country'. 'First we have no intention of abandoning public ownership and accepting for all time the present frontiers of the public sector. . . . Secondly, we regard public ownership not as an end in itself, but as a means – and not necessarily the only or most important one, to certain ends – such as full employment, greater equality and higher productivity. We do not aim to nationalise every firm or to create an endless series of State monopolies.'

Mr Gaitskell then turned to Clause IV, which he described as inadequate. 'It lays us open to continual misrepresentation. It implies that common ownership is an end, whereas in fact it is a means. It implies that the only precise object we have is nationalisation, whereas in fact we have many other Socialist objectives. It implies that we propose to nationalise everything, but do we?' Mr

Gaitskell was 'sure that the Webbs and Arthur Henderson, who largely drafted this constitution, would have been amazed and horrified had they thought that their words were to be treated as sacrosanct 40 years later in utterly changed conditions. Let us remember that we are a party of the future, not of the past.'

The conclusion was the 'hope that the Executive will during the next few months try to work out and state the fundamental principles of British democratic socialism as we see and as we feel it today, in 1959, not 1918, and I hope that in due course another Conference will endorse what they propose.'

This hope was unfulfilled. Mr Gaitskell obtained remarkably little support for his demand for a revision of Clause IV. The demand seemed to infuriate all sections of the Party, except the right-wing intellectuals who supported Mr Gaitskell and who were presumed by many to have misled him into making his proposals. The trade unions as well as the faithful workers in the constituencies, who dominate every Labour Conference, passed resolution after resolution denouncing Mr Gaitskell and reaffirming the sacredness of the text of Clause IV. Within three months of the Blackpool Conference, it was clear that Clause IV was not going to be amended on Mr Gaitskell's lines. So on 16 March 1960 a compromise was arrived at on the following lines.

The National Executive Committee approved a statement on 'Clause IV, Party Objects'. It began by quoting 'the first full declaration of Party Objects in 1918, as subsequently modified in minor respects'. It should be explained that the present constitution of the Labour Party consists of fourteen clauses, numbered with roman numerals. Clause IV deals with 'Party Objects'.

Having set out Clause IV in full, the statement went on as follows:

The following statement adopted in 1960 reaffirms, amplifies and clarifies Party Objects in the light of post-war developments and the historic achievements of the first majority Labour Government.

Twelve objects are then set forth. The only one which concerns our argument is the tenth, which reads as follows:

It is convinced that these social and economic objectives can be achieved only through an expansion of common ownership substantial enough to give the community power over the commanding heights of the economy. Common ownership takes varying forms, including state-owned industries and firms, producer and consumer co-operation, municipal ownership and public participation in private concerns.

K 2

Recognising that both public and private enterprise have a place in the economy, it believes that further extension of common ownership should be decided from time to time in the light of these objectives and according to circumstances, with due regard for the views of the workers and consumers concerned.

The remaining eleven objects in this explanatory reaffirmation are more or less the same as the worthy and blameless objects enunciated in Mr Gaitskell's Blackpool speech; many of them are far from the harsh realities of life and human nature.

This statement on 'Labour's Aims' of 16 March 1960 was followed by this resolution on 13 July 1960, passed by the National Executive Committee of the Labour Party:

The National Executive Committee resolves not to proceed with any amendment or addition to Clause IV of the Constitution but declares that the statement which it adopted on 16th March is a valuable expression of the aims of the Labour Party in the second half of the twentieth century and commends it to the Conference accordingly.

The Scarborough Conference accordingly passed it by a majority of about 2 million votes. By October 1960 the controversey between Mr Gaitskell and his Party on Clause IV had been overlaid by an even more bitter controversy over defence policy. On the latter Mr Gaitskell was beaten at Scarborough and it was thought possible that the statement of aims of March 1960 might also be defeated as it was the result of Mr Gaitskell's initiative. That, however, did not happen.

On 18 January 1963 Mr Gaitskell died and was succeeded by Mr Harold Wilson as Leader of the Labour Party. In the General Election of October 1964 the Labour Party returned to power with a majority of five. Their Election Manifesto repeated the pledge to renationalise the steel industry but with such a minuscule majority that was out of the question. Instead a White Paper, Steel Nationalisation, was issued in April 1965 and debated in the House of Commons on 6 May, when it was passed by a majority of four.

The arguments set forth in the White Paper for renationalising the steel industry are considered in Chapter 6 and will therefore be dealt with very briefly in this chapter. The arguments are three – set out in paragraphs 10 to 12 of the White Paper.

The first is that the existing control by the Iron and Steel Board is 'essentially negative'. That was true and generally admitted. But it did not follow that the only alternative was nationalisation.

The second was the fact that 'difficulties have arisen over the financing of expansion programmes'. The third reason was the restrictive practices of the steel industry in the matter of prices, which had been condemned by the Restrictive Practices Court in June 1964. This third argument might justify the take-over by the State of numerous industries.

The fact was that Labour was committed to renationalisation of steel; it was the reflex of the Conservative denationalisation of 1953. The steel industry was remote from the great mass of the electorate. So when Labour returned to power in April 1966 with a comfortable majority of 99, everyone knew that steel was certain to be renationalised. The Iron and Steel Act 1967 carried out the task and the industry was vested on 28 July 1967. The scope of the industry vested is less than in 1951, but in essential matters the two Acts of 1949 and 1967 do not differ; in fact numerous provisions of the earlier are revived in the later Act.

The Labour Government which took office in 1966 has repeatedly shown an interest in state ownership. Apart from steel, large-scale nationalisation does not appear likely. But the ideas to be found in *Industry and Society*, which was adopted at the 1957 Annual Conference as 'Labour's future policy on public ownership', have been brought forward from time to tlme. Were it not for the constant economic and financial difficulties in which that Government has found itself since taking office it would certainly have produced schemes for expanding the public sector either by taking more industries into public ownership or by taking a government interest in private companies. But the increasing financial pressure on the Government is making it difficult to finance the industries already nationalised, as we have seen in Chapter 9. Labour, coming into power in an expansionist mood after thirteen years in the wilderness, may have thought that the purse of the taxpayer was bottomless. They have discovered otherwise. The accounts of the nationalised industries for 1967–8 will not appear till after this book has gone to the printer. But it is a safe forecast that in that year all the nationalised industries, except electricity, will have incurred deficits. They will also all require massive sums for capital developments. These facts must give pause to any Government.

It is an interesting speculation whether steel would have been nationalised had Mr Gaitskell lived to be Prime Minister in 1964. As this chapter shows, he had grave doubts about further nationalisation, though he was committed to the Labour Party pledge to renationalise. But he would hardly have done it at a time when economic conditions made such a measure irrelevant, if not actually harmful.

Though his efforts in 1959–60 to wean the Labour Party from its devotion to nationalisation were unsuccessful they had some effect in turning the thoughts of the Party to smaller and more selective efforts in the field of public ownership.

Examples of these efforts by the Labour Government are to be found in the Industrial Reorganisation Commission and the Industrial Expansion Bill introduced in January 1968; it had not become an Act when this book went to the publishers. The Commission has concerned itself with advanced technological mergers in the field of automation, computers, etc., which it has helped with loans which might have cost more on the open market or been difficult to obtain. The Industrial Expansion Bill authorises the Government to advance up to £150 million for 'industrial investment'. Such examples as are given, like a larger loan to the Cunard Company for the *Queen Elizabeth II*, are not happy. The Bill provides for the purchase of the Beagle Aircraft Company for £1 million. The White Paper on the Bill (Cmnd. 3509) explains that no shares in any company will be acquired except by voluntary agreement and that 'the Government do not intend to acquire shares freely on the market'. Though the Bill is thus pitched in a minor key, it has been received with suspicion. The Bill claims to help projects which 'are in the national economic interest', but which are held back by a 'divergence between national and private costs and benefits'. There are already agencies available for this purpose: hence the suspicious reception.

But the Labour Party, by its nature, must push forward the bounds of public ownership, whoever happens to be its leader. 'Monolithic' nationalisation on the lines of 1945 to 1949 may not be repeated, if only for financial reasons. But public ownership in some form or other will remain a fundamental tenet of the Labour Party. If that were not so, the Party would cease to be the Labour Party.

14 The Public Corporation in Britain

In this chapter an attempt is made to draw together the facts which have emerged in the preceding chapters, with a view to deciding how far and in what respects the term 'Public Corporation' is applicable to the nationalised industries covered by this book. This is necessary because it has been obvious in recent years that the title 'Public Corporation' has had great influence not only on writers and lawyers, but on Parliament, the general public and the industries themselves.

The concept of a Public Corporation is quite new: the term was first used in 1926. As it became apparent that the State would have to embark on or authorise the embarkation on activities hitherto regarded as outside its purview, it was agreed that some new form of machinery would be required. Certain activities of an industrial or commercial character had been traditionally run by a government department because they were traditional monopolies which naturally fell to be administered by a state agency. Postal services are perhaps the most widespread, to which the nineteenth century added telegraphs and the twentieth century added telephones, though the United States never made these additions. It also became common to put the railways under state administration – though there were and still are many exceptions to this arrangement.

In the U.K. Boards with *ad hoc* functions operating in a defined district with power to levy rates or charges are a long-standing device which has proved quite satisfactory. The Metropolitan Board of Works, the Mersey Docks and Harbour Board, the Metropolitan Water Board and the Port of London Authority are well-known examples of successful administration, carried out with little interference. With the spread of democracy there have occasionally been complaints that these Boards are too aloof because they are not directly elected by ratepayers; but on the whole the absence of complaint has been very striking. The truth is that most of us are almost unaware of their existence and their activities.

Occasionally a large local authority has ventured into strange fields and undertaken a novel enterprise. Manchester, with the confidence of its nineteenth-century greatness, financed the Manchester Ship Canal and waited over twenty years for the first dividend on its £5 million investment.

The Baldwin Government in 1926 was responsible for the creation of two Public Corporations, both of which arose from technical developments which demanded special treatment. By 1926 it was generally accepted that while the distribution of electricity might be left to local agencies – company or local authority – generation of electricity could only be adequately handled on a national plan. So the Central Electricity Board came into being and by 1939 had constructed a high-tension grid which was a major factor in winning the Second World War; the Baldwin Government's decision had been taken only just in time.

During its career the Central Electricity Board was hardly known to 1 per cent of the population. But its fellow Public Corporation became known to all of us and became a direct and major influence in the national life. To hand over broadcasting to a Corporation which enjoyed a monopoly of the new medium was a difficult decision to make. It was safeguarded by the device of a Charter limited to ten years, which has proved a very successful method of regulating from time to time a Public Corporation which was responsible for a new and untried medium developing with bewildering rapidity.

Mr Morrison's London Passenger Transport Board, which followed a few years later, was largely modelled on the Central Electricity Board, with which he had become familiar as Minister of Transport. In essence it was another of the *ad hoc* Boards which London's vast size and special problems had always demanded. But Mr Morrison did not follow the precedent of the other London Boards as regards the appointments to the Board. The other Boards were elected, directly or indirectly; he followed the precedent of the Central Electricity Board and decided that the Minister should appoint. His Conservative successors disliked this and substituted a body of Trustees, a device which proved unsatisfactory and was ultimately dropped.

So in the 1930s we had in this country three Public Corporations, all of them working fairly well. The device obviously had merits. None of these three Boards could have been replaced by a government department. There was a general feeling that a new type of organisation had been devised which would enable Governments to enter the industrial or commercial field with more confidence than hitherto. It is not surprising therefore that in all the plans for nationalising industries the solution should include the transfer of the industry to a Public Corporation. Sometimes, alas, the suggestion that a Public Corporation should take over the industry was the sum total of the plan.

This country was not alone in using the device of a Public Corporation. Indeed the conservative trend of British politics meant that this device was adopted later in the United Kingdom than in other countries more given to experiment and less inhibited by tradition. It has been suggested that the Port of London Authority, created in 1908, was the first Public Corporation in the U.K. But there was nothing novel in the concept of an Authority responsible for operating port facilities and consisting partly of appointed and partly of elected members.

Another fact in British political life which delayed the acceptance of the Public Corporation was our well-developed Civil Service, which regarded itself and was generally regarded by the public as capable of taking on the expanding responsibilities of the State, however novel. When in the First World War it was decided to take over the control of the liquor trade in certain areas, the responsibility was handed over to what in fact was a department of the Home Office, and the Home Secretary – that ultimate repository of unallotted functions – took over this novelty without a murmur. Even the Forestry Commission, which is a Body Corporate, is in effect a minor government department depending on its vote in Class VIII of the Civil Estimates.

But in countries which are not so conservative in outlook and where the public service is not so well developed, it was only to be expected that as Governments were forced to take on additional responsibilities, they should hive them off on to semi-independent corporations or what, at first sight, appeared to be such. The State Governments in Australia in the nineteenth century frequently used such a device for functions which in the U.K. would have been taken over by a government department or a local authority.

Since the 1930s there has been much discussion of Public Corporations and they are now a worldwide phenomenon. Almost every country outside the Iron Curtain – in Europe, Asia, America and Australia – has given birth to Public Corporations. In some countries which are pulling themselves up with their own boot straps they are exceedingly numerous; whenever a problem of economic development appears, a Public Corporation is created to handle it. In 1950, for example, Colombia had no less than seventeen Corporations developing its agriculture while the Philippines had eleven in the same field.

Naturally, therefore, there has developed a considerable literature on the Public Corporation. Political scientists and lawyers have made valuable studies of this new piece of government machinery. Under the auspices of United Nations Technical Assistance, seminars have been held in Rangoon in 1954 and in Delhi in 1960 to discuss the general problems of state enterprise in the economic field, and the Public Corporation figured prominently in these discussions, being regarded on the whole as the most satisfactory method of state ownership of industry.

In many countries the Courts of Law have had difficult questions to resolve arising from the existence and operations of Public Corporations. They are still rather novel and experience of them rather limited; so it is not surprising that lawyers have studied them with care and have tried with varying degrees of success to fit them into the legal conceptions with which they have always been familiar. Later on we shall see why there are exceptional difficulties in these attempts; meanwhile it is interesting to see what the lawyers make of the Public Corporation.

A thorough legal study was carried out in the collection of essays, *The Public Corporation*, edited by Professor W. Friedmann (1954). In that book there are essays dealing with Public Corporations in thirteen countries and Professor Friedmann comes to the conclusion that the Public Corporation is distinguished by the following eight characteristics:

1. They are normally created by State or (exceptionally) by charter·
2. They have no shares or shareholders – either private or public.
3. The responsibility of the Corporations is to a competent Minister, representing the Government, and through him to Parliament.
4. Administration is in the hands of a Board iapponted by the Minister. Neither the Board nor its employees are Civil Servants.
5. Their capital is provided by fixed-interest-bearing stock guaranteed by the Treasury.
6. They have the legal status of a Corporate Body with independent legal personality.
7. They have independent accounting and auditing and some form of public control which varies from Corporation to Corporation.

8. All Corporations are dual in character. They are instruments of national policy but all the same are autonomous units with legal independence and in certain respects are commercial undertakings. The independence varies according to the type and purpose of the Corporation.

We would all readily accept five of these criteria – 1, 2, 3, 4 and 6 – as applicable to the Public Corporations which are responsible for the nationalised industries in the U.K.

As regards criterion No. 5, however, the conception of financing the nationalised industries by fixed-interest-bearing stocks, backed by Treasury guarantee, has faded away. Originally only the National Coal Board was financed by advances from the Treasury, as the miners objected to stockholders, however remote and powerless. Since 1956 all the industries have been financed by Treasury advances as explained in Chapter 9. In the efflux of time the proportion of capital represented by stock will become quite small.

But it is in respect of criteria 7 and 8 that there is scope for discussion. Professor Friedmann admits that the above classification under eight headings is 'broad, tentative and not altogether satisfactory' (*The Public Corporation*, p. 167). The developments since Professor Friedmann wrote have shown that in this country the Public Corporations responsible for the nationalised industries have been undergoing subtle changes and that it is difficult at times to describe their position with accuracy. In particular Professor Friedmann's eighth criterion is so wide that it can cover a very wide range of public control from the slightest to the closest. The legal independence of a Public Corporation is in no doubt, but its independence in policy-making is open to much more serious question.

Twenty years have now elapsed since the industries described in this book became state-owned. Their characters as Public Corporations have changed profoundly in the two decades, though, as we shall see, it is not too easy to assess the full extent of the changes. We still have Public Corporations in the accepted and conventional sense of the term. We can assume that the chairmen of the B.B.C. or for that matter of the Independent Television Authority spend less time in ministerial consultation than the chairmen of the N.C.B. or the British Railways Board. Even in their cases the control of ministers has gradually tightened. For instance, the B.B.C. has met government refusals to agree on the timing of the introduction of a colour television service or on the timing of an increase in licence fee. In the sixties there has been a steady growth in governmental responsibility for the allocation of national resources, and the two broadcasting Corporations have more than once differed from policy decisions by Government in their plans for development. This has been the case both with Labour and Conservative Governments. The ten-yearly review of the activities of the two broadcasting Corporations gives Parliament an opportunity to change relations between the Government and the Corporations. The latest review in the Television Act 1963 strengthened government control over policy. For instance in 1965 the Government decided to ban cigarette advertising on television, which took effect on 1 August. This was a serious blow to the finances of the programme companies, which had received £6·2 million for such advertising in 1963.

As regards the important question of freedom of programmes the B.B.C. can still behave as it always did, from the days of Lord Reith. In the case of Independent Television the I.T.A. was charged by the Television Act 1963 with responsibility for controlling the contents of the broadcasts of the programme companies. Using these powers the I.T.A. has given instructions to the programme companies, for instance, to reduce the number per week of crime stories or Westerns. Today it can be said that the B.B.C. and I.T.A. are clear cases of the standard type of Public Corporation, with powers or duties laid down by Parliament and freedom to act within their scope. If anything, the B.B.C. is the weaker of the two because it depends for its revenue on licence fees, which are, in effect, a tax collected by the Government. All Governments have been most reluctant to increase licence fees.

In the twenty-year life of the nationalised industries there has been a slow and steady erosion of the independence of the Public Corporations. In recent years this erosion has accelerated. Government is taking on more and more responsibility in laying down policy.

In the early days government 'interference' would be of a negative kind; for instance, a refusal to allow an increase in the price of coal. In the fifties gas and electricity charges would be increased by the Boards without restraint or even notification to the Government; under their statutes these Boards were completely free to modify their charges as they wished. But later the position began to change. The coal industry could not sell all its output; the investment programme of electricity began to expand and the railways sank into chronic deficit. So the industries came more and more to rely on government advice and authority; as a result all important questions of policy were settled jointly by Government and Corporations. Such a joint settlement would usually appear as the decision of the Corporation, for which the appropriate Minister might disclaim responsibility.

These consultations behind the scenes were gradually uncovered by the investigations of the Select Committee on the Nationalised Industries and a good example of their attitude is given in the following quotation:

The evidence has shown that there are a great many important aspects of the Corporations' activities which have become subject to the control of the Minister, although there is no statutory warrant for this. In discussing some of these points individually in this Report, your Committee have noted the powerful arguments adduced in favour of the Minister's use of them; it is significant that the Corporations have accepted the assumption of these powers by the Minister, generally without protests. Relations between Ministry and Corporations are clearly good, and the last thing your Committee want to do is to disturb such a relationship. But, faced with the total extent of the Minister's non-statutory powers, they are bound to ask if these do not add up to a degree of control far in excess of that envisaged by the statutes under which B.O.A.C. and B.E.A. were created, and so lead to an undesirable diminution in the authority of the Chairmen and Boards of the Corporations, and in their feeling of responsibility. Your Committee consider it essential to the efficient running on commercial lines of the Air Corporations that there should be a clear-cut division of responsibility between the Chairmen on the one hand and the Minister on the other. When the Minister wishes, on grounds of national interest, to override the commercial judgement of a Chairman, he should do so by a directive, which should be published. (Report on Airline Corporations, para. 218.)

It is desirable, as explained in Chapter 8, that when a Minister takes definite responsibility he should put it in writing in the form of a direction which would then be embodied in the Annual Report of the Board concerned. Parliament would know what a Minister had decided and would be fully authorised to debate the decision. In the case of the Air Corporations, the Civil Aviation (Licensing) Act 1960 went some distance to meet the Select Committee's criticisms. But the Air Corporations, being international and very dependent on government help, are in a different position from the nationalised industries dealt with in this book.

But unfortunately the issue is not always as clear-cut as the Report of the Select Committee makes it out to be. It is not often that ministers make a decision which falls closely within the field of ministerial competence. Usually the decision is more within he competence of the Board whose chairman has obtained the Minister's consent and if necessary the agreement of his colleagues.

As mentioned above, the nationalised industries incurred increasing difficulties in the late fifties and early sixties. That fact alone has tended to drive the chairmen of the Boards into more frequent consultations with ministers and their senior officers. The result is that during recent years ministers and Boards have learned to live together in informal consultations over the ever-increasing problems of the industries. The division of responsibility laid down in the nationalisation statutes is still there. Ministers approve programmes of capital development and research and will refuse to interfere in any question of 'day-to-day administration'. But bridging this division there are these informal contacts, which result in a decision by a Board or, if it is too patently a government matter, by the Minister. In fact, as a result of nationalisation the Government has obtained a great extension of power and responsibility of an economic and financial kind which was never contemplated when the Nationalisation Acts went on to the Statute Book. The Labour Government of 1945 genuinely intended, when drafting those Acts, to follow a policy of self-denial and to set up Public Corporations of the pre-war type. The Conservative Governments since 1951 would have been only too pleased to follow this policy but events have been far too strong for them. Mr Macmillan tipped the balance in 1956 when he brought the financing of these industries within the scope of the Budget. Mr Heathcoat Amory went a long step further in 1960 when he transferred the deficit of the British Transport Commission from 'below' to 'above the line' thus making the Treasury responsible for financing the deficit from taxes and not from savings. This was a striking contrast to the warnings of Mr Watkinson, when Minister of Transport, that the Government would not be prepared to find additional money to finance increases of wages to railwaymen. The water has gone over the dam.

But the large and important industries which were nationalised between 1946 and 1949 presented a special problem which was not solved by putting them under the administration of Public Corporations as the term was then understood. This was much the best arrangement which could then be adopted, but it was self-deception to assume that once these Corporations were launched they would be able to proceed on their independent way on the lines laid down in the Acts. Experiment and development were inevitable, especially as circumstances changed and the assumptions on which the Nationalisation Acts were founded tended to fade out. A Coal Board unable to sell all its output was unthinkable in 1945 or even in 1955, but from 1960 it has been a fact which has dominated the lives of the employees of the Coal Board.

Political and legal writers have noted that Governments all over the world tend to find it difficult to maintain an attitude of self-denial and an avoidance of interference in the affairs of the nationalised industries in their respective countries. In many ways, which are often subtle and difficult to detect, Governments and their officials tend to take part in the running of the Public Corporations which they have created.

The interference comes both from politicians and from their departments. But in the U.K., with its highly developed business and industrial traditions, there is much less belief in the civil servant's capacity to handle economic issues than in countries such as France or the under-developed countries such as India where it is natural for the Civil Service to control Public Corporations. As a result, government departments in this country have stood aloof from the working of these Corporations and (though this may surprise many people) ministers have tried harder than in other countries to maintain self-denial and to allow the Boards, as far as possible, to run their own affairs. But facts have been stronger than theories and in nearly every case infiltration by Government is now taking place on an ever-increasing scale. The Public Corporation in Britain has shown a great power of adjustment and adaptation which is nowhere reflected in the texts of legal documents. But that is how it often happens in the U.K.

There is a school of thought among political theorists who regard the Public Corporation as endowed with superior virtues to any other form of organisation for the task of administering economic affairs in the public sectors. They do not realise that the Public Corporations are not only legal but political creations. However carefully the Acts of Parliament which set up the Corporations are drafted, difficult legal issues crop up when the Corporations get to work. The Courts deliver their judgments and a body of case law is built up, which naturally is of interest to the lawyer and the constitutional historian. But interesting as these cases are, they are only a part – and not the most important part – of the evolution of the Public Corporations. They are in fact part of the political set-up closely geared into the machinery of government; as Professor Friedmann points out, 'they are instruments of national policy'. On the one hand the legal judgments are definite and can be analysed and discussed like other legal judgments. But the political evolution is often obscure and great changes may take place while the façade remains unchanged. It is not easy to penetrate behind the façade because the changes are not in documents and the evolution is so gradual that they might well escape notice for a long time after they have taken place. This is one of the reasons why there is such variety of judgment on the achievements of the Public Corporations. An example of this view is the conclusion of Professor W. A. Robson:

The Public Corporation is in my judgment by far the best organ so far devised in this or any other country for administering nationalised industries or undertakings. Allowing for some teething troubles which are still not entirely cured, the Public Corporation which we have evolved is an outstanding contribution to public administration in a new and vitally important sphere. It is far better than the joint stock company owned and controlled by the State; or than Government departments engaged in business activity; or than State administrations set up to manage commercial or industrial undertakings, such as those existing in the Netherlands, Scandinavia, France and other countries (*Nationalised Industry and Public Ownership*, p. 493).

This is too sweeping and too optimistic a judgement; the second part of the conclusion is very difficult to substantiate. The troubles of the Public Corporations responsible for the nationalised industries can hardly be described as 'teething troubles'; they are far more serious than that. Where the industry is free from troubles, as is the case with electricity supply, for example, the Boards concerned make a moderate success of their task. But that is usually achieved at too great a cost, particularly in capital investment. Technically there may be a great improvement in the quality of the product, as is to be expected from the fact that the influence of the technocrat is so strong in those industries. But where a balance has to be struck between the producer and the consumer of his products, the balance is usually tilted in favour of the producer, who is highly organised while the consumer is not. As a result the climate of public opinion in which the industries live is at the best indifferent and at the worst definitely hostile, with disastrous results on the morale of the workers in the industries; the effect of public opinion is, in the end, overwhelming.

But some of the Public Corporations are in such serious difficulties – particularly coal and transport – that willynilly the Government has to step in and take decisive steps in formulating policy for them. The trouble is due to the absence in the British system of government of adequate machinery for supervising the working of these Public Corporations. The government departments supposed to be responsible have not the powers or the expertise to undertake the tremendous task of supervising these enormous undertakings; so the duty goes by default until a crisis develops. The Government, alarmed at the dangers of a serious crisis, tends to take hasty and ill-thought-out measures which may not improve the situation and may even make it worse.

Since September 1967, when the Government decided that proposals to increase charges must be scrutinised by the Prices and Incomes Board, we have had some Reports from that Board which are of great interest. For example their Report of March 1968 (Cmnd. 3575) on the Bulk Supply Tariff of the Central Electricity Generating Board is a most welcome analysis of that fearsome tariff. It is safe to say that that tariff, which has been operating since 1948, has never been scrutinised by the appropriate government department, which, indeed, would not feel itself competent for that task. In the course of the next few years we shall acquire from these Reports much knowledge of the working of the nationalised industries which has hitherto been sadly lacking.

The Public Corporation can be the right organisation for running industries which are publicly owned provided that their administration should not raise issues of national importance nor incur deficits of such magnitude that the State must provide a subsidy – open or disguised. Once this stage is reached, accountability to Parliament for the expenditure involved tends to make the responsible Minister treat the nationalised industry as if it were an extension of his department. Once the subsidy to British Railways was put above the line and was met by one of the votes for which the Minister of Transport was responsible, he had no alternative but to impose new controls on the Transport Commission and to set about devising some means for controlling the amount of the subsidy.

In the 1960s, therefore, there have been great changes in the status of the Public Corporations. Day-to-day management is, of course, left in their hands and ministers will still refuse to answer parliamentary questions on such management. But as explained in Chapter 9, 'Finances and Economics of the Nationalised Industries', Governments (both Conservative and Labour) have been forced to take a closer and closer interest in the policies of their mammoth Public Corporations. During the sixties there has hardly been a year when the national economy has not been under some strain. Providing finance for the Corporations on an ever-increasing scale and keeping them out of their mounting difficulties have added substantially to these strains.

In April 1961 there was the important White Paper on the Financial and Economic Obligations of the Nationalised Industries which laid down guidelines which have in fact persisted till 1968. In November 1967 there was another White Paper, a Review of Financial and Economic Objectives. In 1962 the nationalised transport industry was reconstructed; in 1968 that is happening again. In 1967 a White Paper on Fuel Policy was issued which led to a bitter clash both with the National Coal Board and the National Union of Mineworkers. Also, as mentioned above, the nationalised industries were deprived in 1967 of their powers to increase charges without prior reference to the Prices and Incomes Board. These are some examples of major government intervention in the 1960s.

It was no doubt these developments that led Lord Reith in an article in *The Times* of 26 March 1966, 'Façade of Public Corporations', to propose that the time was ripe for a Royal Commission on Public Corporations. This would enquire into 'the public corporation system of management' including the relations between the governing Boards on the one hand and ministers and their civil servants on the other. Lord Reith, who has given his views on other occasions, was thinking back to his pre-war experience of the B.B.C. But conditions have changed drastically since he retired thirty years ago.

There is therefore no doubt that after two decades the position of the great Public Corporations which run the nationalised industries has been seriously weakened. They are too large, too important and too expensive to be free from the control or 'interference' (if that word is preferred) of their sponsoring department. They have, of course, most of the trappings of an independent legal status referred to earlier in this chapter. In fact this status has its attractions and the oldest statutory monopoly in the country, the Post Office, is being converted from a government department manned by civil servants into a Public Corporation. The British Steel Corporation, which took over the steel industry in July 1967, is an addition to the list which will also be of great interest. It is a Corporation responsible for a basic manufacturing industry, with substantial markets abroad. It is to be expected that at the start the British Steel Corporation will enjoy a honeymoon period of greater independence than the old-established Corporations. It must be given time to work itself into the controlling seat. But the length of the honeymoon period will depend on its financial success. If it starts, as seems likely, by running at a deficit, it will soon find itself in the same position as the other Corporations. Above all it will find it difficult to bring out substantial schemes of capital development without working closely with the Ministry of Power. It will not be able to imitate the Corporations in the early fifties, which launched large programmes of capital development with little or no consultation with the Government, who at the time were only too pleased that the Corporations were getting down to the job for which they had been appointed.

As an organisation the Public Corporation has great merits. But there does not exist a perfect example which can be quoted for copying. In the U.K. the Public Corporations are huge and vital parts of the national economy, very unlike the pre-war Corporations such as the Central Electricity Board or the London Passenger Transport Board. If a Public Corporation has a limited sphere of operations, and can operate with reasonable chance of commercial success, it can tackle a limited task. In the old days this was possible: Mr Herbert Morrison believed that the new Public Corporations created by the Attlee Government were similar to the Central Electricity Board or the London Passenger Transport Board with which he was familiar. Their chairman would occasionally talk matters over with the Minister; otherwise they went it alone. Those halycon, carefree days for ministers are very much in the past. So the Public Corporations no longer go it alone. They have become very different from what they were planned to be. In the 1970s there will be further changes, which can be foreseen in the Transport Bill, which makes the Minister of Transport a dominating controller over a congeries of overlapping transport undertakings. Yet they will all be Public Corporations. But they will have only a fraction of the powers once associated with that term.

An interesting footnote to this chapter is that the term 'Public Corporation' is unknown in Germany. When an earlier book of the author was translated into German, the term had to be defined in a carefully worded footnote of seven lines of small print.

15 Conclusion

THE Labour Party talked about nationalisation for about half a century. Neither they nor their supporters did the necessary hard work in planning the change-over. Had it not been for Mr Herbert Morrison's efforts in the 1930s, the Party, in 1945, would have been even less prepared; even so, as Mr Shinwell has confessed, there were no plans available on which to act.

One result of this long period of propaganda was that when the opportunity came at last, the industries on which the Labour Government concentrated, were long past their heyday. This was not so obvious in coal but it was very obvious in railways. At the beginning of the century both were dominant industries. By 1945 the internal-combustion engine and the oil industry, which fuelled that engine, were serious competitors. Indeed for railways the competition was so dangerous that the Labour Government, in the Transport Act 1947, envisaged a takeover of the whole of transport. Their belief was that the Transport Commission, with one vast undertaking, would strike a balance between road and rail which would keep the latter healthy if necessary, at the cost of the former. That policy is still with us in the Transport Bill 1967.

The nationalisation of gas and electricity were necessary reorganisations; both industries had an outdated Victorian structure. The take-over of steel – finally carried out in 1967 – also, like coal and railways, harked back to a bygone age, when coal, steel and textiles were the three pillars supporting the national economy and when all three were transported by rail and by rail alone. Latter-day propagandists justify the take-over of steel as one of the 'commanding heights of the economy'. No one has defined that phrase.

The result, therefore, of Labour's delay in coming to power has meant that the two most significant nationalised industries are being propped up by the State as they decline. This has been a great shock, especially for the workers in these industries, as it has always been assumed that the workers were to be the main beneficiaries of state ownership. They naturally demand, therefore, that the Government should take the strongest measures to arrest this decline – regardless of the effects on the national economy. The trouble ahead is that in the 1970s the decline in coal consumption will accelerate; this will in part be due to the unpopularity created by these strong measures forced on the Government by political and trade union pressure.

Since the nationalised industries came into being they have spent thirteen years under Conservative Governments. At first sight that might appear to be to their disadvantage; in fact they fared as well under Conservative as under Labour Governments. Once they had denationalised steel and road haulage, Conservative ministers provided all possible help to the industries for which they were responsible. It is interesting that Lord Citrine in his record of the ten years 1948–57, as chairman of the Central Electricity Authority, criticises only Labour ministers for reducing his capital demands. No one studying the behaviour of Ministers of Transport from 1956 to 1960, when they persuaded Parliament to pour out hundreds of millions of pounds to finance the so called 'modernisation' scheme for the railways, can but be amazed at their patience and tolerance, which finally gave out with the appointment of the Stedeford Group.

The Conservatives were probably not so opposed to the presence of these state-owned industries as their political theories required. By the 1950s all British Governments were converts to Keynesian economics and to the doctrine that the State should take it upon itself to manage demand and so provide full employment. The State's power to carry out this policy was greatly enhanced by the control of several basic industries which had substantial capital programmes and were large employers of labour. It was not difficult therefore for Conservative ministers to establish good relations and work in close co-operation with these industries.

The 1950s were their heyday. They still enjoyed great independence as Public Corporations. On the whole their requirements for capital were met; all the industries reorganised and modernised themselves with massive injections of capital; the one failure was the railways – they were too late. Also, apart from the railways, they had a reasonable control of their own prices. Ministers might demur and occasionally delay as in the 1955 coal price increases; but there was no serious control. Gas and electricity were unhampered, their tariff increases were usually local.

In the 1960s there have been great changes. The White Paper in 1961 on Financial and Economic Obligations of the Nationalised Industries was years overdue. The vagueness about the financial responsibilities of the nationalised industries was directly due to the lack of thought and preparation which went into the Nationalisation Acts. The Treasury, which advanced the large sums for compensation, was mainly concerned to see that the new Public Corporations were sufficiently viable to pay the interest and repay the capital. Hence the emphasis in all the Acts on a central body in each industry responsible for finance. But no thought was given to the financial basis on which the industries would operate. As 'profit' is as dirty a word as 'lechery' to the Socialist (to quote Mr Gunter) the word, of course, does not appear in the statutes; they merely require 'that the revenues are not less than sufficient to meet their outgoings properly chargeable to revenue account, taking one year with another' (Gas Act 1948, Section 41 (1)).

From the 1961 White Paper onwards, all Governments, both Labour and Conservative, have taken more and more steps to control the policy of the nationalised industries. Partly it is due to the difficulties of the national economy. This situation has developed at a time when the Public Corporations are themselves in greater and greater financial difficulties. Either they are declining like coal or railways or they are requiring huge sums for development – such as electricity and lately gas. These difficulties were increased by the compensation to steel shareholders in 1967. By the time this book appears there will probably have been requests for large-scale financial help from the British Steel Corporation.

Finally came the sudden decision in September 1967 to refer all applications for tariff increases by the nationalised industries to the Prices and Incomes Board. Their scrutiny of these applications marks a fresh stage in government control of the Public Corporations. Their Report for instance, on the Bulk Supply Tariff of the Central Electricity Generating Board (Cmnd. 3575) goes much deeper than any previous enquiry into what is the most sophisticated act of pricing policy of any nationalised industry. No government department has shown itself equipped to carry out such a scrutiny. We can expect this kind of scrutiny to continue.

One of the contentions of this book has been the inability of government departments to supervise adequately the Public Corporations for which they are officially responsible. It is out of the question to leave to their own devices a group of industries in the public sector, whose gross fixed capital formation is about 20 per cent of the national total. It is probable, therefore, that by 1970 some machinery will have been developed to work in conjunction with the sponsoring department to supervise the financial and economic performance of the nationalised industries. If not, the results will be serious.

Organisation of the Nationalised Industries

COAL

1. The Minister of Power appoints the National Coal Board. Present members of the Board are:
   Chairman
   Deputy Chairman
   Six full-time members
   Four part-time members
2. From 1947 to 1967 there were eight Divisional Coal Boards.
3. Below the Divisional Boards there were Area General Managers; 48 in 1947 reducing to 38 in 1966.
4. From 1 April 1967 the Divisional Boards were abolished and the Area General Managers reduced to 17, directly responsible to the N.C.B.
5. Below the Area General Manager there were 200 Group Managers and, of course, Managers of Collieries. The Group Managers were also abolished from 1 April 1967.

   A five-tier structure was thus replaced by a three-tier structure. This somewhat simplifies the picture, because officers have been appointed to perform parts of the functions of the Divisional Boards and Group Managers.

ELECTRICITY

1. From 1948 to 1957.
   (a) The Minister of Power appointed the Central Electricity Authority. This consisted of:
       Chairman
       Two Deputy Chairmen
       One full-time member
       Three part-time members
       Four Chairmen of Area Boards serving in rotation
       Chairman of the North of Scotland Hydro-Electric Board
   (b) The Minister also appointed fourteen Area Electricity Boards. These consisted of a full-time Chairman and Deputy Chairman, five to seven part-time members and the Chairman of the Area

Consultative Council. In 1955 the two Area Boards in Scotland were detached from this organisation, to become an independent South of Scotland Electricity Board responsible to the Secretary of State for Scotland. He also appointed the North of Scotland Hydro-Electric Board.

2. From 1958 onwards the Minister of Power appoints:
   (*a*) The Electricity Council. This consists of:
   Chairman
   Two Deputy Chairmen (one full-time and one part-time)
   Two full-time members
   One part-time member
   Three members from the Central Electricity Generating Board
   Twelve Area Board Chairmen
   (*b*) The Central Electricity Generating Board. This consists of:
   Chairman
   Deputy Chairman
   Four full-time members
   Four part-time members
   (*c*) Twelve Area Boards as before; these are now financially autonomous.
3. The Secretary of State for Scotland continues to appoint the North of Scotland Hydro-Electric Board and the South of Scotland Electricity Board.

GAS

1. The Minister of Power appoints the Gas Council; this consists of:
   Chairman
   Deputy Chairman
   Twelve Area Board Chairmen
   Under the Gas Act 1965 the Minister also appoints three additional full-time members of the Gas Council, to help it to carry out the additional functions laid on it by that Act.
2. Twelve Area Gas Boards; these consist of:
   Chairman – full-time
   Deputy Chairman – full-time
   Six to eight members – mostly part-time
   Chairman of the Area Consultative Council

TRANSPORT

1. From 1947 to 1953
   (*a*) The Minister of Transport appointed the Transport Commission consisting of a Chairman and four members.

(*b*) The Minister also appointed the following Executives:
Railways
London Transport
Dock and Inland Waterways
Road Haulage
Road Passenger Services
Hotels
These Executives were subordinate to and responsible to the Transport Commission.

2. From 1953 to 1962
   (*a*) The Transport Act 1953 abolished all Executives except London Transport. The Transport Commission became responsible for managing all its undertakings.
   (*b*) To help it to do so, the Transport set up Area Railway Boards to operate the railway regions.
   (*c*) It set up management boards for docks and inland waterways and for road passenger services. The road haulage activities left to the Commission were organised in companies known as British Road Services.

3. From 1963 to 1968
   (*a*) The Transport Act 1962 abolished the Transport Commission.
   (*b*) From 1 January 1963 it was replaced by:
       (1) British Railways Board
       (2) London Transport Board
       (3) British Transport Docks Board
       (4) British Waterways Board
       (5) Transport Holding Company
   All these were independent of each other and individually responsible to the Minister of Transport.
   (*c*) The Act of 1962 set up six regional railway boards responsible to the British Railways Board. These were reduced to five in 1967.
   (*d*) The Transport Holding Company became responsible for the road haulage companies and bus companies; also other activities such as Thomas Cook & Son.

4. The Transport Act 1968 reorganises all these activities from 1 January 1969.

STEEL

1. The Minister of Power appoints the British Steel Corporation, which consists of a Chairman and not less than seven nor more than twenty other members. The appointments made so far consist of (all full-time):
   Chairman

L

Three Deputy Chairmen
Eight members

2. The Corporation has organised its undertaking into four Groups which will be controlled by a Group Managing Director's Committee. This consists of one Deputy Chairman and three of the members of the Corporation, each of whom is managing director of a group.

3. Each group will be controlled by a board, appointed by the British Steel Corporation. The Chairman of the group board will be the Group Managing Director. The British Steel Corporation have appointed five part-time members to two of the group boards and six part-time members to the other two group boards. These boards are non-statutory.

Bibliography

AFTER twenty years books on the nationalised industries are beginning to accumulate. Many of them are specialist studies on a particular aspect. These are valuable in assembling the data for the specialist study, but they suffer from the inevitable defect that the limitations of the speciality make it difficult to envisage the whole subject. Consequently the conclusions of these studies have a limited range and lose much validity when considered in a wider context.

The basic material for a study of the nationalised industries is the Annual Reports of the Boards, which are now very numerous. There are over five hundred Reports in gas and electricity alone. In addition there are numerous official publications such as Acts of Parliament, *Hansard*, Blue Books, White Papers, etc. Among Blue Books the Reports of the Select Committee on Nationalised Industries contain a vast amount of information. In recent years White Papers in connection with these industries have poured out in a steady stream.

We badly lack books written by persons – particularly middle and senior management – who have worked in these industries. What would be valuable above all would be books by persons who worked in the industries before and after nationalisation; unfortunately a book like Mr Fiennes's *I Tried to Run a Railway* is a rarity.

The volume of basic material is so enormous that in 1960 Professor Robson produced a 'Select Bibliography' of thirty pages. Today that list could easily be doubled. The following bibliography is therefore based on a most rigorous selection. It is hoped that it will be adequate to assist a student to choose some part of this vast field for further study.

1. ANNUAL REPORTS OF THE FOLLOWING:

National Coal Board
British Transport Commission
London Transport Executive
British Railways Board
London Transport Board
Central Electricity Authority
Electricity Council
Central Electricity Generating Board

Area Electricity Boards
South of Scotland Electricity Board
North of Scotland Hydro-Electric Board
Gas Council
Area Gas Boards
Iron and Steel Corporation
Iron and Steel Board
Iron and Steel Holding and Realisation Agency
British Steel Corporation

2. PRINCIPAL NATIONALISATION ACTS

Coal Industry Nationalisation Act 1946
Coal Industry Act 1965
Coal Industry Act 1967
Transport Act 1947
Transport Act 1953
Transport (Railway Finances) Act 1957
Transport (Borrowing Powers) Act 1959
Transport Act 1962
Transport Act 1968
Electricity Act 1947
Electricity Reorganisation (Scotland) Act 1954
Electricity Act 1957
Gas Act 1948
Gas Act 1965
Iron and Steel Act 1949
Iron and Steel Act 1953
Iron and Steel Act 1967

3. PARLIAMENTARY REPORTS AND WHITE PAPERS

Report of Technical Advisory Committee on Coal Mining (Cmd. 6610)
    1945 (Reid Report)
Report of Committee of Inquiry into the Gas Industry (Cmd. 6699)
    1945 (Heyworth Report)
Report of Committee of Inquiry into the Electricity Supply Industry
    (Cmd. 9672) 1956 (Herbert Report)
Reports from Select Committee on Nationalised Industries, October
    1952 and July 1953
Reports from Select Committee on Nationalised Industries (Reports
    and Accounts):
        1956/7/304 (Scottish Electricity Boards)
        1957/8/187 (National Coal Board)
        1958/9/213 (Air Corporations)
        Special Report 1958/9/276

1959/60/254 (British Railways)
1960/1/280 (Gas Industry)
1962/3/226 (Electricity Industry)
1963/4/240 (B.O.A.C.)
1964/5/313 (London Transport)
1965/6/77 (Gas, Electricity and Coal Industries)
1966/7/340 (Post Office)

Report of Committee of Inquiry into London Transport, 1955

Railways Reorganisation Scheme (Cmd. 9191) 1954

Report on the Purchasing Procedure of the British Transport Commission (Cmnd. 262) 1957

Exchange of Correspondence between Minister of Transport and Chairman of British Transport Commission (Cmnd. 585) 1958

Reorganisation of the Nationalised Transport Undertakings (Cmnd. 1248) 1960

Public Investment in Great Britain (Cmnd. 1203) 1960

The Financial and Economic Obligations of the Nationalised Industries (Cmnd. 1337) 1961

Control of Public Expenditure (Cmnd. 1432) 1961

Public Boards; annual lists of members of Public Boards

Public Investment in Great Britain; annual statements

Government Expenditure Below the Line; annual White Paper

Nationalised Industries: a review of economic and financial objectives (Cmnd. 3437) 1967

Fuel Policy (Cmnd. 2798) 1965

Fuel Policy (Cmnd. 3438) 1967

Transport Policy (Cmnd. 3057) 1966

Transport of Freight (Cmnd. 3470) 1967

Railway Policy (Cmnd. 3439) 1967

Prices and Incomes Board; Report on Gas Prices (First Report) (Cmnd. 3567) 1968

Prices and Incomes Board; Report on the Bulk Supply Tariff of the Central Electricity Generating Board (Cmnd. 3575) 1968

Prices and Incomes Board; Proposals for Bus and Railway Fare Increases in London (Cmnd. 3561) 1968

Report of the Tribunal Appointed to Inquire into the Disaster at Aberfan (H.C. 553) 1967

Ministry of Power – Statistical Digest; annual

4. Publications by the Nationalised Industries

Coal

Report of Advisory Committee on Organisation, 1955 (Fleck Report)

Plan for Coal, 1950

Investing in Coal, 1956

British Coal; the rebirth of an industry, 1957
Revised Plan for Coal, 1959

Electricity

Power and Prosperity, 1954
Power for the Future, 1958
Power Progress, 1959

Gas

Fuel for the Nation, 1954
Gas Looks Ahead, 1960

Transport

British Transport Commission; Proposals for the Railways (Cmd. 9880) 1956
British Transport Commission; Reappraisal of the Plan for the Modernisation and Re-equipment of British Railways (Cmnd. 813) 1959
The Reshaping of British Railways, 1963

Steel

British Steel Corporation: Report on Organisation (Cmnd. 3362) 1967

5. *Studies in Nationalised Industry*, published by the Acton Society Trust; these comprise 12 Reports on various aspects of the nationalised industries. The Trust has also published *Training and Promotion in Nationalised Industry, Nationalisation and the Operational Manager*.

6. GENERAL

Baker, R. J. S., *The Management of Capital Projects*, G. Bell, 1962
Baldwin, G. B., *Beyond Nationalisation*, Oxford U.P., 1956
Barry, E. Eldon, *Nationalisation in British Politics*, Cape, 1965
Brady, R. A., *Crisis in Britain: Plans and Achievements of the Labour Government*, Cambridge U.P., 1950
British Iron and Steel Federation, *Stage 1 Report of Development Co-ordinating Committee*, 1966
Burn, Duncan, *Political Economy of Nuclear Energy*, Institute of Economic Affairs, 1967
Citrine, Lord, *Two Careers* (vol. ii of Autobiography), Hutchinson, 1967
Clegg, H., *Industrial Democracy and Nationalisation*, Blackwell, 1951
Clegg, H., and Chester, D. N., *Future of Nationalisation*, Blackwell, 1953
Consumer Council, *Consumer Consultative Machinery in the Nationalised Industries*, 1968
Coombes, D. L., *The Member of Parliament and the Administration*, Allen & Unwin, 1966

Davies, E., *Problems of Public Ownership*, Policy Discussion Pamphlets, No. 3, Labour Party, 1952

Dennis, N., Henriques, F., *et al.*, *Coal is our Life*, Eyre & Spottiswoode, 1956

Federation of British Industries, *Nationalisation, a Report*, 1958

Fiennes, G., *I Tried to Run a Railway*, Ian Allan, 1967

Florence, P. S., *Industry and the State*, Hutchinson, 1957

Foster, C. D., *The Transport Problem*, Blackie, 1963

Friedmann, W. (ed.), *The Public Corporation*, Stevens, 1954

Gaitskell, H. T. N., *Socialism and Nationalisation* (Fabian Tract 300), 1956

Gordon, L., *The Public Corporation in Great Britain*, Oxford U.P., 1938

Hansard Society, *Parliamentary Reform 1933–1960*, 2nd ed., 1967

Hanson, A. H., *Public Enterprise and Economic Development*, Routledge, 1959

Hanson, A. H., *Parliament and Public Ownership*, Cassell, 1961

Hanson, A. H. (ed.), *Nationalisation – a Book of Readings*, Allen & Unwin, 1963

Haynes, W., *Nationalisation in Practice; the British Coal Industry*, Bailey Bros., 1953

Kelf-Cohen, R., *Nationalisation in Britain*, Macmillan, 1st ed. 1958; 2nd ed. 1961

Labour Party Policy Pamphlet No. 1, *British Transport*, n.d.

Labour Party, *Public Enterprise*, 1957

Labour Party, *Industry and Society*, 1957

Labour Party, *The Nationalised Industries – Success Story*, 1958

Labour Party, Reports of Conferences, 1957, 1959, 1960

Little, I. M. D., *A Critique of Welfare Economics*, Clarendon Press, 1957

Morrison, Herbert, *Socialisation and Transport*, Constable, 1933

Morrison, Herbert, *Government and Parliament*, Oxford U.P., 1954

Normanton, E. L., *Accountability and Audit of Governments*, Manchester U.P., 1966

O'Brien, T., *British Experiments in Public Ownership and Control*, Allen & Unwin, 1937

P.E.P., *A Fuel Policy for Britain*, 1965

Polanyi, G., *Comparative Returns from Investment in Nationalised Industries*, Institute of Economic Affairs, 1968

Pollard, S., *Development of British Economy 1914–1950* (ch. 7), E. Arnold, 1962

Robson, W. A., *Nationalised Industry and Public Ownership*, Allen & Unwin, 1960

Robson, W. A. (ed.), *Problems of Nationalised Industry*, Allen & Unwin, 1952

Rogow, A. A., *Labour Government and British Industry 1945–1951*, Blackwell, 1956

Self, Sir H., and Watson, E. M., *Electricity Supply in Great Britain*, Allen & Unwin, 1952

Shanks, M. (ed.), *Lessons of Public Enterprise*, Cape, 1963

Shepherd, W. G., *Economic Performance under Public Ownership*, Yale U.P., 1965

Shinwell, E., *Conflict Without Malice*, Odhams, 1955

Simon, Lord, *The Boards of Nationalised Industries*, Longmans, 1957

Tawney, R. H., *The Radical Tradition* (chs 9 and 11) Allen & Unwin, 1964; Penguin, 1966

Thornhill, W., *The Nationalised Industries – an Introduction*, Nelson, 1968

Tivey, L. J., *Nationalisation in British Industry*, Cape, 1966

Webb, S. and B., *Constitution for the Social Commonwealth of Great Britain*, Longmans, 1920

Weiner, H. E., *British Labour and Public Ownership*, Stevens, 1960

Willson, F. M. G., *Administrators in Action* (ch. 3), Allen & Unwin, 1961

Index